Women's Police Stations

Women's Police Stations
Gender, Violence, and Justice in São Paulo, Brazil

Cecília MacDowell Santos

First published in 2005 by
PALGRAVE MACMILLAN™
175 Fifth Avenue, New York, N.Y. 10010 and
Houndmills, Basingstoke, Hampshire, England RG21 6XS
Companies and representatives throughout the world

PALGRAVE MACMILLAN is the global academic imprint of the Palgrave Macmillan division of St. Martin's Press, LLC and of Palgrave Macmillan Ltd. Macmillan® is a registered trademark in the United States, United Kingdom and other countries. Palgrave is a registered trademark in the European Union and other countries.

ISBN 0–312–24021–X hardback
ISBN 0–312–2402–2 paperback

Library of Congress Cataloging-in-Publication Data

Santos, Cecília MacDowell
    Women's police stations : engendering justice in São Paulo, Brazil / Cecília MacDowell Santos.
        p. cm.
    Includes bibliographical references and index.
    ISBN 0–312–24021–X (HC)—ISBN 0–312–24042–2 (Pbk.)
        1. Women's police stations—Brazil—São Paulo. 2. Women—Violence against—Brazil—São Paulo. 3. Policewomen—Brazil—São Paulo. 4. Sex discrimination in criminal justice administration—Brazil—São Paulo.
    5. Feminist criminology—Brazil—São Paulo. I. Title.

HV8185.S25S26 2004
363.2'082'098161—dc22   2004049769

A catalogue record for this book is available from the British Library.

Design by Newgen Imaging Systems (P) Ltd., Chennai, India.

First edition: February 2005
10 9 8 7 6 5 4 3 2 1

Printed in the United States of America.

In honor of my maternal grandmother,
Maria Anita Amazonas MacDowell (1908–)

In memory of my paternal grandmother,
Helena Fonseca dos Santos (1896–1996)

Contents

List of Figures and Tables

Figures

Acknowledgments

Throughout different phases of the research for this book, as well as the writing and rewriting of the manuscript, which largely draws on original research for my Ph.D. dissertation (Santos 1999a), I benefited from the generous support of several individuals and institutions.

During my graduate studies in the department of sociology at the University of California at Berkeley, I was privileged to receive the guidance of my dissertation advisor, Peter Evans, and the other members of my dissertation committee—Raka Ray, Norma Alarcón, and Sonia Alvarez. They were all very supportive of my project from beginning to end and provided invaluable feedback. Their own research and dedication to their students are very inspiring and have greatly influenced my work. While at Berkeley, I also benefited from an exchange of ideas and moral support from fellow graduate students as well as from my Portuguese students. Thanks are due to Elizabeth Rudd, Naheed Islam, Sheba George, Millie Thayer, Daniel Hoffman, David Whitman, Zach Elkins, Anne Ching, and Dan Littman. I am also thankful to the logistical support I received from the staff members of the sociology department, especially Lucia T. Simons, Elsa Tranter, and Carmen Privat.

Since joining the University of San Francisco in the fall of 2001 as an assistant professor of Sociology, I have been fortunate to count on the support of my colleagues, staff members, and students of the wonderful department of sociology, as well as from other departments and programs at the university. I would like to express special thanks to Stephanie Sears, Aránzazu Borrachero, Dorothy Kidd, Else Tamayo, Michael Webber, and Susan Steinberg. I am also thankful to my research assistants, Deanna Pluma and Laura Lyster. Thanks also to Shona Doyle for logistical and moral support. I have been privileged to also work with Anne Hieber, to whom I am very grateful for the English revisions and constant support.

While conducting fieldwork in Brazil, several feminist activists provided me with interviews, made important comments on my project, and offered me total support. Thanks are due to Maria Angelica Lemos, Márcia Meireles, Fernanda Pompeu, Maria Lúcia da Silva, Maria Amélia de Almeida Teles, Dinalva Tavares, Criméia Alice Schmidt de Almeida, Telma Cavalheiro, Terezinha Gonzaga, Mônica Pitta, Marisa Fernandes, Rosana Zaiden, Sueli Carneiro, Tereza Verardo, Schuma Schumaher, and Maria Aparecida de Laia.

I have also benefited from an exchange of ideas and support from several Brazilian scholars and Brazilianists. In particular, I would like to thank feminist scholars Mariza Corrêa, Suely Kofes, Adriana Piscitelli, Miriam Grossi, Sandra Azerêdo, Maria Luíza Heilborn, Heleieth Saffioti, Sílvia Pimentel, Wânia Izumino, and Ana Cristina Sampaio. I am also indebted to socio-legal scholars, namely, José Eduardo Faria, Alberto do Amaral Júnior, Christina Ribas, and Boaventura de Sousa Santos. In the United States, I am grateful to David Lopez and especially James Green.

In addition to activists and scholars, I also received the support of several policewomen and complainants. I would like to express my great appreciation to those who gave me interviews and allowed me to observe their work. Very special thanks are due to Izilda Ferreira and Ivone de Freire for having welcomed my project unconditionally. I am deeply grateful to all of the female complainants who trusted me, gave me interviews, and agreed to expose their painful lives. To protect their confidentiality, I will not mention any of their names.

Thanks are also due to Daniele Gross Ramos for transcribing most of my interviews conducted from 1994 to 1996. Thanks to Fátima Guimarães for her secretarial assistance in Berkeley. Special thanks go to Adriana Carvalho for her invaluable research assistance in São Paulo from July 2001 to December 2003.

I would like to thank, as well, an anonymous Palgrave reviewer for extensive and helpful comments on an early draft of my manuscript. Thanks are also due to Palgrave assistant editor Gabriella Pearce for her invaluable suggestions and patience.

The following institutions funded the research and writing for the dissertation and later for the book. Conselho Nacional de Desenvolvimento Científico e Tecnológico (CNPq) awarded me a fellowship to carry out graduate studies at the University of California, Berkeley. The field research conducted in 1994 was made possible by a traveling grant from the Center for Latin American Studies, a Carol Hatch Ethnography Grant from the Department of Sociology, and a loan from the International House, all at the University of California at Berkeley. I was able to conduct further research in 1995 and 1996 thanks to a Human Rights Internship Grant from the Doreen B. Townsend Center for the Humanities, and a Humanities Graduate Research Grant from the Graduate Division, both at the University of California at Berkeley; as well as a Mellon Programs in Latin American Sociology Fellowship from the Andrew W. Mellon Foundation. The Mellon Fellowship, along with a Gender Paper Award from the Gender and Feminist Section of the Latin American Studies Association (LASA), supported the writing process of the dissertation as did financial aid for transcription and secretarial assistance from the Disabled Students' Program when I had repetitive stress injury, and a Summer Grant from the Human Rights Center, both at the University of California at Berkeley. From July of 2001 to December of 2003, the Faculty Development Fund of the University of San Francisco supported two research travels, research assistance in San Francisco and in São Paulo, English revisions, and all additional costs to complete this book. Special thanks are due to John Pinelli and the Dean of Arts and Sciences Jennifer Turpin.

Naturally, without the help, encouragement, and love of friends and family, this book would not exist. Among other friends who have sustained me in the United States, I would like to thank Tiana Arruda, Maisa Mendonça, Fátima Wildecy, Regina Camargo, Enid Karpeh, Millie Thayer, Rosa Oviedo, Carmen Lamha, Isabel Amorim, Cristina Ligneul, Bruni D'Avila, Julie Light, and Laura Bandala.

In the summer of 2004, I completed the last revisions on the manuscript while staying in the house of Fernanda Pompeu, Márcia Meireles, and Cida Santos. I am very grateful to their warm support. Thanks also, *mais que tudo*, to Teresa Henriques.

Among members of my family in the United States, I am grateful to my uncle Samuel Wallace Mac Dowell and my cousin Ana Myriam Mac Dowell. In São Paulo, special thanks go to my aunt Dolores Mac Dowell de Figueiredo. Thanks also to my cousins Marcos Mac Dowell de Figueiredo, Carlos Mac Dowell de Figueiredo, Samuel Mac Dowell de Figueiredo, Alexandre de Miranda Mac Dowell, Regina Mac Dowell de Figueiredo, and Isabel de Figueiredo, all of whom greatly facilitated my stay in São Paulo during different phases of the field research. My family in Recife has given me love and strength to follow my own path. I am especially grateful to my mother, Maria Anita Mac Dowell dos Santos, my sisters (Maria Anita, Maria Helena, Teresa, Lulu, Cristina, and Francina), my aunt Francina Fonseca dos Santos, my maternal grandmother, Maria Anita Amazonas Mac Dowell, to whom I dedicate this book, and my paternal grandmother, Helena Fonseca dos Santos, to whose memory this book is also dedicated.

Introduction

Last year in São Paulo, there were 5,470 sexual crimes, and during the first three months of this year, there were 1,400. Only 10 percent of women victims sought police assistance. That is why a women's police station was created. It is the first of its kind in the country. Everything in this police station is different. The environment is calm, and even the staff—from police clerks to the police delegate—are women.

—Police delegate Rosmary Corrêa (quoted on TV Manchete, August 6, 1985)[1]

Over the past ten years, the number of complaints of violence against women has increased dramatically. According to police, this is due to the expansion of women's police stations, which encourage victims to report. But policewomen say that the situation will only get better when there is no need for women's police stations. They say that by then discrimination against women will be over and women will be perfectly integrated into society, fully enjoying all their rights.

—TV Cultura (August 4, 1995)

In the late 1970s and mid-1980s, pressure from social movement actors, such as women's and feminist groups, forced the military regime, established by the 1964 military coup, to initiate a process of redemocratization in Brazil. At the time, diverse social movements mobilized to end the regime and to expand the rights of oppressed groups, including workers, women, blacks, Indians, homosexuals, and transvestites. This political and social climate allowed for the creation of the world's first women's police station in 1985.

The governors of several states where the opposition party Movimento Democrático Brasileiro (Brazilian Democratic Movement or MDB) had been victorious in the 1982 elections responded to the mass women's mobilizations and demands for the recognition of women's rights by creating all-female institutions, such as state councils on women's rights. In the state of São Paulo, in addition to the 1983 establishment of Conselho Estadual da Condição Feminina (State Council on the Feminine Condition or CECF) to design gender-based public policies, the then-governor, Franco Montoro (MDB), created the world's first all-female police station in 1985, named Delegacia de Polícia de Defesa da Mulher (Police Station in Defense of Women). Whereas feminists were appointed to run the CECF, female police officers were appointed to the new all-female police station, commonly known as *delegacia da mulher* (women's police station).

The creation of this unprecedented police station was a direct response to the feminist critique that policemen in regular police stations were sexist and did not take women's complaints of violence against them seriously. The new all-women's police station was inaugurated on August 6, 1985 in downtown São Paulo for the specific purpose of dealing with crimes against women, such as assault, battery, and rape.

The historical significance of this new women's police station in Brazilian culture and society should not be understated. Until very recently, Brazilian society condoned violence against women. In the realm of popular culture, for example, it is worth citing the popularity of the song, "Dá Nela" ("let her have it" or "beat her up") in the early 1930s. Composed by Ary Barroso at the end of 1929, "Dá Nela" brought fortune and fame to Barroso, who at the time was 26 years old and, although a promising composer for musical theater and radio in Rio de Janeiro, had just a handful of successful songs and no money. "Dá Nela" not only won first prize in the competition for the upcoming carnaval, awarding Barroso a fortune of 5 million *réis* (the Brazilian currency at the time), but it also became a huge hit in the 1930 carnaval. Barroso's song was inspired by an incident he had witnessed at Praça XV, a famous square in Rio during that time, where he saw a large crowd almost lynching a woman who had provoked and insulted other women who were waiting for the tram. Barroso used the words of a young man in the crowd, who shouted "dá nela," to write the refrain and the lyrics of his carnaval hit as follows:[2]

Esta mulher	This woman
Há muito tempo me provoca	Has been provoking me for a long time
Dá nela! Dá nela!	Let her have it! Let her have it!
É perigosa	She's dangerous
Fala mais que pata choca	She speaks more than a cackling chicken
Dá nela! Dá nela!	Let her have it! Let her have it!
Fala, língua de trapo	Speak, sewer mouth
Pois da tua boca	'Cause from your mouth
Eu não escapo	I don't escape
Agora deu para falar abertamente	Now she's taken to speaking openly
Dá nela! Dá nela!	Let her have it! Let her have it!
É intrigante	She's an intriguer
Tem veneno e mata a gente	She has poison and kills people
Dá nela! Dá nela!	Let her have it! Let her have it!

Until recently, it was not uncommon to hear Brazilian proverbs legitimizing and normalizing violence against women, such as *mulher gosta de apanhar* (women like to be beaten up), *tapa de amor não dói* (a love tap doesn't hurt), and *em briga de marido e mulher ninguém mete a colher* (fights between husband and wife are nobody's business). These proverbs can even be heard from some of the policewomen working for women's police stations. As a female police clerk expressed in an interview, "Many women are beaten up because they ask for it. I think she should take responsibility and defend herself. She was strong enough to speak up when she was provoking it. So she should fight back."[3] Actually, since colonial times, Brazilian law and justice system have legitimized, and even praised, violence against women as "normal" and deserved by the female victims who "provoke it." A case in point is the legal treatment of adulterous women and the courts' legitimization of wife-murder cases, so-called crimes of passion (see Corrêa 1981; Americas Watch Committee 1991a).

Prior to gaining independence in 1822, Brazil was under the rule of Portuguese colonial law, which allowed a man to kill his adulterous wife and her lover but did not allow the wife to kill her adulterous husband (Corrêa 1981). The first post-independence Brazilian Penal Code, enacted in 1830, revoked this rule; however, the belief that a man could legitimately kill his adulterous wife remained accepted by the dominant culture. The Republican Penal Code of 1890 introduced an exemption from criminal responsibility for those who committed a crime "under a state of total perturbation of the senses and intelligence" (quoted in Americas Watch Committee 1991a, 20). This exemption became the seed for defense attorneys' construction of the "legitimate honor defense" argument in wife-murder cases. Defense attorneys have argued that their clients lost their "sanity momentarily" due to a "strong emotion" caused by the behavior of their adulterous wives. Until very recently, juries accepted this argument to justify the acquittal of wife-murderers (Corrêa 1981; Americas Watch Committee 1991a).

During the Estado Novo, declared by President Getúlio Vargas in 1937, a new Brazilian Penal Code was enacted in 1940. Still in effect today, this code kept "strong emotion" as an attenuation clause to justify the reduction of prison sentences in cases of homicide (see Article 121, Paragraph 1 of the 1940 Brazilian Penal Code). Drawing on this clause, defense attorneys have continued to use the "legitimate defense of honor" argument. Thanks to numerous protests and campaigns organized by Brazilian feminist activists, in 1991 the Brazilian Superior Tribunal of Justice (STJ) decided that the "legitimate defense of honor" argument could no longer be argued. Nevertheless, prison sentences for wife-murderers have hardly been enforced and feminists still must mobilize over wife-murder cases

(Americas Watch Committee 1991a; União de Mulheres de São Paulo 1995; Centro pela Justiça e o Direito Internacional [CEJIL] et al. 2003). The STJ has also contradicted its own decision to disallow the "legitimate defense of honor" argument (Macaulay 2002). In addition, to date, adultery is still a crime (see Article 240 of the Brazilian Penal Code).[4]

For all of these reasons, it is unquestionable that the birth of the world's first women's police station represents an unprecedented recognition by the Brazilian state that violence against women is a crime, a significant advance in the field of women's rights. It created a space where violence against women would be registered, thus encouraging victims of violence to report, as the media's coverage of both the inauguration and the ten-year anniversary of the first women's police station attests. Moreover, the establishment of this women's police station represents a substantive victory for the women's and feminist movements in bringing a gender-based agenda into the state and the police force, and, more specifically, in successfully pressing the state to criminalize an issue hitherto considered "private" and even "normal" (Alvarez 1990). The new women's police station has also contributed to the advancement of a "gendered citizenship," a form of citizenship that values social differences among women and men, granting both of them equality before the law and full access to political, economic, social, and civil citizenship rights (see Walby 1994).

Although feminists did not have the initial idea of creating a women's police station and did not assume that policewomen would automatically treat women clients better than policemen, they supported Montoro's initiative. Acclaimed by feminists of the São Paulo State Council on the Feminine Condition (CECF), most feminist non-governmental organizations (hereafter NGOs), and the female population in general, the first women's police station became a model for the founding of similar stations in São Paulo and throughout Brazil. Today there are 125 women's police stations in the state of São Paulo alone and, as of June 2003, 339 women's police stations exist throughout Brazil (AGENDE and CLADEM 2003). Inspired by this Brazilian phenomenon, eight countries in Latin America have created women's police stations (Corral 1993; Feijóo and Nari 1994; Chinchilla 1994; Nelson 1996; Jubb and Izumino 2002; Santos 1999a).[5] European countries, such as Spain and Portugal, have also established women's desks within regular police stations or some version of women's police stations (Station 1989). In South Asia, hundreds of women's police stations have been created in the main metropolises of India and Pakistan (*San Francisco Chronicle* 1993; War against Rape 2003; Oherald.com 2003).

Nevertheless, research has shown that, as is common in other police stations, very few cases registered in the women's police stations actually go to court (Jubb and Izumino 2002). The infrastructure and quality of services in the women's police stations are also inadequate (Conselho Nacional dos Direitos da Mulher 2001; Massuno 2002; Amaral et al. 2001). Like other police stations, the women's police stations, though part of the state executive power, are a judiciary police auxiliary to the Brazilian criminal justice system. Police officers working in these stations do not patrol and do not wear uniforms. They only have the authority to register criminal complaints and conduct a police investigation (*inquérito policial*), a preliminary administrative proceeding that is sent to the district attorney, who ultimately decides whether or not to file criminal charges (*denúncia*).

According to the legislation on the first women's police station, all police officers working in this kind of police station, as well as the victims, should be women (Decree No. 23,769, August 6, 1985). While the legislation did not explicitly refer to the expression "violence against women," the creation of the first women's police station was aimed at criminalizing and preventing the escalation of violence against women in Brazilian society. In June of 2004, almost twenty years later, the Brazilian National Congress approved a new legislation explicitly criminalizing "domestic violence" and establishing a penalty of detention of six months to one year for this type of crime (Law No. 10,886, June 17, 2004). However, complainants who seek the assistance of police officers in regular as well as women's police stations are not necessarily interested in the criminalization of offenses. Complainants are often poor or come from working-class backgrounds and posses real fears of the police. Despite these fears, complainants utilize the police to resolve civil and criminal grievances, also in part due to the fact that they lack access to the justice system.[6] Complainants use police stations as an arena of alternative dispute resolution, invoking the authority of police officers to mediate their grievances (see Oliveira 1984; Kant de Lima 1994; Muniz 1994). Police end up acting as if they were judges, and they arbitrate arbitrary "sentences." Even during the military regime, lower segments of the population would seek police stations to solve their civil and criminal grievances (see, for example, Oliveira 1984).

In addition to being used like other police stations and sharing similar problems faced by regular police stations, research shows that the women's police stations are also confronted with gender-specific tasks and dilemmas. For example, policewomen and women's police stations continue to be discriminated against by the São Paulo Police Department as well as other police departments throughout Brazil (Conselho Nacional dos Direitos da Mulher 2001; Silva n.d.; Silva 1992; Machado n.d.; Jubb and Izumino 2002; Massuno 2002; Santos 1999a; Hautzinger 1997). The number of women's police stations in the north and northeast regions is insufficient, forcing victims to travel long distances to get to the stations (Amaral et al. 2001). When they do arrive, complainants, especially those reporting cases of conjugal violence, do not necessarily seek the criminalization of their abusers and often request the withdrawal of their complaints in the course of the investigation (Muniz 1994; Brandão 1998; Santos 1999a). Police academies have not included gender-specific training for police officers in general and policewomen in particular into their curriculum (Conselho Nacional dos Direitos da Mulher 2001; Silva n.d.; Silva 1992; Machado n.d.; Jubb and Izumino 2002; Massuno 2002; Santos 1999a). As a result of lack of gender-based training, not all policewomen perceive violence against women as a serious and "real" crime; instead, they tend to emphasize family reconciliation in cases of domestic violence rather than the protection of the victims and the search for justice. Many policewomen also do not necessarily ally themselves with feminist organizations, whose activities and values originally inspired the creation of the women's police stations (Nelson 1996; Santos 1999a, 1999b, 2004; Conselho Nacional dos Direitos da Mulher 2001; Jubb and Izumino 2002).[7]

Existing research tends, however, to focus on micro-level analyses of the women's police stations, neglecting to examine how macro-political processes shape the social interactions between feminists, policewomen, and complainants. In addition, most researchers homogenize the interests and identities of each of these actors, therefore failing to theorize the complex and often contradictory relationship between and among these different groups of women. Finally, existing research has not further examined women's rights from a multicultural perspective on gendered citizenship and justice, and has overlooked the interconnections of race, class, gender, and/or sexual orientation as the basis for granting women the right to live without violence and to claim the enforcement of this right through the state (for exceptions, see Nelson 1996; Santos 1999a, 1999b, 2000).

Feminist theorizing of women's movements, gender, and the state in Latin America has addressed the question of the relationship between women and the state in illuminating ways. Since Sonia Alvarez's (1990) groundbreaking book on feminist politics in the transition to democracy in Brazil, a new and expanding literature on the state and gender in Latin America has emerged. Building on Alvarez's historical and politically contingent (not essentialist) approach to the state, there is a consensus in the literature that the state is not a monolith and does not have predetermined, essential intentions regarding women or gender issues. Moving away from essentialism and structuralism, feminist scholars now conceptualize the state in Latin America as a "differentiated set of institutions" and a "site of struggle" both representing and reconstructing gender relations (Alexander 1991; Waylen 1996; Rai 1996; Schild 1998; Alvarez 1999–2000; Santos 1999a; Molyneux 2000).

Feminist scholars explain the relationship between the state and women as "evolving and dialectic," contingent upon the historical and political conjuncture (Alvarez 1990; Waylen 1996; Rai 1996; Lievesley 1996; Metoyer 2000; Molyneux 2000). The "women's policy machineries" created within the context of redemocratization in Latin America since the 1980s are good examples of how the state can foster both social control and social change in women's lives, depending on the political conjuncture. Scholars have shown, however, that these feminist institutions are fraught with contradictions. In addition to their limited power to influence other sectors of the state, they may disarticulate the women's movement by depending entirely on key women organizers who become constrained by their positions within the state (Alvarez 1997; Schumaher and Vargas 1993; Friedman 1998; Schild 1998).[8] That is why Alvarez (1990; 1997) aptly recommends that feminists develop multiple strategies to work both inside and outside of the state. Molyneux (2000, 67) also points out that the success of feminists in government depends on "strong linkages with those outside." In addition, "The degree of commitment to democracy more generally, the sympathy governments express toward women's issues, and the general direction of policy depend crucially on the party in power" (Molyneux 2000, 66).

Although showing that the state is not a monolith and does not have pre-established, essential intentions regarding women, this new literature has not completely moved away from a macro-level analysis.[9] It is certainly true that the contradictory relations between feminists, policewomen, and their clients in São Paulo are situated within the context of changing state–society relations during the political transition to democracy in Brazil. However, even under governments controlled by the same party, policewomen have held conflicting interests and divergent positions with regard to feminism. As Nelson (1996) asserts, these contradictory relations are the result of the women's police stations being located within the coercive and masculinist arm of the state. Feminists have also diverged among themselves on the meaning of violence against women. And battered women have interacted with the women's police stations in contradictory ways, according to their specific needs and interests, which are shaped by gender, race, and social class.

Therefore, by positing the relationship between the state and women as a function of the political regime or the party in power, feminist state theorists overlook the particular culture of the specific institutions with which women interact. They also ignore the micro-level changes in civil society and the day-to-day interactions between state actors and their clients. Finally, like students of the women's police stations, feminist state theorists have not paid sufficient attention to the interconnections of gender, race, class, and sexual orientation and how they influence the practices and discourses of both state and civil society actors regarding the construction of gendered citizenship and justice (for exceptions, see Alexander 1991; Santos 1999a, 2000).

This book seeks to fill in these gaps in feminist state theory and studies of women's police stations in Latin America by examining the political and social processes shaping the dynamics of the complex and often contradictory relationship between women and the state from both a macro and micro perspective, using the fascinating and unique case study of women's police stations in São Paulo. This study also serves to shed light on the contributions and contradictions of institutionalizing a gender-based agenda through the creation of an all-female space within the repressive arm of the state.

Throughout this book, I explore the construction of gendered citizenship and the processes of engendering justice as a result of the discourses and interactions between specific social actors, such as feminists, policewomen, and complainants. By looking at the interests and identities of these actors and how they relate to each other from both a macro and micro, as well as political and historical perspective, I contend that we can better uncover the interacting forces and processes shaping the contradictions and the changing dynamics of state–society relations, therefore gaining a better understanding of the possibilities and barriers for the full exercising of citizenship rights in Latin America today.

Further, I argue that the state is neither simply a faceless "complex apparatus" nor a "network of contested power relations," but rather an actor in its own right (though multifaceted and contradictory), actively participating in the construction and contestation of hegemonic ideologies in society. Although the state tends to legitimize the ideology of dominant groups in society, different sectors within the state can reinforce diverse hegemonic and counter-hegemonic ideologies, precisely because agents of the state have multiple and contradictory interests as both state actors and social actors embedded in a particular political, economic, and cultural formation.

Figure i.1 represents the relationships that form the core of this book. By "civil society" I mean a sphere of social relations between the economy and the state, composed of voluntary associations, social movements, and NGOs.[10] Figure i.1 also shows that women's movements, as well as feminist and women's NGOs, are part of civil society, whereas the women's

Civil society   State

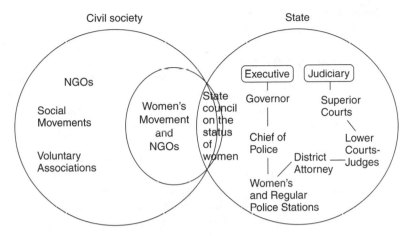

Figure i.1   Civil society and state

police stations are part of the state. By "women's movements" and "women's NGOs" I mean a range of women's activities organizations, grassroots and non-governmental, that are run by women to improve women's living conditions. Although participants in these various women's movements and NGOs may also participate in traditional political groups, such as political parties, the movements and NGOs themselves operate outside of formal politics. In addition, participants in women's movements and women's NGOs do not necessarily identify themselves as "feminist" and may come from various class, racial, and sexual orientation backgrounds. They must have a focus on gender-specific issues, at times intersecting with class, race, and/or sexual orientation-specific issues. Gender-specific issues are those defined in terms of rights of women as women. Such identity may be claimed in conjunction with other forms of consciousness and social categories. For instance, some women's organizations may mobilize around the protection of women (in general) against violence, or the protection of wives, prostitutes, working-class and poor women, black women, lesbians, and so on.

It is important to note that the separation between civil society and the state is not clearly demarcated. Depending on changing political, economic and cultural contexts, this separation is more or less blurred. Political institutions such as state councils, created during the democratization process in the mid-1980s, clearly illustrate that sectors of the state can be embedded in civil society. Figure i.1 shows that the São Paulo State Council on the Feminine Condition (CECF)—staffed by members of women's NGOs, women activists, and government officials—is part of the state while being also embedded in civil society.

Throughout this book, I use the case study of the women's police stations to examine the following questions:

(1) Regarding the dynamics of the relationship between the state and organized, collective actors of civil society, how have policewomen related to feminists, and vice-versa, since the creation of the first women's police station in 1985? What are the social and political forces shaping the relationship between these two groups of women?

(2) How do the discourses and practices of feminist activists, policewomen, and their clients contribute to the construction of gendered citizenship? How does the discourse on gendered citizenship rights (in particular, the right of access to justice) relate to other discourses on citizenship rights based not only on gender, but also on race, class, and sexual orientation? What do policewomen and feminists consider as a legitimate complaint of violence against women? What is the meaning of "violence against women" for feminists, policewomen, and complainants? Does the feminist conception of violence against women take into account not only gender, but also race, class, and sexual orientation as a legitimate basis for women to complain about violence against women? Does the discourse on gendered citizenship incorporate differences not only between men and women but also among women?

(3) Regarding the relationship between the state and civil society actors using the services provided by the state, how do policewomen and female complainants relate to each other in the women's police stations? What are the factors shaping the discursive practices of policewomen with respect to women's complaints? What do policewomen learn from complainants? How do complainants use of the women's police stations? What are their interests and needs? What do they learn from their interactions with the women's police stations?

In sum, how have actors in civil society engendered the state and the justice system? Has the state engendered civil society? If so, has the reciprocal engendering of state and society led to the formation of a discourse on citizenship rights that benefits all women, regardless of their diverse social, racial, economic, cultural, and sexual positions?

Drawing on extensive interviews as well as participant observation and archival research, I argue that through the creation of women's police stations the Brazilian state and society have engendered each other in complex and contradictory ways.[11] Feminists, policewomen, and women clients are heterogeneous groups, having multiple and often conflicting interests. The relationships between these groups of women continue to evolve not only because of the political conjuncture or the political party in power. They also have evolved due to interactions between the political conjuncture, the hegemonic masculinist police culture, developments in the feminist discourse on violence against women, and the impact of the contact policewomen sustain with women clients, all resulting in the construction of a contradictory gendered citizenship.

The hegemonic feminist discourse on violence is contradictory because it defines "gender violence" (for example, conjugal violence and sexual harassment) as the privileged forms of violence against women, therefore silencing other forms of violence against women that are defined not only on the basis of gender, but also social class, race, and sexual orientation. Within such an exclusive and narrow framework of violence against women, multiple forms of violence against prostitutes, black women, and lesbians, for example, are less likely to gain legitimacy in the state or to be taken seriously by legal professionals and police officers in the justice system. Had the woman who inspired Barroso's song "Dá Nela" been lynched, the hegemonic feminist discourse on violence would not consider her case a legitimate complaint to be registered and investigated by the women's police stations.

Policewomen's discourses and practices regarding violence against women are also contradictory. They legitimize the hegemonic feminist discourse on gender violence by considering conjugal violence the paradigmatic case of violence against women. At the same time, they also undermine this discourse through the belief among many policewomen that conjugal violence is not a "real" crime.

Complainants' approaches to the women's police stations are also contradictory. Most complainants are battered women from working-class backgrounds, and many are also poor migrant women from the Northeast. They do not necessarily seek the criminalization of their (male) abusers and use the women's police stations according to their gender and class-based interests and needs. They rely on the force of the police to gain some power in the domestic sphere and in their communities. But police violence, not law enforcement, is what they expect policewomen to exercise in order to help them "fix up" their conjugal relationship. While they develop a gender identity and a sense of women's rights when they go to the women's police stations, they also undermine the authority of the police due to reasons related to gender, class, and culture. The continued and intimate relationship with their partners, the emphasis on the family and community, not on the individual, as the primary subjects of rights, lack of knowledge about the law and legal procedures in police stations, and the fear of police violence against their family and community are all contributing factors shaping complainants' reluctance to pursue a criminal case.

Therefore, this book shows that the discourses and practices of feminists, policewomen, and complainants in the women's police stations have engendered justice in contradictory ways, both challenging and reinforcing hierarchical values and structures as well as the dominant masculinist culture that pervades Brazilian society, state and justice system. To be more inclusive, women's rights must rest on a broad construction of women's interests taking into account social differences and inequalities based not only on gender, but also on race, class, sexuality, and culture.

The book is organized into five chapters and a conclusion, as follows:

Chapter 1, "The Birth of the World's First Women's Police Station," examines the political and historical context in which feminist activists and state managers negotiated the 1985 creation of the first women's police station in São Paulo, showing how gender and politics interacted and how both actors had their interests reciprocally transformed in the process of defining the function, structure, jurisdiction, and scope of this unprecedented institution in Brazil and in the world.

Chapter 2, "Engendering Policewomen's Interests and Identities," discusses, from both a macro and micro perspective, the political and social processes shaping the interests and identities of policewomen and their complex and evolving relationships with feminists, illustrated by their multiple positions of explicit alliance, opposition, and ambiguous alliance regarding feminists and feminism since the creation of the first women's police station in 1985.

Chapter 3, "Feminist Debates over the Meaning of Violence against Women," addresses the feminist politicization of violence against women and the feminist debates over the meaning of violence against women since the late 1970s, showing how the hegemonic feminist discourse has contributed to the construction of a contradictory gendered citizenship that does not take into account the interests and needs of diverse groups of women.

Chapter 4, "Constructing Crimes and Engendering a Contradictory Citizenship," examines the practices of policewomen in the women's police stations, how they construct crimes in the process of applying the law to victims' complaints, how they approach different types of complaints, and what they consider to be a legitimate case of violence against women. Like feminists, though for different reasons, policewomen's practices are also contradictory, because they privilege cases of conjugal violence while also undermining the hegemonic feminist discourse on violence against women.

Chapter 5, "En*gender*ing Battered Women's Sense of Rights," focuses on the experiences of battered women who take their complaints of conjugal violence to the women's police stations, and shows that these complainants' practices are also contradictory. While they gain a gender identity and a sense of women's rights thanks to their contact with policewomen in the women's police stations, they also construct a form of gendered citizenship in their own terms, according to their interests based on gender, class, and culture, and their practices and ideologies depart from the liberal and bourgeoning feminist conceptions of gendered citizenship rights.

In the Conclusion, "Toward a more Inclusive and Grounded Feminist Approach to the State and Gendered Citizenship," I summarize the major conclusions in each chapter and, drawing on the lessons from this book, I suggest some directions for future research and public policies regarding the recognition and enforcement of women's rights, approached from a more inclusive and grounded feminist perspective.

I

The Birth of the World's First Women's Police Station

This is a successful idea. After one year, the police station in defense of women achieved credibility and respect. It has spread all over the neighborhoods and cities in the state of São Paulo. The challenge of running it for the first time was given to this 36-year-old woman [the screen shows police delegate Rosmary Corrêa], who has been working with the police for fifteen years. Throughout the past year, Rosmary was in charge of the delicate task of breaking down the walls that hide violence against women, investigating crimes that not too long ago only concerned husbands and wives.

—TV Cultura (August 6, 1986)

On August 6, 1985, the São Paulo Police Department attracted local, national and even international media attention for reasons other than the usual police corruption, police violence against street kids, or human rights abuses in jails. The media buzz centered on the Delegacia de Polícia de Defesa da Mulher (Police Station in Defense of Women), a specialized police station run exclusively by female police officers, established by the São Paulo state government solely to investigate crimes of violence against women. Created in the context of Brazil's transition from military to civilian rule, this unique institution was made possible through the process of redemocratization. In the mid-1970s, the military-authoritarian regime, in power since the 1964 military coup, had been forced by organized sectors of the civil society to initiate a process of political liberalization known as *Abertura Política* (Political Opening). In the early 1980s, elections for state governors and the redemocratization process opened up new opportunities for feminist activists and other social movement actors to directly participate in designing public policy and legal reform. This culminated in the creation of women's "machineries," such as women's state councils and women's police stations (Alvarez 1990).

Despite Brazil's and specifically the police's dominant *machista* culture, the first women's police station came about in 1985 because of the political conjuncture that allowed feminists to successfully demand of the state to treat violence against women as a serious, public crime. The burgeoning feminist and women's movements effectively argued that the police, almost always men, rarely prosecuted cases of physical and sexual abuse of women. These movements were not seeking the establishment of a women's police station, but by creating an all-female police station to deal with crimes against women, the São Paulo state government responded to feminist claims with the unprecedented recognition that violence against women is a crime (Alvarez 1990). With this action, the state expanded women's rights by redefining an issue hitherto viewed as "private," even "normal," and also created new jobs for women on the police force. Moreover, the first women's police station was judged a success by the thousands of women who became encouraged to report the violence that they had been suffering in silence. By bringing women into the police force and by recognizing violence against women as a crime, state managers in São Paulo claimed both to foster democratization and to provide female complainants with a safe space in which to denounce violence without facing prejudice from sexist policemen.

Although many feminists feared the police—especially because of their experience with the repressive period of military-authoritarianism—most of them embraced the idea of establishing a women's police station. They actively engaged in the debates over the jurisdiction, goals, and functioning of this new institution. While they agreed that policewomen would be better than policemen, they also emphasized that, in itself, being a woman was not enough to understand the problem of violence against women. Furthermore, feminists viewed criminalization as a limited solution to end this problem. They approached violence against women from a holistic and complex perspective, conceiving this issue as a multifaceted social, cultural, economic, psychological, and criminal problem with roots in the male-dominated structure of society. For these reasons, they struggled to change the law and shape the legal culture of those responsible for the women's police station. They also demanded that the state create other services to female victims, such as shelters and psychological, social, and legal assistance.

Despite these demands by feminists, public policy on violence against women focused on the multiplication of women's police stations without providing police officers with specialized training and without the establishment of the additional services. Given this picture, was the first women's police station an instrument to "co-opt" feminist movement actors, or was this all-female police station a positive legal change to truly represent women's interests?

In this chapter, I reflect on this question by looking at the process through which the world's first women's police station was created. I argue that the establishment of the first women's police station—rather than simply "co-opting" feminist movement actors, or "representing" women's interests as if they were not socially constructed—illustrates well how "politics constructs gender and gender constructs politics" (Scott 1988b, 46). I look at the birth of the first women's police station as a historical process of struggles both constitutive of gender and politics, as well as transformative of the state and society. I show that state managers and feminists came together to foster democracy and to challenge Brazil's dominant legal ideology of neutrality and the masculinist police culture. The interests of state managers and feminists conflicted and transformed each other in the process of negotiating the jurisdiction, scope, and functioning of the first women's police station.

Despite the alliance between state managers and feminists, the creation of the women's police station alone was not sufficient to challenge the masculinist police culture that informed the attitudes of both male and female police officers. In fact, the government's "separatist strategy" further exposed this culture and revealed the contradictions of institutionalizing a gender-based agenda through the creation of an all-female institution within the repressive arm of the state.

The Context of "Participatory Democracy"

In March of 1964, Brazil experienced a military coup that established a military-authoritarian regime that lasted for the next twenty years. Based on the doctrine of "National Security and Development" (Couto e Silva 1981), the military regime suspended direct elections for president, governors, and senators; made ineffective the legislature; banned existing political parties, imposing a bi-party political system; suspended constitutional rights; censored the press, the arts, and academia; as well as persecuted, imprisoned, tortured, and killed whoever opposed the regime. Those who could escape left the country in exile. Within this period of political terror in Brazil, sectors of civil society organized resistance and opposition movements.[1]

Various social movements flourished throughout the 1970s in response to increasing military repression, including the students' movement, the movement for amnesty, the workers' movement, the movement against scarcity, the women's movement, the black movement, and the environmental movement.[2] Pressures from these movements and their international allies, as well as divisions among military leaders, instigated a decrease in repression in the late 1970s, leading to the *Abertura Política* (Political Opening). Censorship gradually decreased, amnesty of political prisoners was granted, activists in exile returned to the country, and elections for mayors and state assemblies were restored.[3]

The 1980s brought a period of political, legal, and institutional reform in order to restore democracy in the country. Elections for governors, national congress members, and the president were restored. The focus for social movements shifted from fighting the regime to participation in the redemocratization process from both inside and outside of the state. Diverse social movements lobbied to influence the redrafting of the new democratic Brazilian Constitution in 1988.[4] This constitution ensured new rights for children, adolescents, women, blacks, and consumers, leading to the enactment of new progressive legislation in the following years.[5]

In 1983, the opposition party to the military leadership, Partido do Movimento Democrático Brasileiro (PMDB), gained control of several state governments, including São Paulo. Feminist activists who worked in support of this party in the 1982 electoral campaign were offered the opportunity to work for the newly established women's "machineries," such as the national and state councils on the status of women (Alvarez 1990, 1997). The PMDB won control of the federal government in 1985, thus allowing President José Sarney to create the Conselho Nacional dos Direitos da Mulher (National Council on Women's Rights, or CNDM).[6] Sarney staffed the CNDM with intellectual and middle-class feminists recruited from governmental and non-governmental organizations (NGOs). These councils were asked to design public policy on women's issues in order to promote gender equality in the country.

In the state of São Paulo, the newly elected PMDB governor, Franco Montoro, initiated institutional reforms based on principles of "participatory democracy," which called on social movement actors to work within the state in new hybrid state-society institutions where they would both design public policy and legitimate state authority. In September 1983, Montoro created the State Council on the Feminine Condition (CECF).[7] The CECF was composed of 17 mostly white, middle-class, educated feminists. Nine of them represented civil society, including feminist academics and movement participants; and eight were state actors recruited from the existing state departments of education, health, social welfare, labor, culture, and justice.

It is worth noting that the councils were—and still are—limited to an advisory role, depending on the State Department of Civil Affairs for technical and financial assistance. They did not have their own budget and could not administer any public policy, forcing some feminists, such as sociologist Heleieth Saffioti, who actively participated in the creation of the CECF, to argue for an independent state department rather than a council. Many feminists were already suspicious of the state, fearing co-option of the feminist movement.[8] However, while this and other councils served to legitimate Montoro's "participatory" rhetoric, feminists had been given a real opportunity to influence new state programs and institutions.

Regarding the issue of violence and public security, Michel Temer, secretary of public security during Montoro's term, recalled that:

> The major challenge of Montoro's administration was to reconcile public security with a democratic government elected by the people, having a dialogue with social movements. Montoro's administration was a real participatory democracy, stimulating participation of various social groups in all state departments, especially in the department of public security.[9]

In relation to the police, Temer identified Montoro's politics with "the restructuring of the police, austerity, and originality of ideas."[10] Governed by these values, Montoro created new programs and institutions inside the police department such as Operaçao Povo ("The People's Operation"), a project that resulted in the intense policing of poor neighborhoods located in the periphery of the city of São Paulo; the police station for the protection of authorship rights; the police station for the protection of consumer rights; and finally the police station in defense of women.

According to Temer, these initiatives were responses to complaints of civil society actors. In the case of violence against women, for example, "many women's groups used to complain about how policemen were treating female victims of violence."[11] These complaints were the impetus for his idea to create a police station specializing in crimes against women. But what exactly did feminists demand from the state in relation to the issue of violence against women?

The Feminist Politicization of Violence against Women

The politicization of violence against women in Brazilian society became possible due to the emergence of the second-wave women's and feminist movements in the 1970s.[12] Brazilian feminist groups, composed mostly of middle-class, white, educated women, grew out of Leftist struggles to fight the military-authoritarian regime, class domination in general, and patriarchy in particular (Alvarez 1990, 1997). Coming from a Marxist tradition, these new feminist groups built successful coalitions with the thousands of grassroots (or "popular") organizations originally established by working-class, mostly northeastern migrants, *pardas* (mixed) and black women in the urban periphery of large cities such as São Paulo (Alvarez 1990 and 1997; Teles 1993).

There were important class and race-related differences regarding the needs and interests of feminist groups and popular women's organizations. While access to public services, such as childcare, transportation, education, and sanitation were major concerns of the latter, the decriminalization of abortion was one of the major concerns of the former. Feminist activists were also divided among themselves over forging a "feminist identity in the singular" through maintaining their "autonomy" from political parties, male-dominated unions, progressive sectors of the Catholic Church, and other resistance movements in the Left (Alvarez 1998, 297). Despite these differences, violence against women was viewed as a common issue crossing class, racial, and ideological boundaries. It was one of the most important issues for all activists, bringing these groups of women together (Grossi 1988).

In the late 1970s, feminist activists focused their attention on cases of wife-murder—not rare in Brazilian society—and organized numerous protests and campaigns on the issue.[13] The nationwide slogan Quem Ama Não Mata (One who loves doesn't kill) emerged from their successful mobilization to publicize wife-murder trials, allowing the feminist movement to gain visibility, political strength and respect in the eyes of politicians, the media, and society at large.

In the early 1980s, feminist groups called SOS-Mulher were created all over the country to provide social, psychological, and legal services to female victims of domestic violence. These groups also aimed to attract society's attention to a problem that, at the time, was considered not only private but "normal." Feminists viewed criminalization as one step among others to end violence against women.

Founded in 1981, the now extinct SOS-Mulher of São Paulo served approximately 1,500 women during two years. Most clients of SOS-Mulher were battered women who complained not only about their male abusers, but also about the humiliation they suffered while trying to file their complaints before policemen in regular police stations. As noted by Esther Toledo, then member of SOS-Mulher: "Usually, they [police officers] minimize the problem, advising women to go home, to dress well, and to cook something tasty."[14] Other feminists and women's organizations dealing with violence against women also complained about sexism in police stations. "The lack of a bulletin of occurrence [crime report] is a constant barrier in dealing with the problem," said Márcia Setti, member of Casa da Mulher do Centro, an NGO providing legal services to battered women in São Paulo.[15]

The issue of violence against women was one of the priorities of the CECF. Based on the experience of the women's and feminist movements, feminists of the CECF did not demand that the state created a women's police station. Instead, the CECF proposed a public policy to provide female victims with "integrated services." These included: 1) further politicization of violence against women, coordination of educational campaigns, and consciousness-raising; 2) creation of shelters and new institutions to provide legal and psychological services to victims of domestic and sexual violence; 3) changes in sexist judicial and police institutions, such as anti-sexism training of police officers, as well as hiring of social workers in every police station; 4) reform of sexist legislation;[16] 5) increasing research on violence against women; and 6) incorporation of women's movement's concerns into a gender-based public policy agenda. The CECF conceived of violence against women as a social problem expressed through physical, psychological, and/or sexual abuse. Feminists of the CECF argued that this issue should be addressed from social, psychological, and criminal perspectives. Furthermore, the CECF voiced the concerns of the women's movement by claiming that it was necessary to raise female victims' consciousness.[17]

Based on this agenda, the CECF recommended the creation of the Centro de Orientação Jurídica e Encaminhamento à Mulher (Center for Legal Orientation and Guidance for Women or COJE). Coordinated by the CECF and the Procuradoria Geral do Estado (State Department of Public Attorneys), COJE was inaugurated in March 1984 and was staffed by feminist attorneys and psychologists, who provided psychological and legal advice to battered women on a volunteer basis.[18] COJE was an attempt to give visibility to domestic violence and provide victims with "integrated services," as stated in its first bulletin: "The problem of domestic violence has been treated as a private matter. . . . Although there are several public services providing legal advice, a new service was necessary to deal specifically with women's issues" (Centro de Orientação Jurídica e Encaminhamento à Mulher-COJE 1984).

How victims viewed themselves was an important part of the problem. "Rather than seeing themselves as victims, they feel guilty when they reveal that they have been beaten up," attested the psychologist of COJE.[19] Maria de Fátima Galvanese, member of the CECF in 1984, also expressed that "the major problem in cases of violence against women is lack of adequate services in regular police stations, where it is a common practice to ridicule female complainants who look for protection therein" (quoted in *Contigo*, August 5, 1985).

Therefore, besides demanding social and psychological services, feminists had to force police officers and state managers to recognize violence against women as crime. As journalist Marta Góes explained at the time: "Not all battered women manage to articulate their experience, and even those who do it rarely live without painful memories. That is why some people [feminists] are interested in disseminating the idea that battering is a crime, not a joke" (quoted in *Afinal*, July 23, 1985). Feminist lawyer Zulaiê Cobra, who volunteered to assist women clients of SOS-Mulher and Casa da Mulher do Centro, insisted then that "there must be a consensus that battering is a crime" (quoted in *Afinal*, July 23, 1985).

The state finally publicly recognized that violence against women is a crime in the mid-1980s and also acknowledged the rampant sexism in regular police stations. This unprecedented public recognition was catalyzed by the Montoro administration's announcement of the creation of a Delegacia de Defesa da Mulher (Police Station in Defense of Women). The CECF started then to emphasize criminalization (Conselho Estadual da Condição Feminina de São Paulo 1986b, 1986c). Apart from COJE there was no other governmental organization at the time dealing specifically with the issue of violence against women. COJE's staff was composed of feminist officials working for other state departments. At COJE they provided services on a volunteer basis, spending a few hours per week advising victims of battering or women facing conjugal crises. As these services were offered on a volunteer basis, COJE simply functioned as a referral center and soon lost its initial vigor, and was deactivated in 1987. The first women's police station, though, was able to serve many more women than COJE and SOS-Mulher groups. Whereas 762 women were served by COJE in the course of nine months, 500 women waited in line to initiate complaints the day after the first women's police station was inaugurated. Given this context, the feminists' emphasis on criminalization was unavoidable.

The creation of the first women's police station was intensively covered by the media. At the time, the daily *Folha de S. Paulo*, for example, declared that "sexual violence is a major form of violence against women. It has been hidden due to sexism" (*Folha de S. Paulo*, July 3, 1985). This newspaper also reported the work of feminist organizations in assisting victims of "this most brutal side of oppression suffered by women" (*Folha de S. Paulo*, July 3, 1985). In response to the feminist politicization of violence against women, the redemocratization process prompted an unprecedented legal change in Brazil, giving birth to a new crime. Violence against women was not a "private" matter anymore: it concerned not only husbands and wives, but also society and state authorities—especially the police. The state was also giving birth to a new institution, unique in the world.

Negotiating the Creation of the First Women's Police Station

Who Had the Idea?
Then Secretary of Public Security Michel Temer claims an all-female police station was his proposal in response to the complaints he had received from women's groups about sexism in regular police stations. Temer also found inspiration in the success of other specialized police stations created by Montoro in 1984.[20] Even though the media and some state officials believed that the CECF or the women's movement had made the initial proposal, all feminists I interviewed confirmed that it had been Temer's initiative.[21] As pointed out by Cida Medrado, coordinator of the CECF's Commission on Violence Against Women in 1985: "We never thought of a women's police station. Instead, we recommended the creation of COJE, and that every police station had social workers to attend the needs of female victims."[22]

In the beginning of 1985, after being acclaimed by the Brazilian Association of Writers for designing the police station for the protection of authorship rights, Temer realized that "there should be female police delegates, female police clerks, and female detective inspectors attending the needs of women." As he recalls:

> I left that reception with a lot of enthusiasm. The next day I called the chief of police, asking him to sketch a decree proposing the creation of a police station run exclusively by female police officers. Armed with that proposal, I went to talk with Governor Montoro a few days later. Also excited, he signed the decree creating the first police station in defense of women.[23]

Montoro did not sign the decree immediately. Consuming six months before finally signing the decree, the discussion and negotiation between state managers and feminists built both alliances and conflicts.

Fighting over the Jurisdiction of the First Women's Police Station
In Brazil's legal tradition, police stations are part of the civil police (as opposed to the military police), functioning to help the judiciary—not a jury—in "finding the truth" about alleged criminal facts.[24] "Finding the truth" relies on the interrogation, detection, and investigation carried out by civil police officers in police stations (Kant de Lima 1995). Every police station, and every investigation, is headed by a *delegado de polícia* (male police delegate) or *delegada de polícia* (female police delegate). The *delegado/a* directs the *inquérito policial* (police inquiry) with the help of *investigadores* (detective inspectors) and *escrivãos* (police clerks). While

the *investigadores* go out into the streets to conduct a service, arrest, or to detect evidence, the *escrivãos* perform the administrative tasks of the police station.

Although the work of civil police officers supports the judiciary, they are independent of the judiciary and fall under the jurisdiction of the state's executive power. Both the state executive power and the state legislative power can create new police stations and demarcate the limits of these stations' jurisdiction, though definitions of crimes are found in federal laws and codes. Making use of his executive power, Governor Montoro signed Decree No. 23,769 on August 6, 1985, creating the first women's police station. As established in Article 2 of this decree, the jurisdiction of this new police station included the investigation of crimes defined in the Special Part of the Brazilian Penal Code under Title I (Chapter II and Section I of Chapter VI) and Title VI. The crimes included, among others, actual bodily harm (Article 129), illegal constraint (Article 146), threat of battery (Article 147), rape (Article 213), and violent sexual molestation (Article 214). Although the code does not specify the sex of the victim, it was understood that the new police station would investigate these crimes as long as the victims were women.[25] Homicide (Article 121) and damage to property (Article 163) were not part of the women's police stations' jurisdiction until 1996.[26]

The decree, originally drafted by the police department, proposed that the women's police station investigate only sexual crimes, such as rape and violent sexual molestation. Actual bodily harm—a sign of battering—was not covered, an omission justified by the then head of the police department as follows: "If we process cases such as fights between husbands and wives, the police station will be overloaded."[27] The investigation of homicide (Article 121 of the Brazilian Penal Code) was not included either, based on the argument that there was already a police station specializing in the investigation of this crime.[28]

In response, feminists argued for the inclusion of both crimes. While they did not succeed in persuading the police department to contemplate homicide, actual bodily harm was hard to exclude. At the time, the press reported that "domestic violence" was the major form of violence against women in Brazilian society (see *Afinal*, July 23, 1985). Most cases dealt with by SOS-Mulher concerned domestic violence, 85 percent of which were based on conjugal violence and battering. Most clients of COJE complained about battering as well as 50 percent of the cases at Casa da Mulher do Centro. Feminist educator Maria Amélia Azevedo, who was a member of the CECF in 1985, insisted that "[t]he family is not a safe place for women" (quoted in *Afinal*, July 23, 1985). Indeed, when the first women's police station was inaugurated, most complaints concerned battering rather than rape, further strengthening the feminist argument. These facts also suggested that battered women were more willing to press charges than victims of rape or other forms of violence against women.

The Essentialist Assumptions of the "Separatist Strategy"
In accordance with Decree No. 23,769/85, the staff of the first women's police station was originally composed of women only: Delegada de Polícia (the head) Rosmary Corrêa; Delegada Assistente (Assistant Police Delegate) Clementina de Jesus; eight *investigadoras* (female detective inspectors); three *escrivãs* (female police clerks); and two *carcereiras* (female warders).

State officials justified the creation of an all-female police station based on accounts of prejudice that female victims of violence faced in regular police stations, their justification clearly influenced by feminist discourse denouncing the insensitivity of male police officers toward raped and battered women. Yet, rather than fulfilling the crucial feminist request of training police officers to end sexism, Temer's "separatist strategy" rested on the essentialist assumption that all policewomen, independent of training, would not be sexist. As he expressed: "By having a police station staffed only by women, female victims will not feel intimidated anymore and will tell their stories in detail. The environment in a regular police station is too heavy and hostile" (quoted in *Afinal*, July 23, 1985).

Police officers, such as Pereira Vieira, then head of the civil police in the state of São Paulo, and Delegada Rosmary Corrêa, appointed to head the first women's police station, also viewed the presence of female police officers as the solution to raped and battered women's intimidation before the police.[29] "Everything in this police station is different. The atmosphere is calm and the staff—from the guard to the head—is composed of women," explained Corrêa to a TV Manchete journalist on the inauguration day for the first women's police station (quoted on TV Manchete, August 6, 1985). "We are going to give a feminine face to the women's police station, and this will help female complainants to feel more comfortable," she went on to say to the press (quoted in *Folha da Tarde*, August 6, 1985).

Based on the essentialist assumption that policewomen would naturally be sensitive to raped and battered women, state managers conceived of the women's police station as an instrument to: 1) stimulate female complainants to press charges against male perpetrators; 2) defend women; 3) end impunity of perpetrators; and 4) deter crimes against women. As Rosmary Corrêa assured at the inauguration: "A more personalized service, in a more informal and relaxed environment, makes victims of abuse, especially of sexual abuse, feel more comfortable to speak about

Figure 1.1 Façade of the first women's police station in downtown São Paulo, July 2001. *(Photo by the author.)*

Figure 1.2 Police clerk and investigator on the second floor of the first women's police station. *(Photo by the author.)*

Figure 1.3   Façade of the first regular police station in downtown São Paulo, July 2001. *(Photo by the author.)*

the subject. . . . I think that from the moment they press charges against male perpetrators, we will be contributing to deter this kind of crime."[30]

Besides aiming to help female victims press charges, Montoro's administration and the police department used the women's police station to restore the legitimacy of the police by altering its "repressive" face to a more "democratic" and "humane" face, essentially equating repression with masculinity and democracy with femininity.

Figure 1.4 Waiting room in the first regular police station in downtown São Paulo, July 2001. *(Photo by the author.)*

During the military-authoritarian regime, police officers were predominantly male. Due to their brutal actions toward the poor and people who voiced opposition to the regime, police were viewed as the enemy of the people. Although police brutality, especially against the poor and blacks, did not diminish with the democratization process, state officials, some policemen, most policewomen, and even feminists viewed the new all-female police station as a positive change toward democratization. As mentioned by a policeman at the time: "The presence of a female police delegate in the police forced male police officers to moderate their language and manners, treating the people more politely" (quoted in *Folha de S. Paulo*, August 25, 1985).

According to former head of the Police Department José Osvaldo Pereira Vieira, Corrêa was chosen to head this women's police station due to her "competence, experience in the police, and sensibility" (quoted in *Folha da Tarde*, August 6, 1985). Without questioning Corrêa's competence, it is worth noting that at that time there were only 15 female police delegates in the state of São Paulo. In addition, Corrêa, then 35 years of age, suited the stereotype of a "blond, gentle, and feminine" Brazilian woman, serving to further equate the "feminization" of the police with the democratization of the state.

In contrast to regular police stations, the women's police station had no cells for prisoners, reasserting its feminine image and giving the impression

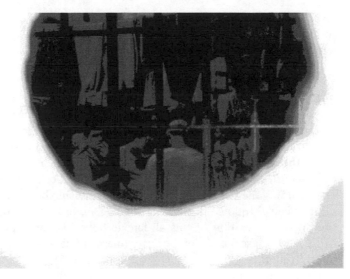

Figure 1.5   Jail in the first regular police station in downtown Sao Paulo, July 2001. Through a small door's opening, the author observed an overcrowded jail with at least 50 detainees. They could not see her on the other side of the door. Their clothes and belongings were hung above their heads due to the lack of sufficient space. The jail's door was made of iron and had several marks from bullets indicating confrontations between the guards and detainees. The jail was located in the back of the police station. The corridor was dirty and smelled. A guard encouraged the author to take a picture of the jail through the small door's opening. The author hesitated but decided to do it. A detainee noticed the flash of the camera and began to scream, saying that someone was taking a picture of them, which was not allowed. Despite the guard's permission, the author felt nervous and managed to leave the police station in a hurry, feeling her heart racing as she walked fast in the crowded streets of downtown São Paulo and entered a restaurant nearby. *(Photo by the author.)*

that policewomen were less repressive than policemen. However, this also gave the impression that policewomen were less effective and had no power to imprison a perpetrator caught in the act. Legally speaking, although the male and female officers work for different stations, there is no difference between the functions ascribed to them; both possess the same power and discretion. Another difference between the first women's police station and regular police stations, which also reinforced a vision of women's police stations as a "feminine" space, was the presence of a social worker and a psychologist who provided services to complainants.[31]

How Feminists Reacted to the "Separatist Strategy"
On July 5, 1985 the CECF organized a meeting with members of several women's organizations to discuss the creation of the first women's police station.[32] As a result of this meeting, they addressed a letter to Michel Temer, expressing the support of both feminist and women's organizations for the creation of a women's police station. They affirmed that "the creation of this women's police station can be an important instrument for the defense and protection of women," also acknowledging the "feminization" of the police as a sign of democratization and humanization of the police.[33] Feminist sociologist Eva Blay, then president of the CECF, reported to the press: "The creation of the police station in defense of women was one step to establish a new relationship between the police and the people" (quoted in *Folha de S. Paulo*, August 12, 1985). Blay also stated that the creation of this all-female police station represented "a change in the consciousness of the Department of Public Security regarding women" (quoted in *Folha de S. Paulo*, August 6, 1985).

Nevertheless, feminists had reservations about Temer's proposal. The country was just emerging from military-authoritarian rule and feminists feared the police and were skeptical of relying on this sector of the state to address issues of violence against women. As Cida Medrado, former member of the CECF, explained:

> How could we think of a women's police station at that moment, when we were just emerging from a dictatorship? That is why some feminists had reasons to hesitate in embracing Temer's idea. But we were aware that social workers did not have the power to register complaints. So we welcomed the creation of the women's police station.[34]

Having struggled against the military regime for most of their lives, it is ironic that in the mid-1980s feminists were working with the police. Especially for those who had been in exile or in prison, it was very difficult to accept the alliance. As Eva Blay remarked at the inauguration of the first women's police station: "I always feared the Department of Public Security. Today I entered here disturbed" (Conselho Estadual da Condição Feminina de São Paulo 1985b, 1).

Feminists also argued that criminalization alone would not solve the problem of violence against women. As co-founder of SOS-Mulher, Rachel Moreno, recalled: "Nobody was against the creation of a women's police station, but Montoro's administration prioritized this police station. There was no proposal to create a shelter, for example. We thought that a women's police station was insufficient to deal with the multifaceted problem of violence against women."[35] According to Moreno,

> It is not enough to prepare bulletins of occurrence [crime reports], because victims need to understand why they [victims] took so long to react against battering. The cause of their submission may rest on economic factors, unemployment, and lack of childcare. Violence is a structural problem, and must be attacked from this perspective.[36]

Furthermore, feminists did not share the essentialist assumption that policewomen would automatically be sensitive to female complainants. "It's not enough to be a woman to be in solidarity with our problems," said Sônia Aparecida de Oliveira, member of the now extinct Coletivo de Mulheres Negras, during debates on the creation of the women's police station (quoted in *Afinal*, July 23, 1985). These reservations prompted feminists to express their concerns to the secretary of public security and to the police department. The letter sent by the CECF to Temer not only supported the creation of a women's police station, it also recommended, among other things, that:

> a) The establishment of this women's police station be monitored by a women's commission; b) policewomen appointed to work with this women's police station reflect about themselves as women; c) the CECF be in charge of monitoring the work of policewomen, serving as a channel to connect the women's police station with COJE, as well as with women's organizations dealing with violence against women.[37]

Successful in guaranteeing their participation in the process of structuring the opening of the first women's police station and in the formation of policewomen's legal culture, feminists were able to address some of their concerns. According to the legislation defining the procedures regarding the launching of this women's police station, its inauguration and the work of policewomen would be monitored by a permanent commission composed of three members, representing respectively, the CECF, the São Paulo Bar Association, and the women's movement. Feminists were particularly concerned about the legal ideology of neutrality and the dominant masculinist culture pervading the Brazilian administration of justice, including the law schools and police academies.[38] Therefore, according to the same legislation, all policewomen selected to work in the women's police station should attend seminars, workshops, and meetings organized by the CECF.[39]

The Legal Ideology of Neutrality and the Masculinist
Police Culture[40]

The Brazilian criminal system is based on the principle of legality, as defined in Article 1 of the Brazilian Penal Code as follows: "There is no crime without a previous law defining it. There is no punishment without a corresponding previous legal standard." In other words, the characterization of a behavior as a crime is a matter of comparing it with the terms of an existing law. As Kant de Lima (1995, 252) explains, "The correct interpretation and application of the general law in any particular case is the main goal of the administration of justice."[41]

Having a judiciary function, police stations must investigate alleged criminal facts and provide the district attorney and the judge—not a jury—with information about the investigation.[42] Following the legality principle, police officers initiate the police investigation once they believe that a complaint matches the legal definition of a crime. As Table 1.1 shows, follow-up police investigations (*inquéritos policiais*) include the crime report, known as Boletim de Ocorrência (literally, a Bulletin of Occurrence, or BO); the *laudo pericial* (medical exam); the *depoimento* (deposition or testimony) of victims, offenders and witnesses; and other pieces of evidence. Only a police delegate (*delegado*), who is required to have a law degree, can direct the police investigation, although in practice

Table 1.1 Follow-up police investigation

Women's police stations			Criminal courts	
Victim initiates a complaint	Police delegate registers the complaint in a Boletim de Ocorrência	Police officers carry out the Inquérito Policial (deposition, medical exam, etc.), which they send to the district attorney	District attorney receives the Inquérito Policial and presses charges	Judge (without a jury) presides over the trial
	Or the delegate prepares a Termo Circunstanciado, which is sent directly to Small Claims Courts			
	Or the police delegate dismisses the complaint		Or district attorney dismisses and closes the case	

police clerks and detective inspectors, who are required to have a high school diploma, also interrogate complainants, perpetrators, and witnesses. By law, the police investigation must last no longer than 30 days. Based on the evidence presented by this preliminary procedure, the *promotor* (district attorney) then decides whether or not to press criminal charges (*denúncia*) before the judge. The creation of criminal small claims courts in 1995 changed some of these police procedures (see Law 9,099, September 26, 1995). For crimes with a prison sentence no longer than one year, police officers must prepare a Termo Circunstanciado (literally, a Term of Crime Circumstances, or T.C.), which is a form of inquiry simplified with a summary of the occurrence, followed by a medical report, when necessary. In lieu of proceeding to criminal investigations, police officers send the Termo Circunstanciado directly to criminal small claims courts.[43]

To enter the judiciary and the police, all judges, prosecutors, public attorneys, and police officers must pass a series of public exams, consisting of written and oral tests on several branches of law (such as constitutional law, criminal law, procedural criminal law, administrative law, etc.), as well as a psychological test. In the case of police officers, they must also take a physical exam. The fact that the judiciary and the police are tenured civil servants is thought to guarantee their impartiality, thus presuming their neutrality (Kant de Lima 1995). This supposed neutrality rests on the separation of law and politics, as well as law and economics, beliefs enshrined in Brazil's legal principles. Thus judges and police officers are presumed free from biases that would result from political pressures, economic interests, even their own gender, racial, or class prejudices. Neither the character of the crime nor the gender, race, or class of the alleged criminal or victim is supposed to influence the practices of police officers. As Delegada Iraci Medeiros says, "We are trained to be police officers, the victim has no sex."[44]

Furthermore, every type of police station must perform the same functions of applying the law to each particular case. As Delegada Rosmary Corrêa points out: "The women's police station is a normal police station. When the case is a crime, we prepare the Bulletin of Occurrence, request the bodily physical exam, hear the parts involved in the crime, and send the criminal investigation to the courts" (quoted in *Notícias de Itaquera*, January 10–16, 1986). However, the dominant masculinist police culture does not consider violence against women a crime, or, if considered a crime, not as serious an offense as robbery, drug trafficking, kidnapping, and so on.

Recruitment of policewomen is not based on expertise on or commitment to reducing violence against women. Once they pass the series of exams to enter the police, all police officers are also required to complete a three-month course at the police academy. This training includes, but is not limited to, classes on criminology, legal medicine, constitutional law, telecommunications, human rights, child and adolescents, self-defense, and shooting. Although the women's police stations must process crimes of violence against women, the police academy, with support from some policewomen, did not—and still do not—see any need to include a course on violence against women in its curriculum. There is no evaluation of policewomen's attitudes of respect or disrespect for their women clients (Massuno 2002).

In July 1985, responding to both this masculinist police culture and the supposed "neutrality" of the police, the CECF proposed to the secretary of public security the organization of a seminar on "Woman and Violence." The goal was to "raise the consciousness of the police department and the judiciary regarding the problem of violence against women."[45] This proposal received the full support of the Montoro's administration. As the press reported at the time:

> Feminism has never been so welcome in the rooms of the São Paulo Department of Public Security. A seminar organized by the Conselho Estadual da Condição Feminina, to be held on July 25 and 26, 1985, will attempt to bring feminism and its reflections on violence against women to police officers. With unprecedented willingness to accept suggestions from women's organizations, the secretary of public security has decided to redefine the contours of the new police station. He has stipulated that all policewomen assigned to work with the new police station receive previous preparation for their new task through participation in seminars such as the one organized by the CECF.[46]

On August 15 and 16, 1985, this unprecedented seminar was attended by two hundred *delegados* and three *delegadas*. Feminists spoke about their analysis that violence against women is a result of patriarchy, as well as about their experience dealing with female victims of violence. Then president of the CECF, Eva Blay, voiced the feminist concern about the culture of police officers: "It is necessary that female victims press charges, but it is also necessary that police officers and judges do not reproduce patriarchal values when women initiate their complaints" (quoted in *Diário Popular*, August 16, 1985).[47]

The alliance between feminists and the secretary of public security favored the participation of feminists in the functioning of women's police stations. Two months after the creation of the first women's police station, the CECF organized a series of meetings with policewomen and functionaries of COJE continuing to meet regularly to discuss the ongoing issue of violence against women. Six months after the creation of the first women's police station, the CECF organized the second seminar on "Woman and Violence," designed to coordinate the work of attorneys and psychologists of COJE with the work of policewomen. "The goal of the seminar is to exchange ideas in order to deal with violence more effectively," said Cida Medrado, then coordinator of the CECF's Commission on Violence against Women (quoted in *Jornal da Tarde*, February 21, 1986). As a sign of feminists' access to build an amicable relationship with policewomen, the CECF sent invitations to the eight women's police stations then created in the state of São Paulo, asking policewomen to suggest the themes they would like to address during the seminar.

Despite the alliance between feminists and Montoro's team, policemen were not receptive to the feminist discourse on violence against women. For example, during the first seminar on "Women and Violence," Delegado Antonio Lopes Filho strongly reacted to feminist Zuleika Alambert's speech on "The Women's Condition," stating to the press that:

> I do not want to become a feminist. They are creating a war between men and women. Since the creation of this women's police station, policemen have been diminished and men have been portrayed as torturers. I think that the family's stability is more important than an actual bodily harm inflicted on a woman (quoted in *Jornal da Tarde*, August 16, 1985).

This statement reflected the dominant masculinist police culture and the discrimination that women faced in the legal professions. Until the mid-1980s, women were often excluded from the judicature.[18] While attending law school in Recife in the early 1980s, I remember female professors commenting that the judiciary considered women to be "crazy" because they always failed the psychological examination for the judicature. At the time, these professors and some successful female attorneys in the city had even planned to take the exam for judges just to attract attention to discrimination against women within the legal professions.

Women were rarely allowed to enter the police force as well, barred either in the physical or psychological test. In São Paulo, the first woman to become an *escrivã* (police clerk) in 1959 received numerous harassing phone calls. Only in 1970 did the state of São Paulo have its first *delegada*, Ivanete Oliveira Veloso, who received "condolences" from one of her instructors at the police academy. Then Secretary of Public Security Erasmo Dias commented: "What are we going to do with this woman?" (quoted in *Folha de S. Paulo*, August 25, 1985).

The creation of the first women's police station and similar stations in the 1980s opened a job market for women on the police force, though it did not eliminate discrimination against policewomen and women's police stations. Before July 1985, only 1 percent of police officers were women. There were 1,622 *delegados* and only 16 *delegadas* in the state of São Paulo.[49] A month before the first women's police station was inaugurated, the police department recruited an unprecedented number of policewomen. While previously no more than one woman would pass the exam for *delegada*, in the exam of July 1985 ten women were approved. In August 1985 in the state of São Paulo there were 26 *delegadas*, 419 *escrivãs*, 628 *investigadoras*, and 229 *carcereiras*—a dramatic increase (see *Tribuna Operária*, August 9–15, 1985).

However, policewomen did not have the option of working for a regular police station; instead they were limited to women's police stations, which were understaffed and devalued by policemen. Whereas a regular police station was usually run by seven *delegados*, twelve *escrivãos*, and twenty-five *investigadores*, the first women's police station, for example, was run by two *delegadas*, three *escrivãs*, and five *investigadoras*. Proportionally, however, the first women's police station processed more complaints than regular police stations. Three weeks after its inception, the first women's police station had registered approximately 400 Bulletins of Occurrence, as opposed to a regular police station that took about two months to register over 300 Bulletins of Occurrence (see *Folha de S. Paulo*, September 7, 1985).

Reflecting their masculinist police culture, most policemen reacted against the creation of the women's police stations, refusing collaboration with the work of policewomen. Doubting that policewomen could perform the "tough" job of a police officer, a policeman expressed to the press: "I just want to see what they [policewomen] will do when a violent man refuses to appear before their station" (quoted in *Folha de S. Paulo*, August 25, 1985). In Brasília, a man sent a letter to the attorney general asking him to take legal action to end the women's police stations on the basis of their alleged unconstitutionality: He claimed that they were discriminating against men (see *Jornal do Brasil*, May 12, 1989). In Curitiba, *delegados de polícia* (male police delegates) criticized the creation of a women's police station there, arguing that there were not enough complaints to file. Furthermore, they were concerned about losing female clerks who were working in regular police stations (see *Jornal de Santa Catarina*, May 7, 1989).

Many policemen considered violence against women to be a "social" rather than "criminal" problem. Erasmo Dias (1990), secretary of public security in the administration that preceded Montoro's, argued that women's police stations were not necessary because women's complaints did not concern the police. Instead, these complaints should be sent to social workers. According to Dias, the state would have spent less money if it had just expanded the number of social workers in regular police stations. Interestingly, some policewomen also shared policemen's prejudice against women's police stations. As pointed out by police clerk Cleonice Ferreira at the time the first women's police station was created: "This police station is about *zica* [literally 'little woman'—police slang for cases that are not considered important]. I think that *tiras* [cops] have more important things to do than working here. I myself used to deal with robbery and drug trafficking. Now I'm here, solving little fights between husbands and wives."[50]

Another police clerk reported to a popular women's magazine that, "to assist victims is easy, because women understand women. The problem will be here [in the women's police station]. If I have the bad luck to be channeled to this station, I will prefer to be in the streets hunting rapists, because in the station there will be lots of gossiping" (quoted in *Contigo*, August 5, 1985).

Some policewomen also shared policemen's vision of sexual violence in marriage as "normal" behavior. A police clerk reported to the leftist newspaper *Tribuna Operária* that she could not accept the fact that a woman had complained about being forced by her husband to have sex with him. "He works and makes money, but she still thinks that she has no obligation as a woman," explained the police officer (quoted in *Tribuna Operária*, August 9–16, 1985). Even those policewomen who considered sexual violence a crime did not see a perpetrator who held a job as a "real" criminal. As Delegada Rosmary Corrêa stated, clearly suggesting her class-based biases:

> Contrary to what happens in other police stations, we respect the defendant because we are conscious that men who abuse women are not delinquents. These few months in the women's police station have showed to me that such a man usually has a job, a family and is respected by his friends. This man beats up his wife because he thinks she is his property.[51]

Overall, however, the few policewomen working in 1985 were more receptive than policemen to the feminist discourse on violence against women. Policewomen lacked the experience dealing with this type of crime and depended on the support of feminists because they faced discrimination in the police department (Ardaillon 1989, 97). But policewomen's willingness to learn from the women's movement did not mean that they had become feminists. As Delegada Rosmary Corrêa explained at the time, "I respect the women's movement, but I think that both feminism and *machismo* are too radical" (quoted in *Afinal*, October 3, 1985).

The "Unhappy Success" of the First Women's Police Station

Despite the prevalence of the masculinist police culture, the first women's police station was considered a success. Its creation led to changes in Brazilian culture regarding the issue of violence against women; an increase in the number of women pressing charges; the rapid founding of similar women's police stations all over the country and elsewhere in the world; the expansion of the job market for women on the police force; and the popularity of policewomen in society.

Campaigns to politicize domestic violence and wife-murder cases in the late 1970s and early 1980s were the first of many challenges feminists faced to the conception of violence against women as a "private" and even "normal" issue. Violence against women was widely accepted in the culture, as illustrated by the popular proverb: *Em briga de marido e mulher, ninguém mete a colher* (fights between husband and wife are nobody's business). Not until the first women's police station was created in 1985 did the state and society at large recognize violence against women as an issue of public concern to be socially and criminally condemned, thus redrawing the limits between the public and private sphere (Alvarez 1990; Sorj 2002; Suárez and Bandeira 2002). The home was no longer viewed as a private and safe space: Fights between husbands and wives became subject to public scrutiny and police investigation. As sociologist Maria Aparecida Medrado expressed: "Domestic violence is not considered an individual and private problem anymore, but rather a public and social problem. This is the major merit of the women's police stations" (quoted in Dias 1985, 136).

Although the legislation on the first women's police station did not mention the term "violence against women," the existence of this all-female police station allowed women to press charges against perpetrators. Once in practice, this led to the unprecedented criminalization of violence against women in Brazil, opening a new chapter in the history of Brazil's criminal justice system. This remarkable legal and institutional change allowed female victims to speak out. In 1984, a year before the creation of the first women's police station, all regular police stations in the city of São Paulo registered approximately 3,000 complaints initiated by female victims of violence, whereas the first women's police station alone registered approximately 7,000 complaints and served 65,000 women from August 1985 to August 1986 (see *Folha de S. Paulo*, August 6, 1986; and *Folha de S. Paulo*, August 7, 1986). This dramatic increase shows that not only was the first women's police station taking women's complaints more seriously than regular police stations, but that more female victims were willing to press charges in this new environment.

According to Delegada Rosmary Corrêa, during the first week the station was open, an average of one hundred women sought their services daily (cited in *Folha de S. Paulo*, August 7, 1985; and *Folha de S. Paulo*, September 7, 1985). It was so crowded with so many women pressing charges that Michel Temer proposed to former Chief of the Police Department José Oswaldo Pereira Vieira the appointment of "one female clerk in every regular police station to help processing complaints of violence against women" (quoted in *Folha de S. Paulo*, August 14, 1985). Temer's goal was the decentralization of the intense service, but his proposal was declined. Instead, new women's police stations were created in the following years, further encouraging more women to speak up before policewomen rather than policemen.[52]

At the beginning of 1986, an average of 208 women per day went to the women's police stations (see *Veja*, April 23, 1986). The high number of cases registered (approximately 6,000 in 1986) was considered a sign of success—though an "unhappy success"—stimulating the creation of more women's police stations in the state of São Paulo and throughout Brazil. By 1989, there were 31 women's police stations in the state of São Paulo, which registered approximately 32,000 Bulletins of Occurrence.[53] With the rapid expansion of women's police stations more women entered the police force and the job market for social workers on the police force gained more visibility.

The *plantão* (daily duty) of social workers in the first women's police station was inaugurated on August 16, 1985 (see *Diário Popular*, August 16, 1985). But while women's police stations expanded, the service of social workers was provided in few women's police stations. Demanding that more social workers be hired in women's police stations, social workers organized the "First National Meeting of Social Workers Working in Women's Police Stations," held in São Paulo from September 6 to September 7, 1990.[54] Regardless of the demands made by both policewomen and feminists in the 1990s, the state did not equip women's police stations with more social workers.[55]

Despite policewomen's fear of segregation in women's police stations, they became popular officials and even role models due to their work there. When Delegada Rosmary Corrêa heard that she had been appointed to head the first women's police station, she thought that her career was over. She expected that her work would be deemed unimportant and that few women would press charges in her police station. Corrêa's expectations not only turned out to be wrong, but soon she became a celebrity, frequently appearing in newspaper articles and on radio and television shows.[56] The largest Brazilian television network Rede Globo, for example, interviewed Corrêa during prime-time shows such as *Fantástico*, *Globo Repórter*, and *Jornal Nacional*. Twice a week, from 8 A.M. to 9 A.M.,

"*Doutora* Rose" (Doctor Rose, as she is publicly called)[57] appeared on a television show about women, *TV Mulher*, which was aired by Rede Globo. Corrêa also appeared on other television networks, giving interviews on popular shows such as *J. Silvestre, Marília Gabriela*, and *A Mulher Dá o Recado*. Thanks to her popularity, Corrêa was elected state assemblywoman in 1990 and was re-elected in 1994. She believes that most of her voters were women.[58]

Like Corrêa, other policewomen became very popular. On occasions such as the celebration of the International Women's Day on March 8, policewomen were and continue to be invited by women's governmental and non-governmental organizations, unions, neighborhood associations, and religious groups to speak about violence against women and the work of women's police stations. Policewomen—rather than feminists—became the most influential experts on the issue.[59]

The first women's police station itself became as popular as the policewomen. In 1986, the work of this women's police station was covered three times a week by the radio show *Programa Rádio Barbosa* (produced by the network Rede Globo), surpassing the popularity of other popular radio shows on crimes, such as *Gil Gomes* and *Afanázio Jazadji* (see *Veja*, April 23, 1986).

The culmination of the women's police stations' popularity was achieved at the national level in 1990, when Rede Globo aired a weekly TV show inspired by the women's police stations aptly titled *Delegacia de Mulheres* (Women's Police Station). Regardless of the popularity the show brought to this new institution, at the time, policewomen complained that the show ridiculed them. But the show's screenwriter, Maria Carmen Barbosa, argued that her intention was the opposite. She wanted to portray "strong women who are respected for their work" (quoted in *Diário Popular*, December 8, 1990).

In July 1990, Rede Globo devoted its weekly documentary show *Globo Repórter* to the problem of violence against women, offering its solution through women's police stations. As the show stated:

> In the past, battered women had two choices: either to silence violence against them, fearing more harm at home; or to go to a police station, running the risk of being subject to prejudice and humiliation. Thanks to the women's police station, this situation changed altogether. Women have gained a place that guarantees their protection and provides them with advice (*Globo Repórter*, July 1990).

The immediate success of the first women's police station was also illustrated by the media's extensive coverage of testimonies given by female complainants, who expressed their preference for women's police stations over regular police stations. "I felt better here than in the police stations for men, because there I didn't find the support I found here," said a female victim who appeared on TV Manchete the day the first women's police station was open (quoted in TV Manchete, August 6, 1985). Another female complainant expressed her view of the women's police stations to the reporter of TV Cultura as follows: "The police station in defense of women was the best accomplishment of Governor Montoro. Whenever I have a grievance, I will come to this police station. I don't want any other station, I will only come here" (quoted in TV Cultura, August 8, 1985).

The first women's police station's "unhappy success" instigated the creation of new women's police stations all over São Paulo, the nation, and even the globe. One year after the creation of the first women's police station there were six women's police stations in São Paulo and 36 throughout the country. These women's police stations became so popular among the female population that every politician—even in small and remote towns—requested that the police department create a women's police station in their town. As of December 2003, 125 women's police stations had been created in the state of São Paulo alone and every state had established at least one. There were 339 women's police stations throughout Brazil. However, only 10 percent of the municipalities had women's police stations and most of these stations were concentrated in the capitals and large cities of the country's south and southeast regions (Conselho Nacional dos Direitos da Mulher 2001; AGENDE and CLADEM Brasil 2003).

Since the mid-1980s, the women's police stations have also gone global. Inspired by this "successful" Brazilian invention, eight countries in Latin America—Argentina, Colombia, Costa Rica, El Salvador, Ecuador, Nicaragua, Peru, and Uruguay—have created women's police stations (Corral 1993; Feijóo and Nari 1994; Chinchilla 1994; Nelson 1996; Jubb and Izumino 2002; Santos 1999a). European countries, such as Spain and Portugal, also launched women's police stations during the late 1980s (Station 1989). In 1990, while participating in a seminar on violence in Brazil, the director of the Institute of Criminality in Wiesbaden, Germany liked the idea and considered copying it (*Diário Popular*, December 8, 1990). In 1993, the Pakistani Prime Minister Benazir Butto opened a women's police station in her country (*San Francisco Chronicle*, December 21, 1993). In 1992, India's Chief Minister J. Jayalalitha established the first women's police station in the state of Tamil Nadu, followed by the creation of numerous similar stations there and in other states, such as in Panjim-Goa, where 188 all-women police stations have been set up (Oherald.com 2003).

Despite their unhappy success, the advent of women's police stations, though important for the advancement of women's rights in Brazil, has not been sufficient to assist the social and psychological needs of female victims. Aware of the limitations of criminalization, since the early 1990s Brazilian feminists have pressured the state to create more shelters, as well as provide more psychological and social services (Grossi 1994). Echoing the feminist urge for shelters, some policewomen, such as Delegada Terezinha de Carvalho, head of one women's police station in the city of Campinas, have also publicly expressed the limitations of women's police stations in dealing with the problem of violence against women (see *Correio Popular*, April 5, 1991). Yet, with the exception of progressive mayors from the leftist Workers' Party (PT), most state representatives have only paid lip service to shelters. Until 1998 there were only seven shelters in the country (see *Veja*, July 1, 1998). Thanks to feminist pressure, this number jumped to 59 in 2003—a dramatic increase, though still insufficient to fulfill the needs of victims.[60]

In the state of São Paulo, with approximately 22 million people and 125 women's police stations, there are only 14 shelters. However, the state government has created only one, Centro de Convivência para Mulheres Vítimas de Violência Doméstica (Center for Female Victims of Domestic Violence or COMVIDA). Established in 1988 by the departments of welfare, public security, and justice, COMVIDA has the capacity to host 50 people (15 battered women and their children), for a period of three months. Due to lack of infrastructure and staff workers, this shelter was closed in 1989. Reopened in 1991, it still faces the same problems. Run by two psychologists with the help of four policewomen and one housekeeper, COMVIDA is now subordinated to the department of public security.

The other shelters have been created at the municipal level by either private foundations or progressive mayors from the Workers' Party (PT). In November 1990, the mayor of Santo André, José Augusto da Silva Ramos (PT) created a shelter coordinated by feminists in the city's Assessoria dos Direitos da Mulher (Advisory Council on Women's Rights). This shelter had the capacity to host 20 people (see *O Estado de S. Paulo*, November 28, 1990). On August 29, 1991, then-São Paulo Mayor Luíza Erundina (PT) created the first shelter of the city, Casa Abrigo Helenira Resende de Souza Nazareth, with the capacity to host 25 people for a period of four months.[61] This shelter was coordinated by feminists of the Casa Eliane de Grammont, a governmental organization also created by Erundina on March 9, 1990 to provide battered women with psychological, social, and legal services. This organization was the first of its kind at the municipal level and became a national model of public services for women in situations of domestic and sexual violence. In 1991, the mayor of Diadema (PT) created an organization similar to Casa Eliane de Grammont, called Casa Beth Lobo, also coordinated by feminists (*Diário Popular*, May 11, 1991).

The São Paulo's shelter Helenira de Souza Nazareth was, however, closed at the end of 1992 for security reasons—its address had been disclosed. The new mayors, Paulo Maluf (1993–1996) and Celso Pitta (1997–2000), both from the conservative Social Democratic Party (PDS; changed to PP-Progressive Party in 2003), ignored the issue of violence against women.[62] Only on March 8, 2001, eight years later, was the shelter reopened, by newly elected Mayor Marta Suplicy from the Workers' Party (PT). Since then, Suplicy has established partnerships with the private-owned shelter Casa da Mamãe and three other private organizations that are similar to Casa Eliane de Grammont. On November 24, 2003 the mayor opened a new organization, Casa Brasilândia, to provide social and psychological services to victims of domestic and sexual violence.

Outside the state of São Paulo, other progressive mayors, mostly from the Workers' Party (PT), have also created shelters run by feminists, such as the governmental organization Casa Maria in Porto Alegre. Unlike other cities in the São Paulo state, where the political climate has conditioned the coordination of shelters, Porto Alegre has been unique in the sense that feminists there have been able to secure by law that they coordinate Casa Maria independent of the political party in power. This solution, depending on the local power of feminists, is far from being reached in most Brazilian cities.

In addition to their limitations to address the social and psychological needs of women in situations of violence, women's police stations have also faced material difficulties that affect the administration of justice as a whole. Policewomen and feminists have reported that these stations lack the minimum infrastructure to adequately serve their clients, especially in the impoverished northeast region (Conselho Nacional dos Direitos da Mulher 2001; Amaral et al. 2001).

Furthermore, policewomen are still a minority and face discrimination within state police departments throughout the country. Even in the state of São Paulo, where most of the country's women's police stations are concentrated, by April 1999 policewomen comprised only 22.9 percent of the entire state's police force, according to a study conducted by Delegada Elisabete Massuno (2002, 30). Considering each of the three positions normally performed in women's police stations—police delegates, investigators, and police clerks—Massuno's study shows that sexual prejudices shape the recruitment of police officers. Whereas 45.5 percent of all of São Paulo state's police clerks are women, only 12.5 percent of the police delegates and 9.3 percent of the investigators are female (Massuno 2002, 30). Massuno suggests that women are more likely to be accepted into the police force to perform administrative tasks, considered more feminine than heading the police station or hunting "criminals" in the streets, jobs that are viewed as masculine and associated with the "real" police identity.

Conclusion

As Alvarez (1990) asserts, the creation of state councils, the national council on women's rights and women's police stations emerged from the redemocratization process during the 1980s. This political conjuncture contributed to open "access points" in the state, allowing organized sectors of civil society direct participation in state politics. After a twenty-year period of military-authoritarianism, state managers and feminists developed a relationship of political alliance. In the process, feminist mobilizations to end violence against women politicized gender. In the early and mid-1980s, the feminist and women's movements in Brazil were well-organized, gaining the leverage to bring their perspective into the state. The politicization of violence against women by feminist and women's groups began in the 1970s and was further politicized through the creation of SOS-Mulher groups in the early 1980s. Once the CECF was launched, feminists had gained direct experience in dealing with battered women and therefore were well equipped to influence public policy on the issue.

In response to the feminist critique of sexism in regular police stations, state managers literally *gendered* the police force and, likewise, the criminalization of violence, forcing feminists to emphasize the criminal aspect of violence against women. Aspects of the feminist approach to end violence against women were selectively absorbed by the state, though not recognized as feminist ideas. The state's emphasis on women's police stations as the major public policy addressing violence against women narrowed the feminist approach to this issue, raising questions about the limitations of the state in advancing gendered democratization and citizenship rights. In this sense, both state actors and feminists had their interests transformed in the process of creating the first women's police station. They negotiated over the jurisdiction, scope, and functioning of the first women's police station.

The first women's police station was considered a success for stimulating female victims to press charges and for giving visibility to violence against women as crime. This visibility amplified the work of policewomen, generating a rapid increase in the number of women's police stations. The first and subsequent women's police stations opened the job market for women on the police force. However, despite the alliance between state managers and feminists to challenge the dominant masculinist police culture, discrimination against policewomen did not end. In fact, the first women's police station, though contributing to expand women's rights and to bring more women to the police department, further exposed the masculinist police culture of both policemen and policewomen.

The "feminization"—rather than "feministization"—of the police through the creation of the women's police stations continues to be an issue of feminist concern. Since the inception of the first women's police station, feminists have struggled to shape the legal culture of policewomen but have been unable to include a course on violence against women in the curriculum of the police academy. Do policewomen consider violence against women a crime? Do they see themselves as "real" police officers? Do they see male perpetrators as "real" criminals? Are they in favor of receiving a gender-based training? This training and how policewomen relate to feminists have a major influence on the ways policewomen conceive of their work, approach violence against women, and deal with complainants. In the next chapter, I examine these questions by looking at the dynamics of the relationship between policewomen and feminists since the mid-1980s.

2

Engendering Policewomen's Interests and Identities

During the first days of work, journalists would ask me: "Are you a
feminist?" I would reply assertively: "No, I'm not. I'm a police officer."
I feared the sound of the word "feminist."

—Delegada Rosmary Corrêa (Interview, São Paulo,
June 16, 1994).

From the inception of the first women's police station, feminists in São
Paulo have been challenging the legal ideology of neutrality and the
masculinist police culture. They maintain that the work of the women's
police stations must be informed by the women's movement. Feminists
have further demanded from the state that policewomen receive gender-
based training. But are policewomen interested in this type of training?
Do they favor continuous contact with feminists? How have policewomen related to feminists and feminism since the creation of the first
women's police station in 1985? Have their gender identities and interests
as women and police officers been influenced by feminists?

As discussed in chapter 1, feminists embraced the creation of the first
women's police station but remained skeptical of its functions because
they did not assume that policewomen would be natural allies with their
women clients. It is not surprising that research in Brazil and in other
Latin American countries shows that this feminist-inspired institution is
fraught with contradictions. Studies have challenged the government's
(not feminists') initial "separatist strategy," which assumed that all female
police officers, independent of training, would be more sensitive to female
victims of violence than male police officers and would not oppose making
violence against women a crime.[1] The existing research, however, tends to
homogenize the interests and identities of policewomen (for exceptions,
see Nelson 1996; Hautzinger 1997; Santos 1999a). Most importantly,

researchers tend to overlook and undertheorize the political forces shaping the complex and often contradictory relationship between police-women and feminist organizations (for exceptions, see Nelson 1996; Hautzinger 1997; Santos 1999a).

Based on ethnographic research and extensive interviews in women's police stations and the women's movement, I found that policewomen assumed three basic positions regarding feminism.[2] In the first instance, I met policewomen who made explicit alliances with feminists, fully embracing the feminist definition of violence against women as a crime, and favoring continuous contact with feminists. In other words, they became *feminist policewomen*. This position was predominant in the 1980s and regained prominence in 1994 as well as from 1998 to 2000. Second, I encountered policewomen who opposed any contact with feminists. These policewomen did not view violence against women as "real" crimes; some were against the very existence of women's police stations. Their position held sway in the early 1990s, reflected the hegemonic masculinist police culture, and can be categorized as a *masculinist female police*. Finally, I met policewomen whose alliances with feminist organizations were indirect and ambiguous; they embraced aspects of the feminist approach to "gender violence" but did not, or could not, make explicit alliances with feminists. This position was predominant in the mid-1990s and has prevailed since August 2001, and can be identified with a *gendered police*. Frequently, I also found that individual policewomen held at least two of these positions over the course of a career.

What explains the emergence of these different positions and the shifts between them? More broadly, this question refers to the relationship between the state and women's movements. According to the literature, the state is more or less friendly to women's movements, fostering either social change or social control in women's lives, depending on the political conjuncture (Alvarez 1990, 1997; Waylen 1996a, 1996b, 1998; Lievesley 1996; Metoyer 2000; Molyneux 2000). It is certainly true that relations between policewomen and feminists in São Paulo are situated within the context of changing state-society relations during the political transition to democracy and the post-authoritarian regime in Brazil. It is also true, however, that these contradictory relations are the result of the women's police stations, and policewomen, being located within the coercive and masculinist arm of the state (Nelson 1996). In fact, considering Brazil's history of military rule and police repression of resistance movements, it is not surprising that the role of women's police stations in Brazilian society is politically ambiguous.

In this chapter, I argue that additional forces interacted with the political conjuncture and the hegemonic masculinist police culture to shape the contradictory dynamics of the relationship between policewomen and feminist organizations. The developments in the feminist movement and in the feminist approach to end violence against women have also played a role in shaping the culture of policewomen; in turn, policewomen's daily contact with female victims of violence has affected policewomen's individual identities and interests. In light of these interactive macro and micro forces and processes, I discuss the emergence of a feminist police in the 1980s; the coexistence of a masculinist and feminist female police in the early 1990s; and a feminist *versus* gendered police since the mid-1990s in the city of São Paulo. As this chapter will demonstrate, although the political conjuncture is important and shapes the practices of state actors, the dynamics of state-society relations must be captured at both levels of analysis.

1980s: The Emergence of a Feminist Police

In the early 1980s, feminist organizations dealing with violence against women, such as the SOS-Mulher, focused on practices of *conscientização* (consciousness-raising) of women's oppression. Violence against women, basically defined as domestic violence, was viewed as the quintessential expression of male domination or patriarchy. Women would only liberate themselves from violence and male domination once they were able to become conscious of that domination. Building on this approach, feminists in the CECF expected policewomen to become sensitive (*sensibilização*) to the problem of violence against women and to be in solidarity (*solidariedade*) with female complainants, thus raising complainants' consciousness (*conscientização*) of this problem as an expression of male domination. The criminalization of violence against women was not the major goal or an end in itself, but rather it was part of a larger struggle to end patriarchy. According to this perspective, the women's police stations should be women-friendly spaces of "solidarity," having pedagogical roles (as opposed to simply law enforcement roles).[3] As feminist sociologist Heleieth Saffioti explained:

> We wanted to get rid of men [male police officers], because the victim was already fragile and harmed by another man. We wanted to create a space of solidarity. It was an illusion, of course, because the space [of the police] is not one of solidarity at all. But I remember that we wanted to build a space of solidarity for women only, in order to avoid harassment by men.[4]

Feminists knew, however, that policewomen would not automatically be in solidarity with their clients. To raise female complainants' consciousness, policewomen themselves would have to be *conscientizadas* (conscious) of their female condition. Feminist training was crucial for the women's police stations to achieve what feminists believed should be the goals of these stations—to raise women's consciousness of their oppression and to build solidarity among women. Feminists successfully lobbied to include in the legislation on the first women's police station a paragraph that required policewomen to participate in seminars and workshops organized by the CECF and the São Paulo Bar Association.

As noted in chapter 1, the first workshop organized by the CECF, in collaboration with the Department of Public Security, took place on August 15 and 16, 1985, ten days after the first women's police station was inaugurated. This two-day workshop, titled "Woman and Violence," was the first attempt by feminists to bring their perspective on violence against women and patriarchy into the police department. Feminist sociologist Eva Blay, then president of the CECF, emphasized the importance of this kind of meeting in her opening remarks: "There is nothing more just than unearthing, through debates, a violence that has been covered for thousands of years, because it is necessary to raise the awareness [*sensibilizar*] of all those who work on this problem."[5] Male police officers, however, strongly reacted against this type of speech made by feminists, confirming their opposition to the creation of a women's police station. Some policewomen as well shared the policemen's views on feminism and held prejudices against the women's police station.

Given the resistance of the police, feminists were very concerned about how different the women's police stations would be from regular police stations. Feminists also wanted to raise women's consciousness, and therefore strived to maintain connections between the women's police stations and the women's movement. Right after the inauguration of the first women's police station, the Conselho Nacional dos Direitos da Mulher (National Council on Women's Rights, or CNDM), based in the country's capital, Brasília, demanded from the Brasília Secretary of Public Security that the CNDM be granted free access to women's police stations to maintain the bridge between the stations and the women's movements.[6] As more women's police stations were established, both the CECF and the CNDM began to organize meetings and workshops to evaluate the work of policewomen, in an attempt to bring their feminist perspective to bear on the role of women's police stations.

In August of 1986, the CECF organized, along with the department of public security, the "First Meeting of Women's Police Stations." The speech of Zuleika Alambert, president of the CECF at the time, illustrates well the feminist perspective on the role feminists attributed to the women's police stations. This perspective combined Paulo Freire's approach to *conscientização* with the American and French approach to women's consciousness-raising. As Alambert said, "It is necessary to come together to fight violence [against women] through constant work on women's education and *conscientização*, to establish their true image in society—an image of subject, not of object" (Conselho Estadual da Condição Feminina de São Paulo 1986d, II).

Following the meeting in São Paulo, the CNDM organized in Brasília the First National Meeting of Policewomen Working in Women's Police Stations as part of its campaign *Diga Não à Violência Contra a Mulher* ("Say No to Violence against Women"). At the time, there were 10 women's police stations in the state of São Paulo and 22 throughout the country. Besides feminists of the CNDM and of the state councils, academia and the women's movements, 60 policewomen attended this meeting. In her opening speech, Jacqueline Pitanguy, then president of the CNDM, characterized the women's police stations as "territories of solidarity and repression, in which violence becomes visible for the victim, for the perpetrator and for society. And in which violence can be erased through the reformulation of the relations between men and women."[7]

As a result of this meeting, participants concluded that the women's police stations not only had to differ from regular police stations—functioning in separate buildings and being staffed by female police officers only—but that, in addition to its law enforcement role, the women's police stations should have a pedagogical role. Moreover, policewomen should educate both victims and perpetrators about the consequences of conjugal violence and should treat female complainants in a respectful manner, creating a "new form of assistance, where physical and verbal aggression must be replaced with a human practice, characterized by dialogue, respect and solidarity."[8] While having only female police officers was a necessary condition to differentiate women's police stations from regular police stations, it was not sufficient to differentiate women's police stations from regular police stations. Thus, feminists recommended in the meeting that "[P]olicewomen have more contact with the community at large, especially with women's organizations working on the issue of violence against women."[9] They also recommended that police officers participate in "courses to raise their awareness [*sensibilizar*] about the problem of violence against women and the women's condition [of oppression]."[10] Finally, they proposed "a dialogue between the women's police stations and state councils to fight violence against women."[11]

In São Paulo, the dialogue between feminists in the CECF and policewomen developed within the context of participatory democracy. Backed by Montoro's team, the CECF was able to organize several meetings and workshops with policewomen (but not policemen) from 1985 to 1989.

Despite policewomen's initial resistance, persistent discrimination by the police department favored the burgeoning alliance between policewomen and feminists. As noted in chapter 1, in August of 1985 there were only 15 female police delegates in the state of São Paulo. The first women's police station attracted enormous attention from the media and society at large, and Montoro established 12 additional women's police stations in the remaining 16 months of his term, which ended in December 1986 (see Table 2.1). Other states across the country immediately followed in the footsteps of São Paulo and by September 1986, one year after the creation of the first women's police station, there were 23 women's police stations throughout Brazil. The rapid expansion of these stations opened up new jobs for policewomen; however, women officers were still in the minority and faced continued discrimination within the police department. This state of affairs made it possible, or necessary, for policewomen to seek out the support of feminists. But the dominant masculinist police culture was hard to challenge and feminists were not able to institutionalize a course on violence against women in the curriculum of the police academy.

The alliance between feminists in the CECF and policewomen prospered under the leadership of Delegada Rosmary Corrêa, appointed to head the world's first women's police station. Corrêa entered the police force in 1972, as a clerk, under the military regime. She was 22 years old. In 1976, she graduated in law and passed the exam to become a *delegada*, the third female police delegate in the state of São Paulo. "At that time, it was not common to have women in police stations," informed Corrêa.[12] After passing the exam, she was channeled to an office in the police department, assisting a male police delegate with clerical work, instead of investigating crimes in police stations. In 1983, the police department finally allowed her to preside over police investigations. Just two years later, she was appointed to organize and head the first women's police station. She worked there until August of 1989, when she was selected by the police department to be the first head of the Assessoria Especial das Delegacias de Polícia de Defesa da Mulher do Estado de São Paulo (Special Advisory Committee on the Police Stations in Defense of Women, or the Assessoria), created to coordinate the work of policewomen in the state of São Paulo. At the end of 1989, she left the Assessoria to run for elective office. Due to her popularity as the first head of the first women's police station, she was elected assemblywoman for the state of São Paulo in 1990 and was re-elected three times (in 1994, 1998, and 2002) for the same position.

Like most policewomen, at first Corrêa did not want to work for the new women's police station. As she recalls: "I was working in a regular police station for four years, doing very well. Professionally, I was moving up. I was very happy. When I was transferred to the first women's police station, I must confess that I felt very angry. I thought that my career was over at that moment."[13]

Although Corrêa had dealt with complaints initiated by women in a regular police station and was aware that her gender had played a role in attracting female complainants, she did not consider violence against women to be a visible problem in Brazilian society. She believed, as the police asserted, that regular police stations did not discriminate against women clients. In short, she did not think that a police station specializing in crimes against women was necessary. As she explains:

> Perhaps because I was a woman, I would process more complaints by women than male police officers. But my vision was that the case of violence against women was like any other criminal case coming to a regular police station. I thought it was not necessary to open a specialized police station for women, because there were not many cases of violence against women, and regular police stations could process them very well.[14]

As soon as Corrêa started running the first women's police station, however, her viewpoint changed. The day after the first women's police station was inaugurated, Corrêa found herself facing a line of 500 women waiting to file complaints. "I joke," says Corrêa, "that *o povo vestia a camisa* [literally, 'the people were wearing the shirt,' meaning that the people had embraced the idea]."[15] Then "I saw that women lacked basic knowledge about their rights, and they were not heard anywhere else. I saw how important that work was, and I fell in love with it."[16]

In the beginning, Corrêa was not clear about the role of the new police station. Because she believed feminists had instigated the opening of this police station, as many complainants usually assume, she sought contact with feminist organizations already dealing with the issue of violence against women.[17] She was receptive to the help of feminists and did not resist the contact with the CECF. "I looked for them," she says, "to find out what they expected from us, how we should approach complainants, what our purpose should be."[18] Until this time, she had no involvement with feminists; in fact, she was prejudiced against them, believing that her image would be at risk if she were associated with feminists. As she recounts, "At that moment, in my view, as in the view of everybody I knew, a feminist was, let's say, a homosexual, a woman who dresses like men and acts like men in order to compete with men."[19]

It is interesting to note that the stereotype of policewomen, as described by Corrêa, was not very different from the image she had of feminists: "A tall woman, strong like men, wearing big shoes, size 44 [in Brazil, lesbians are called *sapatão*, which in English literally means big shoes], and holding a gun at her hip."[20] The appearance of Corrêa—feminine, blond, gentle, and somehow maternal—did not fit this stereotype. Her gender, sexuality and race played an important role in creating the image of the women's police station as a feminine rather than feminist institution, run by a gentle, maternal, and educated white woman. Although this feminine image served to dissociate Corrêa from feminists, it also devalued the work of policewomen in women's police stations, considered by the police department to be less important and demanding than the work of policemen in regular police stations.

Through contact with feminists, Corrêa did not overcome her prejudice against homosexuality, but gradually she changed her views on feminism and started to value the women's movement—a movement she originally believed was "too radical" and "against men."[21] "My contact with women's groups," says Corrêa, "showed that the so-called feminists were married women, with families, leaving their partners and children to fight for other women who are less privileged."[22] She saw the importance of feminism and understood why feminists had to be "radical" in the 1970s. "Otherwise, they would not be heard," she says.[23] Besides changing her perception of feminists, Corrêa also redefined feminism and started to publicly identify herself as a feminist:

> After knowing what feminism was about, although still fearing the word, I would tell journalists: "Yes, I am a feminist, if feminism means fighting for women's rights, for the end of discrimination and violence against women, for women to occupy a position in society." Notice that I was still careful, always explaining the meaning of feminism. Not because of myself, but because in our society the word feminism/feminist still has a pejorative meaning.[24]

From feminists she learned that the women's police station had been created "to encourage women to denounce violence against women, to speak about their problems in a place where they could find other women."[25] She also learned from feminists to differentiate the women's police stations from regular police stations in the following terms: "A women's police station was much more than simply a place to register complaints, it was the open door for women to spell out their suffering and questions which cannot be addressed through police investigations."[26] As a place for women to speak and be heard, policewomen in the women's police stations, according to Corrêa, should learn to listen and understand the problem of violence against women. In Corrêa's words: "Listening is like being a mother, a social worker, a friend, a police officer, in short, everything."[27] The work of policewomen should be "humanized." As she explains:

> A women's police station demands that policewomen do more than performing a legal task, it demands that they demonstrate sensibility, solidarity, and humanity. The task of policewomen is indeed one of investigating crimes, but solidarity, friendly words and good reception, although necessary for the work of both female and male police officers, are crucial in a women's police station.[28]

Besides providing an environment of trust for women to speak, a women's police station should offer an "integrated service," meaning that legal advisers, psychologists, and social workers should be available to complement the work of policewomen.[29] According to Corrêa,

> We need legal advisers to inform complainants about their rights, in case of divorce for example. We need psychologists to talk to the victim and her husband, following up the situation of the family. We need social workers to assist complainants, because every time poverty and unemployment increase, all sort of problems and violence at home also increase. And where do they end up? In the hands of policewomen.[30]

In addition, Corrêa believes that the goal of the women's police stations should be "to prevent the escalation of violence."[31] Corrêa reminds us, however, that a "women's police station is like any other police station, with a police delegate, police clerks, police investigators, all of them well equipped with legal skills and able to work in any kind of police station."[32] Thus, "enforcing the law," she points out, "was the mission of policewomen." After all, "this was the best formula we had to really reduce the incidence of violence against women. And that is why the women's police stations became a success."[33]

Corrêa knew that many female police officers shared her initial conception of the women's police station and they did not consider the women's police station a "real" police station. Women who entered the police force at that time—and even today—would only be assigned to women's police stations instead of regular police stations. Although there was no choice, many would have preferred not to work in the women's police stations because they wanted to be "real" police officers; consequently they would not *vestir a camisa* (embrace the idea). She learned, as the feminists taught, that being a woman was not enough to understand the situation of female victims: "The Police Department was discriminating against policewomen; we had a problem, but we had no choice, and the solution was to raise the consciousness of these women, showing the importance of their work."[34] By 1987 there were 15 women's police stations in the state of São Paulo, and all *delegadas*, *escrivãs*, and *investigadoras* were encouraged by Corrêa to attend meetings and workshops organized by the CECF. Ultimately Corrêa believes that "they have stayed in the women's police stations because they have fallen in love with their work."[35]

Corrêa also saw the CECF as an ally to policewomen as they endeavored to empower themselves as policewomen vis-à-vis policemen. As she explains:

> We fought for a long time, because everywhere there are obstacles to a new kind of work. I myself achieved recognition and projection, but it was very difficult for an institution predominantly masculine to become internationally known for the work of women's police stations. It was very difficult for us, policewomen, because the police have a hierarchy. We could not go directly to the head of the Police Department and make our demands. Since the CECF is not subordinated to this hierarchy, it could help us to address our demands. With the help of the CECF, and after many meetings, we could make our proposals. Among these proposals, there was always one concerning the training of those policewomen channeled to work in women's police stations.[36]

As there was no official course to teach policewomen, they depended on their own experience in the women's police stations. According to Corrêa, "even if we had a course, the women's movements would not be able to train policewomen, because there were not many women's groups working on the issue of violence against women and they did not have the experience of dealing with complainants in a criminal space such as the women's police stations."[37] During meetings with feminists, policewomen realized that their experience was adding to the feminist experience not only in quality but in quantity, since the number of women victims going to the women's police stations was much higher than the number of women looking for women's groups. The CECF and policewomen mutually benefited from the alliance they built while Corrêa was the head of the first women's police station.

In 1988, the police academy finally included in its curriculum a course called *vitimologia* (study of victims), which was taught by Corrêa. Although the title of the course did not suggest that it concerned violence against women per se, she took the opportunity to teach this subject and her experience in the women's police station. Gradually, policewomen gained power and visibility in society and in the police department, particularly within the female population. As Table 2.1 shows, the number of these stations multiplied, jumping from 13 to 58 during the administration of Montoro's successor, Governor Orestes Quércia (PMDB 1987 1990).

In 1989, during Quércia's administration, the police department created an Assessoria Especial das Delegacias de Polícia de Defensa da Mulher (Special Advisory Committee on the Police Stations in Defense of Women, or the Assessoria) to coordinate the work of the women's police stations in the state of São Paulo. Corrêa was selected to head the Assessoria, and in that capacity she strengthened policewomen's ties with the CECF. In October 1989, Corrêa and all female police officers working for women's police stations in the state of São Paulo attended the first meeting of *delegadas* and their assistants, which was organized by the CECF and the State Department of Public Security. At the time, there were over 100 female police officers working for 42 women's police stations.

During her tenure in the Assessoria, more women's police stations were established throughout the country, and Corrêa was always invited to attend their inauguration to speak about the experience of São Paulo. She would also speak about women's organizations, always connecting the women's police stations to the women's movements, and bringing the feminist perspective to the police all over the country. Because she was also a member of the police, other police officers began to listen and form

Table 2.1   Number of women's police stations created by governors of São Paulo, 1985–2003

Year	Governor (political party)	Political context	Women's police stations	Total
1985–1986	Franco Montoro (PMDB)	Participatory democracy	13	13
1987–1990	Orestes Quércia (PMDB)	Formal democracy	45	58
1990–1994	Luiz Fleury (PMDB)	Formal democracy	58	116
1995–2001	Mário Covas (PSDB)	Formal-participatory democracy	9	125
2002–Present	Geraldo Ackimin (PSDB)	Formal-participatory democracy	0	125

Source: Assessoria Especial das Delegacias de Polícia de Defesa da Mulher do Estado de São Paulo (Special Advisory Committee on the Police Stations in Defense of Women in the State of São Paulo).

respect for feminists. As Corrêa recalls:

> As a *delegada* and someone who had become engaged with the women's movement, they [police officers] could see that the movement was serious, whereas feminists knew that I was their ally. I was privileged in this sense, because I was a professional like other police officers, and sometimes they resisted the idea of opening women's police stations in their states. So I could speak with my colleagues and raise their sensibility.[38]

Corrêa left the Assessoria in November 1989 to run for the São Paulo state Assembly. She was elected twice, because of her popularity with women as head of the first women's police station. After she left the Assessoria, the alliance between policewomen and feminists floundered. Corrêa was replaced with Delegada Carlinda de Almeida, who had never worked in a women's police station and did not favor the existence of women's police stations, let alone any contact with feminists in the CECF. Corrêa had recommended that Almeida replace her in the Assessoria, but in the end this recommendation confirmed that it was not enough to be a woman, in and of itself, to represent women's police stations. "Unfortunately, Carlinda, although an excellent police delegate, was not able to *vestir a camisa* [embrace the idea]," says Corrêa.[39]

> There were no more meetings; she [Almeida] did not have the sensibility to put together policewomen and tell them that their work was beautiful and necessary, and that later they could go to a regular police station. Besides, she was practically an enemy of the CECF. Not because the CECF had no interest in the Assessoria; feminists tried many times, but were not successful. And I could not do anything, because I did not have the political power to change that situation.[40]

Almeida remained in the Assessoria until 1994, after which the alliance with feminists was re-established for a period of one year by her successor, Delegada Izilda Ferreira. These two divergent positions of opposition and alliance were shaped by changes in the feminist discourse on violence against women, the nature of the democracy adopted by the local government, and the continued increase in the number of women's police stations.

1990–1994: The Masculinist versus Feminist Women Police

In São Paulo in the early 1990s, feminist discourse on violence against women changed in three major aspects, both facilitating and hindering alliances between feminists and policewomen. First, Brazilian scholars, influenced by U.S. and French debates, started to replace the term "woman" with the term "gender," which they defined as a socially constructed category created through power relations between the sexes—therefore, not determined by biological differences between men and women (Heilborn 1992). "Gender violence" was seen as emerging from asymmetric and unequal power relations between the sexes (Saffioti 1994; Teles and Melo 2002). The use of "gender violence," a more neutral and scientific term than "violence against women," helped to facilitate the incorporation of gender claims made by feminist organizations into public policy.

Second, the practice of consciousness-raising (a grassroots process of acquiring a feminist consciousness and a gender identity) was replaced by the method of *capacitação* on gender (technical training with a critical perspective on gender aimed more at professionals).[41] The enactment of new and progressive legislation in the 1980s influenced social movements to focus their practices on citizenship—meaning access to justice and legal enforcement of civil rights. In the 1990s, this new focus on citizenship, combined with the emergence of academic feminist discourse on gender (rather than woman), shaped the feminist approach to the role of women's police stations. This approach shifted from *conscientização* and women's solidarity to *capacitação* on gender and law enforcement. In the context of the women's movements in Brazil, *capacitação* is a combination of professionalization, empowerment, and consciousness-raising, often emphasizing training providers of public services, especially in the areas of health and security. For feminists, policewomen are already *capacitadas* on the law, but not on gender. As feminist sociologist Heleieth Saffioti remarked:

> No professional [state agent] has a gender perspective. Obviously, they need it, all of them, in any area, such as health care, education, and in women's police stations as well. We need to create strategies to provide these professionals with *capacitação* from a gender perspective. They have never received any course in that direction. So how can we expect them to behave properly? Some non-governmental organizations and centers for gender studies in the universities can provide courses of *capacitação*.[42]

Feminists expected policewomen to perform their legal task as police but also believed that policewomen should understand the problem of violence against women from a gender perspective. As Maria Aparecida Schumaher, member of the CECF until 1994, explains:

> Police officers must be professionals, must be police. However, this is a specialized police station and police officers must be *capacitadas* [enabled with technical skills and critical knowledge] to have an understanding of, and the

sensitivity to deal with, the specific phenomenon of violence against women. They do not need to identify themselves as feminist or join the feminist movement. An understanding of violence against women already implies a feminist perspective.[43]

While feminists would like policewomen to enforce the law, they also intend, through courses of *capacitação*, to "humanize women's police stations and to teach policewomen to listen to complainants," just as the discourse on women's *conscientização* emphasized in the 1980s.[44]

The shift from *conscientização* to *capacitação* happened within the context of what Alvarez (1998) identifies as the "NGOization" and "transnationalization" of feminist movements in Latin America. In the 1990s, a growing number of feminist organizations professionalized and specialized, transforming themselves into non-governmental organizations (NGOs), increasingly dedicating themselves to intervening in policy processes on the national and international levels (Alvarez 1998). These trends proved to be a double-edged sword. For example, the emphasis on the preparatory meetings preceding the United Nations conferences of the 1990s temporarily distanced NGO professionals from local feminist mobilizations. At the same time, the participation of feminists in the 1993 United Nations Conference on Human Rights held in Vienna helped to revitalize local anti-violence struggles and launched the now internationally recognized assertion that "women's rights are human rights." In Vienna, violence against women was the center of the transnational feminist agenda (Keck and Sikkink 1998).

A third shift in the local feminist discourse on violence related to the emergence of a medical-therapeutic approach to the issue. In São Paulo, some local feminist NGOs working in the area of health, such as Coletivo Feminista Sexualidade e Saúde, incorporated violence against women into their agenda and began to offer a series of courses of *capacitação* on gender targeting mostly health care providers and social workers. From 1993 to 1995, Coletivo Feminista Sexualidade e Saúde, in conjunction with the Medical School at the University of São Paulo-USP, offered a series of annual courses called Capacitação para Atendimento a Mulheres em Situação de Violência (*Capacitação* for Assisting Women in Situations of Violence). These courses emphasized a therapeutic model, focusing on self-esteem, empowerment of women in situations of violence, and ability to negotiate with male partners. Most participants in these courses were professional women working for the state in health and social work—only a few policewomen attended.

These three changes were accompanied and shaped by two other important changes in the national and local political situation: the adoption of neoliberal policies, also known as structural adjustment policies (SAPs),[45] and a move away from participatory to a more formal democracy. In 1989, Brazilians chose Fernando Collor de Melo to be their first civilian president elected by direct ballot since the military coup 25 years before.[46] Collor opened the economy to foreign capital and cut public expenditures, especially in social areas such as education, health, and public security. Collor also depoliticized instances where participatory democracy brought together state actors and social movement actors. Feminist members of the CNDM, for example, were replaced with women completely disconnected from, or opposed to, feminist movement organizations.[47] Yet despite these unfavorable conditions, the number of women's police stations continued to grow, and policewomen in São Paulo continued to hold two positions—opposition and alliance—regarding feminism.

Opposing Feminism (1990–1993)
The governor of São Paulo, Luiz Antônio Fleury (1990–1994) did not facilitate the participation of social movement actors in the state. Even though he belonged to the same political party (PMDB) as governors Montoro and Quércia, Fleury was a former *delegado* and prosecutor who made it difficult for feminists to challenge the masculinist police culture.

Delegada Carlinda de Almeida headed the Assessoria during this period and, as previously mentioned, opposed any contact with feminists in the CECF. Almeida worked as a lawyer for ten years before joining the police force in 1982, during the transition from military to civilian rule. She was the fourth woman in the state of São Paulo to pass the exam to become a *delegado* working in a regular police station until the end of 1989 when she was appointed to replace Corrêa as head of the Assessoria. She left the Assessoria in April 1994 to do administrative work for a *delegado* in a division of the police department.[48]

Almeida had never worked for a women's police station before and was not familiar with the work of policewomen, but nonetheless was still selected to head the Assessoria because this position had to be occupied by a female police delegate in at least the second phase of her career and she was the only woman in that position at the time. Like most policewomen, Almeida never wanted to work in women's police stations and managed until this time to avoid doing so. This means that Almeida had never worked directly with female victims. She could not, however, avoid the Assessoria: "Orders are made to be obeyed, not discussed," she explained.[49]

Throughout her tenure, Almeida's views on the women's police stations and on feminism did not change. When I interviewed her in 1994, she claimed that the women's police stations had been created as a tool for feminists and politicians to empower themselves politically. "To say that men harm women is not true," explained Almeida.[50] "Men have much more patience with women, they cannot bear to see women crying. Women are not harassed in regular police stations. Feminists invented that for political reasons. The proof is that the first head of the first women's police station abandoned everything to become an Assemblywoman."[51]

Almeida also believed that women's police stations discriminated against and segregated both policewomen and complainants. As she explained: "First, there is discrimination against policewomen who are forced to work in these women's police stations. Secondly, there is discrimination against female complainants who end up having fewer places to file their complaints."[52] Making use of the legal ideology of neutrality to explain her position, Almeida claimed that, "We must be concerned about the human being, independent of sex, color and age. When you create a distinction, you discriminate. Can't women deal with men? Why can't they speak with men? Feminists are inventing foolish things to segregate women even more."[53]

In addition to segregating women, Almeida believed that the women's police stations diminished the role of policewomen because the cases they processed were not criminal cases and did not belong to the police. Unlike Corrêa, she did not think that policewomen should learn to listen like a mother, a psychologist, and a social worker. Policewomen should investigate crimes only; what arrived in the women's police stations were not crimes. As she put it:

> Women go there to complain about lack of money, custody and alimony. These are not problems for the police, these are problems concerning family law, for lawyers, not for police officers. Thus, besides dealing with the Penal Code, policewomen end up having to give information on civil law. They have to behave like psychologists or social workers. But there is a specific career of social workers for these cases.[54]

Almeida did not perceive violence against women as a crime but rather as a social problem to be dealt with by social workers. "I agree that women should denounce this situation," she said, "but instead of creating women's police stations, we should have more social workers in regular police stations."[55] Besides not treating violence against women as a crime, Almeida assumed an individualistic approach to this problem, based on a free-choice model. As she explained:

> Women are beaten up because they allow it. Women are stronger than men, they give birth, they can do everything they want, as long as they have the will. So they do not react against eight or ten years of beating because they

are afraid of having to work [outside the home]. I can't stand women who use their tears as an excuse [not to face their own problems].[56]

According to Almeida, feminists patronized women and treated them as fragile; however, she defined herself as a feminist in her own way: "I'm a feminist in my way. I believe in women; they [feminists in the CECF] don't. I believe that women can do everything as long as they want to."[57] Thus, unlike Corrêa, she redefined feminism to *oppose* the perspective of feminists in the CECF.

Given Almeida's view that violence against women is not a crime, it is not surprising that she did not see a need to include a course on violence against women in the curriculum of the police academy. "Police delegates are well trained in law schools and in the police academy," argued Almeida.[58] Even if she favored such a course, feminists, in her view, should not be the teachers: "These feminists [in the CECF] do not have a law degree. They do not know what is right and wrong."[59] Hence, she never encouraged policewomen to attend seminars or workshops on violence against women organized by the CECF. As she recalled:

> In the beginning, they tried to intervene in the women's police stations, because they thought the women's police stations were subordinated to the CECF. They would demand that policewomen attended their meetings. But policewomen are not subordinated to them. We even went to the first meetings, but we realized it was a waste of time. These people in the CECF never worked in women's police stations, they do not know anything about the work of policewomen. It is more productive to have policewomen advising feminists in the CECF than feminists advising policewomen.[60]

Almeida's contact with the CECF never influenced her views on women's police stations and feminists; Almeida "was not able to embrace the idea," as Corrêa put it.[61] When she left the Assessoria, it was a relief, not only to the CECF but also to her: "I had the opportunity to do other things and to be a police officer again. You know, I entered the police to do everything men do, to be a police officer. Most women do not like to work with women's police stations, because they enter the police to do everything, to investigate crimes such as homicide."[62]

Despite the Assessoria's lack of interest and support, the number of women's police stations continued to grow. Because of the popularity of these police stations among the female population, politicians saw them as a tool to attract votes and the government began to open new stations indiscriminately. In just three years, Governor Fleury created more women's police stations than any other São Paulo governor (46.4% of the total 125 women's police stations established from 1985 to 2003). Yet the police department's disinterest had a great impact. The department did not provide the new stations with the minimum resources, human and material, needed to do the job, much less specialized training for police-women. In this context, it was not surprising to hear statements from policewomen that clearly undermined the original goals of the women's police stations. For instance, police clerk Mila Duarte expressed that, "Problems between husband and wife must be resolved at home. I'm very concerned about the family, I may regret the registering of a case later, because this may cause damage to the family."[63] Duarte did not view rape in marriage as a crime either. She even blamed women for their situation. As she put it, "Many women are beaten up because they ask for it. I think she should take responsibility and defend herself. She was strong enough to speak up when she was provoking it. So she should fight back."[64]

Hearing stories about this type of attitude, feminist activists felt disenchanted, and the CECF vocalized criticisms of the services offered by the women's police stations (Conselho Estadual da Condição Feminina de São Paulo 1993, 7). As Teresa Verardo, then coordinator of the CECF's Commission on Violence against Women, expressed:

> Policewomen in the first women's police stations attended workshops organized by the CECF, and they treated clients from a feminist standpoint. As politicians are opening more and more women's police stations without any concern about training, we have a problem rather than a solution. Policewomen are extremely *machistas*.[65]

Bringing Feminism Back In (1994)

In April 1994, an election year, the CECF had the opportunity to work closely with the Assessoria again. Corrêa, running for state assembly for the second time, was able to use her political influence in the police department to replace Delegada Carlinda de Almeida with Delegada Izilda Ferreira, an old ally.

Ferreira entered the police force as a police clerk in 1973 during the military regime. She became a *delegada* in 1983 and worked in a regular police station. In March 1986, still under Montoro's administration, a new women's police station was opened on the west side of São Paulo. Ferreira was immediately transferred there where she worked for eight years until named to head the Assessoria in April 1994, a position she held until January 1995, a meager nine-month term.

Like Corrêa, Ferreira did not think women's police stations were necessary at first. "When I was working in a regular police station, there were some cases of threat, but I did not believe them, I thought that was not important. I thought that other police officers would not initiate the police investigation afterwards either."[66] Overwhelmed by the number of cases after working in the women's police station a short time, she altered her position: "I changed a lot my way of seeing these cases, especially after I faced a case of threat that resulted in the actual behavior. But we didn't know that until we had this kind of contact."[67]

Ferreira's experience in a women's police station also affected her perception of it as a police station that should be different from regular police stations. According to Ferreira, the main role of the women's police stations is to provide female complainants with "moral support" by recognizing her complaint as a crime:

> A woman goes to a women's police station, rather than to a regular police station in her neighborhood, because she wants not only to register her complaint, but also to get this kind of support [i.e. moral support]. She wants to hear that what she's doing is not bad, that she is not harming her husband. Sometimes, she doesn't even want to register the complaint. So we talk to her and try to explain that what he did was a crime and that she shouldn't feel ashamed. He is the one who should feel ashamed. In our society, nobody questions the fact that a victim of robbery files a complaint in a police station; but when a woman is harmed by her husband, everybody says "Ha, he was just nervous! Filing a complaint will destroy the marriage." She is surrounded by these stories and we must say that she shouldn't feel ashamed for coming to the women's police station.[68]

Ferreira's position was also affected by her ongoing contact with feminists in the CECF. Although not identifying herself as a feminist, her understanding of violence against women was clearly influenced by the feminist perspective that this problem is a result of a patriarchal social structure rather than deviant behavior. As she explained:

> I don't know if I am a feminist, there is a lot of prejudice against this word. But I make trouble, you know, when I hear someone saying that *mulher gosta de apanhar* ["women like to be beaten up," a popular proverb in Brazil], I get really upset and react back. Some people even say that women like so much to be beaten up that they go to the women's police station and ask to close their cases. But the reality is that these women depend on their husbands economically, and they were raised hearing that they should be housewives. Once they get information, they will leave their husbands.[69]

Ferreira saw the relationship between policewomen and the CECF as "very fruitful for both sides."[70] As she recalled, "In the beginning [in the mid-1980s] we didn't know that reality [the reality of female complainants], and we had to learn from experience. The CECF helped a lot; we would meet there and discuss our work."[71] But, at that time, she still believed feminists were "too radical," meaning that they were not willing to negotiate.[72] Although the meetings organized by the CECF were informal and not mandatory, Ferreira and some other policewomen—not only *delegadas* but also *escrivãs* and *investigadoras*—would "sacrifice our free time to be able to share our experience and learn from each other, because during our work time we had no chance to phone each other."[73]

In contact with the CECF again in 1994, Ferreira found feminists "more mature and realistic about the possibilities for meeting their demands."[74] The CECF's new "gender perspective," which first appeared in the 1994 bulletins of the CECF, helped to neutralize the "radicalism" of feminists in Ferreira's eyes. In the early 1990s, in an attempt to gain better access to the police department, feminists in the CECF emphasized their professional knowledge on gender issues instead of their ideological feminist vision of patriarchy. They took care in framing their language in ways that would not make police officers feel accused. "We want police officers to learn about gender violence, by discussing our values with them and making clear that we, women, are not enemies of men," explained Tereza Verardo.[75]

The CECF and the Assessoria, with Ferreira at the head, created the Grupo Gestor da Política Estadual de Prevenção e Combate à Violência Contra a Mulher (Working Group on Public Policy to Prevent and Fight Violence against Women). One of the proposals of this Working Group focused on the gender *capacitação* for those providing public services to female victims of violence. Although the Working Group tried to include a course on violence against women in the curriculum of the police academy, they only managed to create workshops. Had they actually offered the proposed course, "it would have to have been taught by a police delegate rather than a feminist anyway," said Ferreira.[76] In her view, the training of policewomen had become a very important issue, not because policewomen lack legal knowledge, but rather because they need to better understand the problem of violence against women. Like Corrêa, Ferreira thinks that, "[i]t is not enough to be a woman in order to work in the women's police stations. It is necessary to become involved with this problem [of violence against women], understanding and accepting its reality. Those who do not know this reality cannot understand the reasons why a woman who is beaten up for twenty years does not fight back, and does not want to separate from her husband."[77]

Policewomen's lack of understanding of the problem of violence against women was not the only reason for specific training. It would also help to confront the prejudices endured by women who entered the police force during the 1990s. Many women still did not want to work in women's police stations, feeling they were put there as a form of "*castigo*"—a "punishment" that would keep them from moving up professionally. Thus, another objective of the proposed course was to attract policewomen to work for women's police stations.

Like Corrêa, Ferreira saw the CECF as an ally in the struggle against the discrimination that policewomen still faced within the police department. "We need each other," she said, "because the women's police stations were the result of a struggle initiated by the CECF, and there are many things we [policewomen] cannot say, whereas they [feminists in the CECF] can. Thus, we need them to express our demands. But they also need us, because we are the source of statistics and information."[78]

Ferreira's positive view of the relationship between feminists and policewomen bore fruitful outcomes. In June 1994 the State Department of Public Security sponsored a seminar, "A Delegacia de Defesa da Mulher Frente à Realidade Social" (The police station in defense of women and social reality). The seminar brought together the majority of *delegadas* from the 117 women's police stations in the state of São Paulo for the first time as well as the Secretary of Public Security, state assemblywoman Rosmary Corrêa, Ferreira as the head of the Assessoria, and the president of the CECF.

Around the same time, the 1 Curso de Capacitação para Atendimento a Mulheres em Situação de Violência (First Course of *Capacitação* for Providers of Services to Women in Situations of Violence) was offered by Coletivo Feminista Sexualidade e Saúde—one of the most important São Paulo NGOs focusing on women's health and reproductive rights. However, only two policewomen attended this course, Izilda Ferreira and her assistant, police investigator Ivete Ramos.

It is worth noting Ramos's transformation of her gender identity and interests as a police officer after her interaction with clients in women's police stations and with feminists in the CECF. Ramos comes from a working-class family and identifies herself as black. She entered the police force during the military regime, in 1977, as a police investigator, when she was 29 years old. She worked in a regular police station until 1986, when she was transferred, along with her chief, Ferreira, to the women's police station that opened on the west side of São Paulo. Five years after their initial transfer, both women were again transferred to the women's police station located in downtown São Paulo. In April 1994, when Ferreira became the head of the Assessoria, Ramos followed her chief.[79]

While working in a regular police station, Ramos did clerical work for the male police delegate instead of actually working as a police investigator, for example, looking for criminals in the streets. "We always had a man in the forefront, and we had to perform bureaucratic tasks only," said

Ramos.[80] The head of the police station where Ramos worked would leave notes on the desk of other policemen saying: "Send *zicas* [police slang for cases of violence against women] to Ramos."[81] Although Ramos was not allowed to perform the tasks of policemen, she still considered herself a "real" police officer. With her transfer to the women's police station, she felt, as Corrêa and Ferreira had, a change in her career:

> I felt like I was not a police officer anymore. My colleagues, after knowing that I was in the women's police station, would say: "Are you crazy? You only have *zicas* there." I also felt different in a police car with women only. I was not used to driving a police car before, because usually male police chiefs do not allow policewomen to drive. And people in the streets would look at us as if we were animals behind bars. The people were not prepared to see policewomen either.[82]

Yet, Ramos's position changed once she started to face long lines of women waiting to file their complaints in the women's police station. "Although we had seen some cases in regular police stations, we had no idea about the gravity of the problem. It seems that all women decided to file complaints when the first women's police station was created, the lines were always enormous."[83]

The meetings and workshops on violence against women organized by the CECF were important tools for Ramos and other policewomen to learn about a problem they had not thought about before: "In the beginning, all policewomen would meet with feminist groups and they would help us to understand the problem of violence against women. The oldest policewomen have not left the women's police stations, because we all ended up embracing the idea."[84] Ramos considered these meetings very important "to raise policewomen's consciousness,"[85] allowing her to "embrace the idea" and start differentiating women's police stations from regular police stations. "Women have more patience to listen, though we know that not everybody likes to work there. Not all policewomen treat complainants the way we would like to."[86]

Like Corrêa and Ferreira, Ramos favored alliances with feminists "to raise policewomen's consciousness," and attempted to reestablish those meetings and workshops in 1994, when she followed Ferreira to the Assessoria.[87] Ramos advocated the close connection between women's police stations and the women's movements:

> I tell Lígia and Tereza [feminists working in the CECF in 1994], "we need to organize meetings, we need to bring everybody together." This will raise policewomen's consciousness. There are one hundred and some more

regular police stations in the Capital of São Paulo. If we do not differentiate our work, let's close the women's police stations. That is why we want workshops. We need the CECF. Without it, without these women, Lígia and Tereza, we cannot work.[88]

Fully embracing the feminist discourse on *conscientização* (consciousness-raising), Ramos considered raising policewomen's consciousness a necessary step to raising complainants' consciousness. In her view, "the main role of the women's police station is to raise women's consciousness."[89] She spoke passionately about the transformation some complainants went through while filing complaints in the women's police stations: "It is hard to help all battered women, to raise their consciousness about their own problem, and to solve it. The woman comes in under horrible conditions and we tell her: 'You have to struggle, you have to get up.' It is interesting when a few days later, the woman comes back as if she was another woman. I have seen cases like this. I couldn't recognize the woman, well dressed, more beautiful, wonderful."[90]

Challenging both the masculinist police culture and the legal ideology of neutrality, Ramos viewed the role of the women's police stations within a broader context of democratization of the police: "Nowadays, any public service is political. Today the people don't see our group as members of the police force anymore. Instead, they see us as *companheiras* [comrades, a word used by the Left]. This is very gratifying."[91] By "our group," Ramos meant Ferreira, Corrêa, and other policewomen who had made alliances with social movements and organizations fighting for democracy. It is worth reproducing here one of the stories Ramos vividly recalled during our interview:

> We [Ramos and Ferreira] were in the Computer Workers' Union to celebrate International Women's Day. There were women from all over the country. A few years ago, when would you hear that a *delegada* and a police investigator were together in the same room with unionists? Never! Neither they nor us wanted it. Nowadays, they receive us with their doors open. When they passed the microphone to *Doutora* Izilda, she was hesitant, because there were women from different political parties. But, to my surprise, she stood up and addressed the audience by saying: COMPANHEIRAS! I couldn't control my emotions, I stood up and clapped enthusiastically. Everybody in the room did the same. Can you imagine a police delegate in a union with all those women from different political parties, suddenly calling them *companheiras*? That was my major glory! It is a sign that we are really together for one cause; and I feel touched because they are not viewing us as repression anymore.[92]

Since the Assessoria, under the leadership of Ferreira and her team, did not have the political leverage to make participation in workshops organized by the CECF and feminist NGOs mandatory, or to succeed in getting a course on violence against women included in the police academy's curriculum, it was not able to directly challenge the ideology of neutrality and the masculinist culture shaping the discourses and practices of the new policewomen working in the growing number of women's police stations in the mid-1990s. Ferreira and Ramos became outspoken critics of this masculinist culture; their criticisms were not appreciated, and they were removed from the Assessoria in January 1995 by the newly elected governor, Mário Covas. The police department sent them to work in a regular police station.

1995–2003: The Feminist *versus* Gendered Police

Since the mid-1990s, relations between policewomen and feminists have developed in the context of a transnational feminism—a post-Beijing world—in which international feminist politics impacts local feminist politics, and vice-versa. Policewomen and feminist relations have also developed within a national and local conjuncture of neoliberal policies and a hybrid formal-participatory democracy.

At the Fourth United Nations World Conference on Women held in Beijing in 1995, violence against women was at the center of the feminist agenda, further contributing to the strengthening of local feminist politics regarding this issue. In the footsteps of the Vienna Conference, the issue was framed as a violation of human rights and, therefore, as an object of international criminal law (Keck and Sikkink 1998; Macaulay 2002). However, given the complexities of understanding and using international law to fight violence against women on a local level, feminist activists also framed it as a health issue (Keck and Sikkink 1998). In the post-Beijing period, these two discourses—human rights and health—complemented each other, influencing the Brazilian government and local feminist organizations.[93]

Further shaping feminist politics during this period was the presidency of Fernando Henrique Cardoso. Cardoso headed the ticket for a new party—Partido Social-Democrático Brasileiro (Social-Democratic Brazilian Party or PSDB) and was elected for two terms (1994–1998 and 1999–2002). The PSDB was founded in São Paulo in the late 1980s by Cardoso, Franco Montoro and Mário Covas, who all came out of the more social-democratic sectors of the PMDB. Despite the social-democratic name, the Cardoso government continued to implement the PMDB's neoliberal policies as dictated by the IMF, favoring the privatization of publicly owned companies and the retreat of the state from social responsibilities. On the other hand, Cardoso adopted a hybrid formal-participatory democracy that included the participation of social movement actors in the design of social programs emphasizing human rights and racial issues. The CNDM, for example, was re-staffed by highly regarded feminist scholars and activists.

In São Paulo, Governor Mário Covas (PSDB) also favored the participation of social movement actors in state councils. He received unanimous support from feminist organizations when he nominated a black woman (a first), Maria Aparecida de Laia, to the presidency of the CECF. However, because of his neoliberal policies, he also cut the staff of the CECF to less than one third of its original strength. The Assessoria received a new name, Serviço Técnico de Apoio às Delegacias de Polícia de Defesa da Mulher do Estado de São Paulo (Technical Service in Support of the Police Stations in Defense of Women in the State of São Paulo, hereafter referred to as Serviço Técnico), but its role did not change. In this paradoxical political climate, the new head of the Serviço Técnico, Delegada Maria Inês Valenti, moved from an initially ambiguous relationship with the CECF to an explicit alliance. Under the administration of the PSDB, Valenti's explicit alliance with the CECF ultimately led to her removal from the Serviço Técnico.

Figure 2.1   Maria Aparecida de Laia, the first black woman to become president of the CECF (1995–2003). *(Photo by the author.)*

From Ambiguous to Explicit Alliances (1995–2001)
Maria Inês Valenti, who identifies herself as middle-class and white, graduated from law school in 1988 when she was 42 years old. She passed the exam to become a *delegada* in 1989 during the administration of Quércia. Valenti divorced while attending law school, raising her two children alone. She knew that she suffered through a terrible time, but only after working for the women's police stations was she able to name the conditions that led to her divorce—she came to realize that her husband had inflicted psychological violence on her.[94] Like most policewomen, Valenti was assigned to a women's police station as soon as she concluded the three-month course in the police academy. She worked for six years as head of the women's police station of Osasco, a town near the city of São Paulo. In January 1995, when newly elected Governor Mário Covas (PSDB) took office, she was selected to replace Ferreira's position in the Assessoria.

Like many other policewomen, Valenti did not initially favor the existence of specialized police stations for women, believing that they discriminated against women. She also believed that violence against women was not as serious as other crimes, such as robbery, drug trafficking, and kidnapping. However, just as Corrêa and Ferreira found, her experience in dealing with complaints initiated by female victims persuaded her that the women's police stations were not only necessary but that one of their main goals was "to make it possible for women to denounce violence against women."[95] But unlike those policewomen who "embraced the cause," Valenti did not agree with the feminist critique that policemen mistreated women clients. In her view, policemen could not give priority to cases of violence against women because they had "more serious" crimes to process. As she explained in August 1995:

> In a regular police station, police officers must process crimes such as homicide, robbery, drug trafficking, and of course a woman who makes a complaint against her husband is going to wait. It is a matter of setting priorities. We have other crimes that harm society with more brutality than fights between partners. So that is why the women's police stations were created, for women to have a place where they feel comfortable to make a claim. These specialized police stations must deal only with this kind of problems, because you have to be patient and female complainants are tiring.[96]

Valenti did not think that female victims of violence would necessarily feel more comfortable talking to policewomen rather than policemen. "This story that women don't feel comfortable talking to a man. . . . I don't agree. It's not true, most women choose a male gynecologist, for example. Is there a situation more embarrassing than this one? Now, women do feel uncomfortable when [the person] who is listening to them does not take them seriously."[97]

Valenti also considered that: "The only role of women's police stations was to investigate crimes."[98] She was "absolutely against" having psychologists and social workers providing services in the women's police stations' precinct. She reasoned that,

> They [the psychologists and social workers] are not part of the police force. They will never become part of the police force, because their career does not have a hierarchy. I can't order them to act in this or that way, because their work is completely subjective. It's similar to the work of a physician. Also, the women's police stations' precinct is not a place to deal with victims' health or social life. There are other state departments for these issues.[99]

When she entered the police force in 1989, Valenti attended a few workshops organized by the CECF but felt that the feminists leading the workshops acted as if "they were in a war."[100] Whenever the meetings were not mandatory, she did not attend, believing that they were not useful or practical for policewomen. "I think they were somehow necessary, because the women's police stations were just starting, but Rose [Corrêa] had her own political agenda. We would feel like marionettes. Policewomen were sent to work anywhere, regardless of where they lived."[101]

In 1995, newly appointed to head the Serviço Técnico, Valenti still harbored some prejudices against feminists, establishing an ambiguous alliance with the CECF illustrated by her responses to the debates on the redrafting of the legislation on the women's police stations. In December 1995, state representatives, judges, policewomen, and a few feminist activists met to discuss whether abortion and infanticide (as well as a few other crimes) should fall under the jurisdiction of the women's police stations. It is important to note that this would represent a significant shift since, in the cases of abortion and infanticide, women are perpetrators not victims.

The discussion was sparked by new legislation establishing criminal small claims courts (Law 9,009, September 26, 1995), which defined "small claims" as those crimes carrying a prison term of up to one year. Since most cases processed in women's police stations fit this definition, policewomen feared that this legislation would force the closure of the women's police station. In their defense, policewomen lobbied to expand the jurisdiction of their stations. With a few exceptions (such as Corrêa) the majority of policewomen, including Valenti, favored the change. For them, it did not matter that the women's police stations had been created to serve female *victims* rather than process female *perpetrators*.[102]

Despite her misgivings, Valenti began to absorb aspects of the discourse on gender violence, prompting other policewomen who entered the police in the 1990s to also embrace aspects of this discourse. This shift, influenced by changes in the discourse of both feminists and policewomen in the 1990s, illustrates one of the trends Alvarez (1998) points out in feminist politics in the 1990s. As Valenti pointed out: "The feminist discourse was very critical and not constructive. This was not stimulating, because we [policewomen] work 24 hours per day, we are the only institution in the justice system that serves women, and they [feminists] criticize only us. More recently the CECF has changed its discourse. Policewomen have also changed, becoming more confident about their work."[103]

Indeed, as noted above, the CECF changed its discourse on violence against women during the 1990s: instead of insisting on feminist *conscientização* (consciousness-raising) of policewomen from a feminist perspective, the CECF fought for policewomen's *capacitação* on "gender violence." This new feminist language was first presented to policewomen in 1994, when Ferreira replaced Almeida in the Assessoria (now Serviço Técnico). At first, there was a negative reaction on the part of many policewomen who did not favor—and still do not favor—the idea of receiving any kind of training other than the legal training provided by the police academy. Once she became the head of the Serviço Ténico, Valenti was immediately contacted by state representative Bia Pardi (Workers' Party), who asked Valenti to promote policewomen's *capacitação* on "gender violence," a new term Valenti was just starting to hear from feminists. Valenti was outraged by the proposal. As she recounted:

> I don't understand this whole thing about *capacitação* very well. This is a technical expression. Just to give you an idea [of my ignorance], as soon as I came here [to the Serviço Técnico], I received a letter from a state representative asking for *capacitação* of policewomen. I was furious; . . . legally speaking we are all *capacitadas* [entitled to work as police]. So I refused to work on this kind of training. Nowadays, I wouldn't react the same way.[104]

Valenti's resistance to the kind of training known as *capacitação* was due in part to a semantic confusion. In Portuguese, *capacitar* literally means to enable someone to do something. Since policewomen are already trained by the police academy on legal knowledge, Valenti felt insulted when feminists demanded the *capacitação* of policewomen, assuming feminists were insinuating that they were unable to perform the task of police officers. In addition to her confusion about the semantics of *capacitação*, Valenti also reacted against the idea of *capacitação* because she did not believe—like the majority of policewomen—that working in women's police stations should require specific training to better understand the problem of violence against women or of gender violence. Furthermore, her reaction against *capacitação* was indicative of the lack of contact she had with feminists in the CECF, as well as women's NGOs.

Valenti started to change her ideas about *capacitação* after participating in a seminar on violence against women, children, and adolescents held in São Paulo in 1995. In our interview, she recalled how the speech of Maria Amélia Azevedo, former member of the CECF's Commission on Violence against Women, taught her not only about the meaning of *capacitação*, but also about the need to *capacitar* policewomen on "gender violence." As Valenti recounted:

> I was listening to Maria Amélia Azevedo's speech, which was on violence against children. And she said the following, without even defining *capacitação*: "Without believing the child, how can you hear him? If you assume that he is lying, you cannot hear him, you arrive at your own conclusions without taking into account what he is saying." Oops, I thought, how can you deal with a woman [victim of violence] if you assume that she likes to be beaten up? This assumption discredits the victim's problem. Most policewomen do not take seriously female complainants, do not believe their stories, and think that these women want and deserve to be abused. So I understood what *capacitação* was about. It's not the same as *capacidade* [being able to perform a task, or being licensed to practice law, for example]. Now we will try to establish a course of *capacitação* for both [policewomen and policemen].[105]

Valenti also began to absorb the new feminist language on "gender violence." In a 1995 interview, she explained this term based on what she had learned from feminist sociologist Heleieth Saffioti:

> [Saffioti] says that there is no hierarchy in same-sex relations, only between men and woman. Gender violence, she says, is a result of women's subordination to men. A child is socially transformed into a man or a woman. And women are socially subordinated to men, hence the hierarchy and gender violence. This is a new world for me. I never had thought about this. And I agree with her.[106]

In October 1995, Valenti attended, and encouraged all policewomen to attend, the II Curso de Capacitação para Atendimento a Mulheres em Situação de Violência (Second Course of *Capacitação* for Providers of Services to Women in Situations of Violence), offered by the feminist NGO Coletivo Feminista Sexualidade e Saúde and the Medical School of the University of São Paulo. This three-month course, though emphasizing a medical-therapeutic approach to violence, helped Valenti and the

other police delegate, Delegada Maria Tereza G. Rosa, to further understand the meaning of "gender violence" and the importance of policewomen's *capacitação* from a gender perspective.

It is worth noticing how this course affected Delegada Rosa who had then
been assigned to head the women's police station located in the neighborhood of Butantã, which I regularly observed over the period of three months
in 1995. One day, shortly after I arrived in that women's police station,
Delegada Rosa asked me, almost in despair, whether I could help her to
understand battered women. She had just talked to a female complainant
who had begged her to close the police investigation. Rosa seemed really wor-
ried about the complainant, and wanted to understand her situation. "I hope
this course will help me," she said pointing to the *II Curso de Capacitação para
Atendimento a Mulheres em Situação de Violência* reader on her desk.[107]

Rosa had first heard about "gender violence" during the celebration of
the 10th anniversary of the first women's police station, when Heleieth
Saffioti gave a speech on the subject, but this course had further shaped
her views on violence against women. On the one hand, she started to read
about "gender" and she expected to learn about "gender violence." On the
other hand, Rosa was exposed, for the first time, to the feminist discourse
on "women in situations of violence." It was interesting to observe how
Rosa's language changed after having attended that course. Our first interview took place at the beginning of the course and she rarely used the term
"women in situations of violence." After the course, when I interviewed
her for the second time, she consistently referred to female complainants
as "women in situations of violence."

Figure 2.2 Delegada Maria Tereza G. Rosa, head of the first women's police
station in 2001. *(Photo by the author.)*

Finally, this course made Rosa see—as Corrêa, Ferreira, Ramos, and Valenti had through their interactions with feminists—that "it is not enough to be a woman to work in the women's police stations."[108] In addition, Rosa learned about services provided to women by the state outside of the criminal system (e.g., Pérola Byton Hospital), and by women's NGOs (e.g., Coletivo Feminista Sexualidade e Saúde). In Rosa's perspective, interacting with social workers and other professionals during the course was an enriching experience. She did not know about these services and the problems they face. She also came to realize the need of governmental and non-governmental organizations to learn about the problems facing the women's police stations. The exchanging of experiences is important, in her opinion, to better advise complainants. Speaking enthusiastically about the course during our interviews in 1995 and 1996, Rosa was hoping that similar courses would be offered, not only to policewomen, but also to policemen.

Although Rosa and Valenti were the only policewomen who ended up attending the course, it is important to note that Rosa's decision to attend was strongly supported by Valenti. The head of the Serviço Técnico had become more open to establishing an explicit alliance with feminists not only in the CECF but also in NGOs and academia.

In the post Beijing context, Valenti "absorbed" aspects of the discourse on women's human rights and began to favor an explicit alliance with feminists. In May 1998, as part of the Campaign for the Human Rights of Women, the CECF organized, in partnership with the State Department of Public Security (and the Serviço Técnico), the Primeiro Curso de Capacitação para Delegadas das Delegacias de Defesa da Mulher: Violência de Gênero (First Course of Capacitação for Female Delegates Working for Women's Police Stations: Gender Violence).[109] This ten-week course was mandatory for all delegadas of the then 124 women's police stations in the state of São Paulo. Throughout the course, feminist scholars and activists from the CECF, CNDM, and feminist NGOs gave lectures addressing gender issues in relation to human rights, health, media, and the like.[110]

By 1999, Valenti's explicit alliance with feminists was undeniable when she became the first policewoman to join the CECF, doing so as a "representative of civil society" (Conselho Estadual da Condição Feminina de São Paulo 2003). Then CECF president, Maria Aparecida de Laia, described their relationship as "good and harmonious."[111] By joining the CECF, Valenti challenged the separation between her supposedly politically "neutral" role in law enforcement and her political-feminist role in civil society. The neutral-legal ideology and the masculinist culture of the police department would not tolerate such a challenge and in May 2001, she was removed from the Serviço Técnico, sent to perform administrative duties in a politically insignificant sector of the police department.

Back to an Ambiguous Alliance (2001–2003)

The new head of the Serviço Técnico, Márcia Buccelli Salgado, entered the police force in 1980 as a police clerk and worked in regular police stations until 1988, when she passed the exam for police delegate. After the three-month training period in the police academy, she was immediately channeled to a women's police station. Like the women before her, she also participated in the first meetings organized by feminists in the CECF. As she recalls,

> The number of women's police stations was small. Unlike today, there were not many in the interior of the São Paulo state. The few of us who started working for women's police stations in the mid-1980s would meet in the CECF to discuss the problems of the women's police stations. At the time we even had a closer contact with the secretary of public security.[112]

Like Valenti and other policewomen who absorbed aspects of the feminist discourse on violence against women, Salgado learned from feminists that the women's police stations should provide a specialized service more attentive to the needs of their women clients. As she explains, "the major difference between regular police stations and women's police stations is that the former investigate crimes but do not listen to the victims as we, in the women's police stations, do."[113] According to Salgado, the Serviço Técnico must provide not only technical assistance to policewomen but also bring awareness and motivation to them, so the women's police stations distinguish themselves from regular police stations. But, like the majority of policewomen, Salgado does not identify herself as a feminist: "I have more of a vision of social equilibrium than what the feminists advocate. I fight for women, but I don't share that extreme concept of feminism."[114]

Like the policewomen in alliance with feminists, Salgado favors the capacitação of policewomen from a gender perspective, but believes feminists need to be less critical of the women's police stations. Overall, her relationship with feminist organizations, such as the CECF and União de Mulheres de São Paulo, is amicable. But, according to her, other sectors of the criminal justice system, including in the judiciary, do not treat women with the same respect that women's police stations offer. Yet feminists, she says, tend to first blame women's police stations. She recalled that in a meeting a member of the feminist organization Casa Eliane de Grammont said that the services provided in women's police stations were worse than in regular police stations. Salgado felt this was a harsh critique and a gross generalization. In response to this criticism and because her colleagues had heard similar critiques, she asked the president of the CECF to organize a meeting with the police delegates.

While Salgado is receptive to gender *capacitação* and has established an amicable relationship with the CECF, she is also reluctant to "embrace the cause," as Corrêa and Valenti did during their tenure in the Serviço Técnico. In July 2003, the newly appointed president of the CECF, Aparecida Maria de Almeida, invited Salgado to participate in the CECF's monthly meetings. As a result of Salgado's lack of interest in attending, the CECF's president sent a memo to the police chief and the secretary of public security soliciting her presence. Salgado is now forced to attend the meetings.[115]

Salgado's reluctance to attend the CECF's meetings should not be interpreted from an individualistic perspective or as a free decision. The dominant masculinist culture of her institutional base may play a role in how she approaches feminists in the CECF. Valenti's fate may remind Salgado to be careful in establishing a too amicable relationship with the CECF. According to some policewomen, Valenti's removal from the Serviço Técnico was a sort of "*castigo*" (punishment) for her strong position in defense of women's police stations as well as her close ties with the CECF. For many, Valenti "went too far."[116] Valenti was further punished by being forbidden to give interviews. In August 2003, I asked my research assistant in São Paulo to approach Valenti for a follow-up interview. Valenti asked my assistant to make a written request to her superior, explaining that she could not speak without his authorization. I faxed a letter formally asking for the interview, but my request was denied. This was the first time I had to write such a letter to interview any female or male police officer and the first time I was denied an interview.

Conclusion

This chapter corroborates the assertion that the state is not a monolith, as much of the new literature on gender and the state has observed (Alexander 1991; Waylen 1996a, 1996b, 1998; Rai 1996; Schild 1998; Alvarez 1999–2000; Santos 1999a; Molyneux 2000). As Waylen points out, "it [the state] is not a unitary structure but a differentiated set of institutions, agencies and discourses, and the product of a particular historical and political conjuncture" (1998, 7). But, even within the same institution, such as the police, state actors have multiple, often conflicting, interests. Policewomen's interests and identities, for example, are not homogenous, and policewomen relate to feminists in multiple and contradictory ways.

Feminist scholars have emphasized that the nature of the government or the political conjuncture is a major factor in shaping the relationship between gender and the state (Waylen 1998; Alvarez 1990, 1997, 1999–2000; Molyneux 2000). Indeed, the multiple and shifting positions assumed by policewomen regarding feminists in São Paulo must be understood within the context of the local political conjuncture and the larger political process of democratization. But by positing the relationship between the state and women solely as a function of the political conjuncture, or of the party in power, feminist scholars have ignored micro-level changes in civil society and the effects of the interactions between non-feminist state actors, feminist actors within and outside of state institutions, and the clients of the state. The case of women's police stations shows that, even under political regimes controlled by the same party, policewomen have held conflicting and changing positions and interests with regard to feminism.

In addition to the macro political conjuncture, policewomen's interests and identities have been shaped by the legal principle of neutrality and by the masculinist culture of their concrete institutional base—the police. Both internal and external actors, such as policewomen and feminists, have challenged this culture, even under the same political regime. Policewomen's daily experience working with female victims of violence has transformed, for some more than others, their conception of the criminal nature of violence against women. Their legal culture has also been transformed by their interactions with feminists in the CECF and by the changing feminist discourses on gender violence, *capacitação*, and women's human rights, all within the context of the professionalization and transnationalization of feminism. The growing number of women's police stations has also empowered policewomen as a distinct gendered actor within the police department. In short, the relationship between the state and women is more than a function of the political regime: it evolves due to multiple and interactive macro and micro, local and global processes.

Alvarez suggests that a successful feminist lobby would require the constant questioning of any "gender-based policy" adopted by a given state or the United Nations, a "re-translation" from inside and outside of the institutional lobbies (1999–2000, 63–4). This constant "translation" is indeed needed in all levels of the state, from inside and outside of each specific state institution with which feminists interact. In the case of the police, it is necessary to expose the dominant police culture, understand the constraints policewomen face in women's police stations, and use the inside-outside strategy recommended by Alvarez to have the feminist agenda, or at least aspects of it, incorporated into the police. The feminist efforts to shape police officers' understanding of violence against women have important consequences for the construction of a gendered citizenship in Brazil. Women's access to the criminal justice system depends, in part, on the success of civil society actors to bring their discourse into the state.

But, just as policewomen, we should not assume that "feminists" and "women" are homogeneous. Before examining what policewomen consider as a "legitimate" case of violence against women, it is necessary to dissect how feminist activists and scholars have defined "violence against women" since the 1970s. This will be examined in the following chapter, which will help us to see, in the consecutive chapter, what aspects of the feminist definitions of violence against women have been absorbed by policewomen in their daily contact with clients in the women's police stations.

3

Feminist Debates over
the Meaning of Violence
against Women

Considering various actions that comprise violence against women, it
can be affirmed that among them one category receives more social
acceptance: the crimes practiced within marriage.

—Maria Luíza Heilborn, feminist anthropologist (1986, 13)

The phenomenon of gender violence traverses society, ignoring frontiers
of social class and race/ethnicity.

—Heleieth Saffioti, feminist sociologist (1994, 454)

Geledés has been forcing the [women's] movement to accept the idea
that racial violence is an aspect of violence against women as serious and
important as domestic violence. But the dialogue is not easy.

—Sueli Carneiro, co-founder of Geledés-Instituto da Mulher Negra
(Interview, São Paulo, January 15, 1996)

These statements clearly buttress Brazilian anthropologist Miriam
Grossi's argument that "[w]hat today is considered 'violence against
women' in Brazil is the result of a historical construction by the feminist
movement over the past 15 years" (Grossi 1994a, 482). Grossi made this
same point in a paper that she presented in 1994 during a meeting in São
Paulo organized by the State Council on the Feminine Condition (CECF)
and the women's movement in preparation for the 1995 United Nations
Fourth World Conference on Women held in Beijing (Grossi 1994b). Her
paper addressed different forms of violence against women, as defined by
the women's movement since the 1970s. But in addition to conjugal violence, Grossi examined "new" forms of violence against women, such as

sexual abuse of children, sexual harassment, and violence against women from nonwhite ethnic groups in Brazil. In other words, Grossi illuminated forms of violence defined on the basis not only of gender but also racial oppression (Grossi 1994b). As an attendee to this meeting, I observed the refusal of some feminist scholars and activists to accept expanding the definition of violence against women to include a racial perspective (see also Conselho Estadual da Condição Feminina 1994a). The meeting and the conflicts that arose over particular issues illustrate Grossi's point that the definition of violence against women is socially and politically constructed.

This chapter builds on Grossi's work to examine how feminist activists and scholars in São Paulo have defined the issue of violence against women since the 1970s. It is worth noting that, in addition to the feminist movement, academics have participated equally in the historical construction of the meaning of violence against women. Moreover, the women's policy machineries (e.g., the CECF and the National Council on Women's Rights or CNDM) run by feminist academics, activists, and government officials have also contributed to defining this issue. In fact, these institutions have been key actors in the establishment of hegemonic feminist frameworks for understanding and acting upon the social reality of violence against women.

As noted in chapter 1, the Brazilian second-wave women's and feminist movements emerged in the mid-1970s and have been consistently comprised of diverse groups of women from various racial, class, and sexual orientation backgrounds. Women activists and scholars also come from different regions, including rural and urban areas, and have different social needs. Despite these differences, activists and scholars have recognized violence against women as a major problem facing all Brazilian women, approaching it as a multifaceted problem, involving social, economic, cultural, political, and psychological dimensions of human relationships. Over the past thirty years they have approached violence against women as a political issue to be addressed as part of a the larger feminist struggle for democracy and gender citizenship in Brazil.

However, scholars and activists have disagreed over two major points regarding the meaning of violence against women. First, they have debated over what specific violations should be included within the definition of violence against women. While some have defined this issue from an exclusive gender perspective, others have attempted to also use a race, class, and/or sexuality perspective to broaden the meaning of violence against women. Second, scholars and activists have developed competing approaches to explain the power relations between perpetrators and victims. Some scholars and activists have approached these relations from

a structural perspective, as an expression of male domination and patriarchy, emphasizing the unequal power relations between women and men
in situations of violence. In contrast, other scholars and activists have
rejected the concept of "victimization" altogether and have approached
violence against women from an inter-subjective rather than structural
perspective.

Drawing on in-depth interviews and informal conversations with
feminists, personal participation in the women's movement, as well as
newspaper articles, texts written by feminist academics and activists,
booklets, pamphlets, reports, and other documents, this chapter examines
these feminist debates and shows that the shifts in feminist approaches to
violence against women since the 1970s are situated within the local,
national, and international political contexts in which Brazilian feminist
activists and scholars operate. The first feminist mobilizations around
violence emerged in the mid-1970s during the military dictatorship,
focusing attention on political violence, wife-murder cases, and police
violence against prostitutes, blacks, and homosexuals. By the beginning of
the 1980s, during the redemocratization process, the hegemonic feminist
discourse on violence against women focused primarily on conjugal
violence, portraying women as passive "victims" of male domination. In
the early 1990s, with the increasing diversification, professionalization,
and transnationalization of the women's movement, feminist activists
debated over competing definitions of violence against women to include
not only gender but also race, class, and sexual orientation. The hegemonic
feminist discourse assumed, however, an exclusive gender perspective,
adding only the issue of sexual harassment and emphasizing women's
agency from a medical-therapeutic rather than criminal perspective. Since
the mid-1990s, in the context of post-Beijing and other international
conferences, violence and discrimination against women have been
viewed as human rights violations. Discrimination against different
groups of women, especially black women, has also entered the feminist
agenda. However, the hegemonic feminist discourse on violence against
women remains solely based on a gender perspective addressing primarily
conjugal and family violence.

1975–1980: Initial Feminist Mobilizations to End
Violence against Women

Political Violence against Women
According to Brazilian feminist scholars, the first feminist and women's
mobilizations over violence against women began in the late 1970s around
cases of conjugal violence (Goldberg 1985a; Verardo 1992; Pontes 1986),

police violence against prostitutes (Gregori 1993a), or sexual harassment (Grossi 1988, 1994). Yet it can be inferred from feminist and women's newspapers, as well as historical accounts of the feminist and women's movements, that by the mid-1970s Brazilian women had already mobilized against political violence (e.g., illegal imprisonment, torture, assassination, and forced exile). This is not surprising. As pointed out by Alvarez (1990) and Teles (1993), the Brazilian second-wave women's movement emerged in the 1970s when feminist and women's groups were formed to fight both the military-authoritarian regime and discrimination against women, challenging traditional female roles in the family and in society.[1]

Along with working-class and poor women who mobilized massively over child care and fought for better material conditions in poor neighborhoods, the feminist movement—mostly composed of white, middle-class, educated women—was rooted in the politics of the Left. The women's and feminist movements faced repression from the military regime and the private sector.[2] Yet, despite their basis in the leftist-Marxist tradition, feminist and women's groups also faced resistance from emerging Leftist unions and clandestine political parties to the legitimation of women's specific struggle and political autonomy.

The United Nations' Declaration of 1975 as the International Woman's Year had an enormous impact on the mobilization of Brazilian women and feminists, empowering and prompting the emergence of various women's *grupos de reflexão* (equivalent to consciousness-raising groups in the United States). After the conclusion of the International Woman's Year, two important feminist newspapers appeared in the mid-1970s: *Brasil Mulher*, founded in October of 1975; and *Nós Mulheres*, founded in June of 1976. *Brasil Mulher* was linked to the *Movimento Feminino pela Anistia* (Women's Amnesty Movement), strongly focusing on the struggle for amnesty of political prisoners and exiled political leaders. *Nós Mulheres*, while focusing on the specific struggle of women, did not separate the struggle women faced from the general working-class struggle (Alvarez 1990; Teles 1993).

The most important feminist concerns at the time were political repression, autonomy from political parties, as well as specific working-class and middle-class women's issues (e.g., child care and sexual discrimination at the workplace). Thus, political violence was the principal form of violence politicized by feminists in the mid-1970s. Oddly, the first issue of *Nós Mulheres* (June 1976) published the testimony of a black woman from Rio de Janeiro denouncing racism. But this testimony and future cases of racism politicized by black women did not reflect or affect the hegemonic feminist discourse on violence against women either in the 1970s or in the 1980s.

By the end of the 1970s, the military-authoritarian regime was facing a major crisis due to internal disputes and a total lack of social legitimacy, thus forcing the regime, as discussed in chapter 1, to initiate the *Abertura Política* (Political Opening). In 1979, Ato Institucional No. 5 (Institutional Act Number Five), which supported institutional repression during the military regime, was abolished. The repealing of legal, institutionalized repression allowed for the free assembly of political parties as well as for the banning of press censorship. The Lei da Anistia (Amnesty Law) enacted in August of 1979 released most political prisoners and allowed the return of exiled political leaders to the country.

As Alvarez (1990) and Teles (1993) assert, feminists actively participated in the process that led to the Abertura Política and to the Lei da Anistia, organizing the Movimento Feminino pela Anistia and promoting their specific women-oriented political agenda. It can be inferred from these historical accounts of the women's and feminist movements that in the late 1970s, while feminists still emphasized political violence,[3] they began to use the adjective "sexual" in reference to violence against women, referring to the cases of police violence and sexual violence in prisons and at the workplace. For instance, during the Congresso Nacional pela Anistia (National Congress for Amnesty) that took place in January of 1979, a women's commission proposed the unification of the campaign for amnesty with the movements that addressed women's specific issues. Among other things, this commission strongly recommended that police brutality and acts of repression in general be denounced by making visible cases of violence at the workplace; sexual violence; police violence against women; as well as the imprisonment, torture, and killing of minors (Teles 1993, 83).

Domestic Violence and Wife-Murder Cases

With the enactment of the Lei da Anistia, leftist political leaders returned from exile in Europe and the United States, altering the progression of feminist and women's mobilizations against violence. Leftist women in exile had "discovered" feminism and returned to Brazil influenced by the European and North American discourses on domestic violence, battered-women shelters, and consciousness-raising. These discourses were then adapted to the Brazilian context and, while political repression was lifting, Brazilian feminists were "discovering" domestic violence and its most extreme manifestation, wife-murdering.

During the late 1970s and throughout the 1980s, wife-murder cases, not rare in Brazilian society, became the focus of numerous feminist protests and campaigns from which emerged the nationally widespread slogan Quem Ama Não Mata (One who loves doesn't kill).[4] Feminists mobilized intensively against the discriminatory response of the judiciary to wife-murder cases. Wife-murderers were usually acquitted by juries on the basis of the "legitimate defense of honor" argument, a holdover from Portuguese colonial penal law that allowed a man to kill his adulterous wife and her lover. Anthropologist Mariza Corrêa (1981) shows in her study of the legal discourse on wife-murder cases that, despite the abolishment of this rule with the enactment of the first Brazilian Penal Code in 1831, defense attorneys and prosecutors continually constructed the "legitimate defense of honor" argument by opposing "honest" women (e.g., non-adulterous wives) to "dishonest" women (e.g., adulterous wives, prostitutes), and "honest" men (e.g., workers) to "dishonest" men (e.g., the unemployed, thieves). This dichotomy highlights the historical construction of sexism and classism in Brazilian legal culture.[5]

The first wife-murder trial reported by mainstream media occurred in the early 1970s in Belo Horizonte.[6] Because feminist and women's organizations began to flourish only after the mid-1970s (Alvarez 1990, 83), there was no feminist mobilization to protest the Belo Horizonte jury's decision to acquit the murderer of Josefina Lobato on the basis of the "legitimate defense of honor" argument. But by the late 1970s the expanding feminist movement would not rest until this argument was abolished from Brazilian legal culture.

In 1979, the first trial of the playboy Raul Doca Street, who in 1976 killed his famous upper–middle class girlfriend, Angela Diniz, in the resort town of Búzios, attracted enormous attention from the media and caused a strong national feminist mobilization.[7] In this trial, Doca Street was virtually acquitted by the jury on the basis that he was defending his honor.[8] Feminists repudiated this judicial decision so vehemently that they formed in Rio de Janeiro the Núcleo de Mobilização Ângela Diniz (Ângela Diniz Mobilization Center). With the support of feminist organizations from all over the country, the Núcleo vehemently organized around the second trial of Doca Street in 1981 and was able to successfully influence the jury, who ultimately found him guilty.[9]

In the same year that Doca Street was found guilty, another wife-murder case, this time in the city of Rio de Janeiro, attracted attention from the media and was targeted by new feminist mobilizations.[10] German citizen Christel Arvid Johnston, who worked at the German Consulate in Rio, was killed by her ex-husband Eduardo Johnston. During (and after) the trial, 24 feminist organizations from Rio de Janeiro, São Paulo, Belo Horizonte, Porto Alegre, and Salvador once again successfully influenced the judiciary through education and awareness to find Eduardo Johnston guilty and to keep him in jail.

Also in 1981, the killing of Eliane de Grammont in São Paulo by her ex-husband and popular romantic singer, Lindomar Castilho, attracted enormous attention from the media and was extensively politicized by feminist organizations throughout the 1980s.[11] Equipped with the same methods they had used in the case of Doca Street, feminists organized demonstrations, distributed open letters, and protested during the singer's concerts. During Castilho's 1984 trial, feminists also organized a vigil and a demonstration in front of the court, resulting in another successful guilty verdict.[12]

By the early 1980s, thanks to the feminists' successful mobilizations over wife-murder trials, the feminist movement gained enormous visibility, political strength, and respect in the eyes of politicians, the media, and society at large. In fact, by the late 1970s, as a sign of this visibility and recognition, Rede Globo aired a weekly television series, *Malu Mulher* (Malu, a woman), which was clearly influenced by feminist ideas.[13] In the early 1980s, Rede Globo also produced a daily television program, titled after the feminist slogan, Quem Ama Não Mata (One who loves doesn't kill). This slogan became so popular in the country that one of the feminists I interviewed expressed less pessimism about the power of feminism in the 1990s by recalling that once she had seen the phrase Quem Ama Não Mata on the back of a truck. In her view, this proved that feminists had an impact on Brazilian culture at large, especially considering that in general *caminhoneiros*(truck drivers) are *machistas* (sexists).

As proof of the influence of feminist pressure on the criminal judicial system, the Brazilian Superior Tribunal of Justice (STJ) decided in 1991 that the "legitimate defense of honor" argument could no longer be argued. Nevertheless, prison sentences for wife-murderers have hardly been enforced, and feminists still need to pressure the courts to find wife-murderers guilty (Americas Watch Committee 1991a; União de Mulheres de São Paulo 1995; Centro pela Justiça e o Direito Internacional or CEJIL, et al. 2003). Furthermore, the STJ has on occasion contradicted its own decision to disallow the "legitimate defense of honor" argument (Macaulay 2002). In addition, to date adultery is still a crime (see Article 240 of the Brazilian Penal Code).[14]

Police Violence against Prostitutes, Transvestites, Homosexuals, and Blacks

Although political repression has abated since the late 1970s, police violence in both Brazilian rural and urban areas has increased, targeting specifically poor people, street children, blacks, prostitutes, transvestites, and homosexuals (see Americas Watch Committee 1991b; Adorno 1995). For example, in 1980 in the city of São Paulo, there was a wave of police violence resulting in the unjustified arrest of thousands of people. Leading what the police called Operação Rondão (Rondão Operation),[15] Delegado José Wilson Richetti arrested, within a period of fifteen days, approximately four thousand people—mainly prostitutes, transvestites, homosexuals, and vagrants in downtown São Paulo. Richetti's intention was to close every brothel and slum tenement-house in downtown São Paulo, and began his project with "cleaning up" the streets. Although not defined as crimes by Brazilian penal codes, prostitution and homosexuality have been culturally associated with criminal or deviant behaviors, leading to the subjection of street prostitutes and gay men to police violence.

The media and social movements—including the feminist movement—protested and denounced Richetti's brutality.[16] On June 13, 1980, gay organizations (e.g., Grupo Somos, Grupo Eros, Grupo Libertos, Ação Homossexualista), feminist and women's organizations (e.g., Ação Lésbico-Feminista, Grupo Nós Mulheres, Grupo Feminista 8 de Março, Associação de Mulheres, Núcleo de Defesa à Prostituta), and the black rights' organization Movimento Negro Unificado organized a huge and historic demonstration in downtown São Paulo denouncing "police violence against homosexuals, transvestites, blacks, prostitutes, and unemployed people," as stated in the open letter signed in June of 1980 by the Comissão Pró-Comando contra a Violência Policial (Commission against Police Violence). This letter described the police brutality led by Richetti, and invited the people to sign a petition addressed to the judge in charge of controlling police arbitrariness. The letter also explained why blacks, homosexuals, transvestites, feminists, and prostitutes had organized the mass demonstration to protest against police violence.

Although feminists participated intensively in this historic demonstration, police violence against prostitutes did not become part of the hegemonic feminist discourse on violence against women in the 1980s. Instead, conjugal violence remained the only form of violence against women politicized by the feminist movement throughout this decade.

1980s: Defining Violence against Women as Conjugal Violence

The Experience of SOS-Mulher
During the Second Congress of Women held in March of 1980 in São Paulo, feminists intended to set the agenda to fight violence against women. But political divisions within this Congress hindered the planned discussions, forcing feminist groups to call an emergency meeting in June of 1980 in Valinhos.[17] At this meeting, violence against women (along with reproductive rights) was acknowledged as one of the movement's priorities, resulting in the creation of a Commission on Violence against Women.[18] While wife-murder cases were largely the focus of this meeting, the demonstration that had occurred a few days earlier to protest police violence against prostitutes, transvestites, and homosexuals was not even

mentioned (Gregori 1992, 30).[19] Specific forms of violence against black women and lesbians did not become an important issue either. With their silence, the feminist movement ignored the support of black women and lesbian groups for feminist struggles against conjugal violence, and denied support for black women's and lesbians' struggles against specific forms of oppression and violence against them as well.[20]

The meeting in Valinhos launched new feminist non-governmental organizations (NGOs) focusing on political mobilization and providing services related to violence, reproductive rights, and communication.[21] The Commission on Violence against Women was transformed in October of 1980 into the feminist organization SOS-Mulher, with the purpose of raising the visibility of violence against women, providing services to women who had suffered violence, and raising victims' consciousness.[22]

Most members of SOS-Mulher were lesbians from a white, middle-class, educated background. Some were participants in the emerging lesbian movement, but considered feminism to be a larger struggle and chose to participate in groups like SOS-Mulher, focusing on women's issues but not on lesbian-specific issues. One of SOS-Mulher's founders was mixed-race, but told me in an interview that she did not identify herself as "black" until the early 1990s. Although these members of SOS-Mulher were personally dealing with varying forms of oppression, the organization focused on the politicization of only two forms of violence against women: conjugal violence and wife-murder cases.[23] In part, this was due to racism and homophobia within the feminist movement and in the larger Brazilian culture. It was—and still is—easier to fight only against sexism than to also challenge homophobia and racism in Brazil. However, the lack of recognition regarding homophobia and racism rarely affected SOS-Mulher's clientele, who mostly came from a working-class background, and generally complained about conjugal violence (85 percent of the 1,500 women SOS-Mulher served during a three-year period) (Gregori 1993a).

Although SOS-Mulher provided psychological services and referred clients to free legal advice provided by feminist lawyers, the main goal of the organization was to create a "space of solidarity" among women, raising clients' consciousness as women. Within SOS-Mulher, violence against women was framed as the result of women's oppression. Women in general and battered women in particular were viewed as "victims" of male domination.[24] And clients' *conscientização* (consciousness-raising) was the feminist way to end oppression and domination. "What we want from these women is that they become conscious," explained one of SOS-Mulher's members (quoted in *Diário Popular*, October 11, 1981).[25]

Despite its limitations in helping clients, SOS-Mulher's discourse on conjugal violence and women's oppression was instrumental in the construction of an essentialist and universalist feminist discourse based on a binary oppositional gender perspective, that is, male-versus-female (see Gregori 1993a, 45; Pontes 1986; Grossi 1988). Ultimately, this discourse was crucial in unifying and building the political strength of the feminist and women's movements as a whole—at the cost, however, of covering up differences among women. Although SOS-Mulher in São Paulo, like those in most cities, had a short life (1980–1983), it was the most popular women's organization at the time, attracting enormous attention from the media.[26] Its closure after only three years was the result of internal problems and changes in the broader political conjuncture (Pontes 1986; Gregori 1993a), as well as the numerous difficulties that arise when offering services on a purely volunteer basis. According to a member of SOS-Mulher, the organization failed to receive financial aid from international donors, which would have allowed it to continue on a more professional basis. Still, as noted in chapter 1, SOS-Mulher directly influenced the state discourse on violence against women through the Conselho Estadual da Condição Feminina (CECF), created in 1983 during the period of participatory democracy inaugurated by the governor of São Paulo state, Franco Montoro.

Hegemony of Conjugal and Sexual Violence in the CECF

From its inception, the CECF considered violence against women one of its priority issues and strongly incorporated the discourse of SOS-Mulher. The first issue of the CECF's bulletins published an article that used the SOS-Mulher slogan for a title: "O Silêncio É Cúmplice da Violência" (Silence as Accomplice to Violence) (see Conselho Estadual da Condição Feminina de São Paulo 1984, 9).[27] For the CECF, violence against women basically meant conjugal and sexual violence. *Conscientização* (consciousness-raising) was the means to fight it.

To better coordinate its actions, in the mid-1980s the CECF created commissions to deal with priority issues, such as violence against women, health, education, work, and racial discrimination. At the time, feminist and women's NGOs were diversifying and becoming professionalized (Alvarez 1994). The 1985 United Nations World Conference on Women in Nairobi contributed to both processes. Professionalization was a result of international financial aid transforming women's volunteer groups into professional NGOs.[28] Diversification was a result of black women, lesbians, and rural women workers increasingly participating in the feminist movement (Alvarez 1990, 1994, 1997; Soares et al. 1995; Ribeiro 1995; Roland 2000).

Since its creation in 1983, the CECF has benefited from the participation of members of black women's organizations. However, as black feminist Edna Roland recounts, "at first the relations [of black women] with white women and the feminist movement were tense, often characterized by a paternalistic posture [on the part of white women]" (Roland 2000, 238; my translation). Roland (2000) points out that all of the 30 members nominated by Montoro to create the CECF were white women. In reaction, black women formed the first black women's organization of São Paulo, the Coletivo de Mulheres Negras de São Paulo (Collective of Black Women of São Paulo) and successfully demanded the inclusion of two black women into the CECF. Roland (2000, 238) further explains that black women were active participants in the black movement, not the feminist movement, but their mobilization as an autonomous social actor emerged out of gender struggles, though in reaction to racial discrimination. Because of their gender, black women were successful in establishing a dialogue with the state before black men did.

Black women indirectly and directly framed racial discrimination against women as a specific form of violence against women. In 1986, the CECF's Commission on Black Women's Issues published extensive research on racial discrimination, listing addresses of existing women's police stations and advising that "complaints about racial discrimination can be registered in any police station" (Conselho Estadual da Condição Feminina de São Paulo 1986a, 28). However, the CECF did not alter its hegemonic discourse on violence against women until the early 1990s. All written and audiovisual materials produced in the 1980s by the CECF's Commission Fighting Violence against Women framed this issue from an essentialist and universalistic women/wives perspective that did not take into account differences among women.

SOS-Mulher and other groups within the feminist movement had borrowed the concept of violence articulated by Brazilian philosopher Marilena Chauí. In her famous article on violence, Chauí (1985) defines violence as an action that transforms differences into inequalities with the goal of dominating, exploiting, and oppressing the person who is object of violence. This action, she asserts, treats the dominated human being as an "object," not a "subject," who is silenced and becomes passive. Chauí argues further that the differences between women and men were historically transformed into inequalities and male domination. According to her, women, as opposed to men, are not autonomous subjects. Their femininity is defined by the culture to serve others, and their dependency is enforced by the use of ideology and violence in ways that prevent them from gaining autonomy. In line with Chauí, SOS-Mulher conceived men as autonomous subjects and women as dependent subjects, victims of male domination, reproduced by the culture and secured through symbolic or concrete violent means.

Accordingly, the CECF represented violence against women as the result of male domination exerted over women. Violence against women could be expressed through psychological, physical, or sexual violence. This exclusive male-versus-female dichotomous perspective, exemplified by cases of conjugal violence or sexual violence, represented women essentially as victims of male violence (see Conselho Estadual da Condição Feminina de São Paulo 1985a, 1986b, 1986c; Conselho Estadual da Condição Feminina de São Paulo and IDAC 1986; Goldberg 1985b). As Maria Amélia Azevedo Goldberg, coordinator of the CECF's Commission Fighting Violence against Women in the 1980s, expresses in the CECF's booklet titled *Violência Contra a Mulher* (Violence against Women): "We speak of the violence expressed through sexual, psychological or physical abuse, practiced by a man with the explicit purpose of subjecting a woman to his will (Goldberg 1985b, 4)."[29]

As noted in chapter 1, due to pressures from the CECF, in July of 1984 Governor Montoro created a center to provide legal and psychological advice for battered women: Centro de Orientação Jurídica e Encaminhamento à Mulher or COJE(Center for Legal Orientation and Guidance for Women). Domestic violence, and more specifically conjugal violence, was the form of violence that corresponded to COJE's discourse on violence against women. COJE's first bulletin stated that,

> The problem of domestic violence has been treated as a private matter. . . . Although there are various public services providing legal advice for free, a new service was necessary to deal specifically with women's issues. That is why COJE was created in March of 1984. (Centro de Orientação Jurídica e Encaminhamento à Mulher-COJE 1984)

The feminist consciousness-raising approach also informed COJE's project. With the creation of the first women's police station in 1985, the CECF's discourse on violence against women began to emphasize criminalization (Conselho Estadual da Condição Feminina de São Paulo, 1986b, 1986c). Apart from COJE, there was no other institution dealing specifically with the issue of violence against women at the time. COJE's staff was composed of feminist public attorneys and psychologists working for other state agencies. Therefore, they worked for COJE on a volunteer basis, spending only a few hours advising victims of battering or women facing conjugal crises. The Centro de Orientação Jurídica e Encaminhamento à Mulher (COJE) primarily functioned as a referral center and soon lost its initial vigor, which led to its dismantling in 1987.

Contrary to COJE, the first women's police station attracted enormous attention from the media and from society at large upon its inception. As noted in chapter 1, while 762 women attended COJE in nine months, 500 women waited in line to initiate complaints of violence against them the day after the first women's police station was inaugurated. Given this context, a feminist emphasis on criminalization was unavoidable, regardless of the emphasis the feminist discourse stressed for consciousness-raising and psychological services. Throughout the second half of the 1980s the CECF attempted to bring its hegemonic feminist discourse on conjugal violence and consciousness-raising to women's police stations, as discussed in chapter 2.

1990s: Gender Violence and "other" Forms of Violence against Women

The New Gender Discourse
As Brazilian feminist scholars have noted, contrary to women's studies programs in the United States, Brazilian women's studies centers (*núcleos de estudos da mulher*, hereafter *núcleos*)emerged in the early 1990s as research (not teaching) centers within universities and private foundations, such as the Carlos Chagas Foundation (Costa 1994; Lima Costa 1997; Bruschini and Unbehaum 2002a). As Bruschini and Unbehaum explain: "Here [in Brazil], feminist academics, rather than creating alternative spaces [for teaching], attempted to integrate themselves into the academic community through the recognition of the scientific value of their intellectual preoccupations" (Bruschini and Unbehaum 2002b, 21). Since the late 1980s, under the influence of U.S. feminist debates on gender as a "useful category of analysis" (Scott 1988b), Brazilian feminist scholars have increasingly abandoned the category "woman" in their research and replaced it with "gender." With this change in terminology, the *núcleos* created in the late 1980s were named "gender" (rather than "women") studies centers (*núcleos de estudos de gênero*). Within Brazilian gender and women's studies, "gender" replaced the category "woman" to define relations between men and women as socially constructed—rather than determined by biological or natural differences (see Saffioti 1990, 1994; Souza-Lobo 1991; Heilborn 1992, 1993). Bruschini and Unbehaum point out that "the adoption of the analytical category of gender favored the acceptance by the academic community at large of this area of research because it depoliticized a problematic [women's studies] that used to provoke established prejudices" (2002b, 21).

Despite broadening women's studies with more accepted scientific research goals, some feminist scholars have raised several critiques of gender studies. Costa and Sardenberg (1994) argue, for example, that the shift from women to gender studies served to silence feminism and depoliticize research within academia. They also claim that the gender language of academia entered many segments of the women's movements (e.g., unions, political parties) but they incorporated gender claims without making women visible participants. Moreover, Costa and Sardenberg (1994) argue that there was only a shift in language, not in conceptualization, because gender studies continued to take an essentialist perspective on women. Azerêdo (1994) goes further by claiming that gender studies still relies on a binary hierarchical perspective (male versus female) that does not take into account racial differences among women. Lima Costa (1997, 10) suggests that the resistance of the *núcleos* in the 1980s to incorporate post-structuralist debates on multiple subject positions (except for sex and class) was linked to the fact that most theorists were white, liberal, economically privileged feminists. More recently, Sorj has also pointed to the limitations of an exclusive gender-based perspective within gender studies: "The enormous social inequalities between women and men in the country require a more qualified concept of gender, less homogeneous and twice as relational—a concept that can simultaneously contrast the feminine and the masculine and the feminines and the masculines produced by the effects of social inequalities. The result of this analytical effort would be to formulate a variable system of domination in which gender positions are not always fixed" (2002, 101; my translation).

Gender Violence and the Question of Victimization
The new gender perspective affected feminist conceptualizations of violence against women, raising the critiques mentioned above as well as other debates especially those regarding victimization. Since the early 1990s, the language of "gender violence" has gradually replaced "violence against women" to illuminate the problem of violence as a social and cultural construct based on unequal power relations between men and women. As feminist anthropologist Maria Luíza Heilborn explains, "[g]ender violence emerges from asymmetric and unequal relations between the sexes in Brazilian society" (quoted in Conselho Estadual da Condição Feminina de São Paulo 1994a, 21). Scholars and activists have moved away from essentialism and victimization, broadening their attention to examine not only women but also men in situations of violence. But while some have used an inter-subjective rather than structural perspective, others have adopted the "gender violence" concept without abandoning a structuralist approach to violence against women as an expression of patriarchy and male domination.

The feminist critique of victimization emerged from anthropological studies conducted in the 1980s on the discourse and practice of SOS-Mulher (Pontes 1986; Gregori 1993a, 1993b). According to these studies,

SOS-Mulher's approach to clients was problematic because it assumed that battered women were essentially victims of male domination as expressed through violence. Such a victimization approach neglected to take into account women's agency and their participation in the dynamics of the violent relationships in which they were involved. Based on a constructionist approach to violence against women, Gregori (1993a, 1993b) suggested that the clients of SOS-Mulher in São Paulo were active participants in the cycle of violence and somehow became "accomplices" to their own situation. In the early 1990s, other feminist analyses of conjugal violence incorporated Gregori's framework (see Grossi 1994; De Oliveira and Vianna 1993). Psychoanalytical studies of incest and sexual violence further suggested the complicity of victims of violence, emphasizing an intersubjective approach to gender violence (see, for example, Cromberg 1994).

However, some scholars and activists reacted strongly against this conception of battered women as "accomplices" to violence. Renowned feminist sociologist Heleieth Saffioti, a pioneer in women's studies in Brazil, criticized Gregori for implying women's complicity and therefore denying the existence of gender violence. According to Saffioti (1994), gender violence is a structural rather than inter-subjective problem, part of the social organization of gender, which is integral to the hierarchical social structure. Men and women occupy unequal positions in the social structure of gender and they do not exercise the same power. Although women are not passive victims of male violence, Saffioti asserts that men are the dominant group and women are the subjugated group. She further explains that because women and men do not occupy the same position of power, women's participation in violent gender relationships is informed by threat and concrete violence, rather than "consent" and knowledge to make conscious decisions. In short, women are not "accomplices" to violence (Saffioti 1994, 446).[30]

During the 1994 National Seminar on Violence against Women, organized in São Paulo by the CECF in preparation for the 1995 United Nations Fourth World Conference on Women in Beijing, panelists and the audience firmly rejected Grossi's suggestion, who supported Gregori's claim, that battered women should be viewed as accomplices to violence. One of the commentators in response to Grossi's presentation, feminist anthropologist Maria Luíza Heilborn, forcefully expressed that, although it is necessary to move beyond victimization, it is also problematic to characterize battered women as accomplices to the violence perpetrated against them. As explained by Heilborn,

> It seems to me that this term "accomplice" attributes to women a degree of responsibility over relations in which they are involved, somehow neutralizing

Figure 3.1   Maria Amélia de Almeida Teles and Criméia Alice Schmidt de Almeida, the founding members of União de Mulheres de São Paulo. (*Photo by the author.*)

the role after all played by men as perpetrators. I am not suggesting that women are naturally good and men are necessarily bad. I just want to call attention to the fact that men and women participate in unequal gender relations.[31]

On a similar note, Maria Amélia Teles, co-founder of União de Mulheres de São Paulo, further explains:

This idea that a woman is an accomplice reinforces her own doubts. Because she looks for services asking herself: "Am I guilty? Am I stupid for continuing to live with this man? Why is he beating me up?" Then the provider tells her: "You are responsible." Of course, the victim is going to feel stupid. And this is the kind of treatment provided by the women's police stations because the feminist movement itself has doubts about women's responsibility for the violence perpetrated against them. There is a crisis in the movement. Many feminists are losing their perspective on why we started to struggle against violence in the first place.[32]

The Therapeutic Approach to Gender Violence
Critical of both the perspective on victimization and the notion of accomplice, some feminist activists began to develop an alternative approach based on their experience providing psychological services to battered

women at the governmental organization Casa Eliane de Grammont, which was created in 1990 by then mayor of São Paulo Luiza Erundina (PT). Influenced by psychoanalytical approaches to violence against women, the feminist staff of this new institution, such as Tereza Verardo, who later went to work for the CECF's Commission Fighting Violence against Women, started to formulate the alternative approach of "women in situations of violence." As outlined by Verardo in an interview,

> Sometimes [during the interview] I'm going to use the term "women victims of violence," but most of the time I'll use the term "women in situations of violence." We're increasingly abandoning the term "victim" and using "in situations," because the former suggests a very strong character of victimization. We want to avoid that because if you deal with women as victims they cannot become subjects. You treat them as miserable and helpless. By doing so, they can't picture themselves as subjects and change their situation. Obviously, at the time they are beaten up, they are "victims." But it is necessary to see them as subjects, telling them that they are in a temporary situation, that they can escape the situation.[33]

Although several activists resisted accepting this alternative approach, some adopted the discourse on women "in situations" of violence. That was the case of Coletivo Feminista Sexualidade e Saúde, whose members actively participated in the Erundina's administration, establishing and monitoring new institutional women's spaces, such as Casa Eliane de Grammont. During Erundina's term (1989–1992), Casa Eliane de Grammont became for feminists what women's police stations had meant for them during Montoro's term: the primary site to address violence against women. More than that, this new organization had the advantage of being staffed by feminists themselves. But both in number of cases and visibility, Casa Eliane de Grammont was far less powerful than women's police stations. Whereas there were 500 women waiting to file complaints in the first women's police station the day after its inauguration, only 358 women benefited from services provided by Casa Eliane de Grammont during all of 1991 (see Casa Eliane de Grammont 1991). This organization lost strength once conservative mayor Paulo Maluf (PP, former PDS and PPB) took office in March of 1993. Maluf's successor, Celso Pitta (1997–2000) was from the former PDS and PPB as well and did not support Casa Eliane de Grammont or other public services that attend to the specific needs of women. In this context, feminist members of Coletivo Sexualidade e Saúde resumed their work at Casa Eliane de Grammont. In 2001, this organization regained its original vigor when another female politician from the Workers' Party, Marta Suplicy, was elected mayor of the city of São Paulo.

The work experience of feminists at Casa Eliane de Grammont in the early 1990s providing psychological services to battered women launched a new approach to women's position and subjectivity with respect to male perpetrators, further problematizing victimization. In addition, Casa Eliane de Grammont reinforced the hegemonic feminist discourse on gender violence, especially conjugal violence.[34] Finally, the experience of feminists at Casa Eliane de Grammont also contributed to the development of an alternative medical-therapeutic approach to gender violence that focused on self-esteem and *empoderamento*, a translation of the English word empowerment. As Diniz expressed,

> We tried to empower clients within the limits and contradictions of their situation, feeling the need to abandon the juridical-rational model. Dealing with this problem in the police is very limited, because our clients had expectations about their partners and their relationships. But these relationships were not good and that's why we started to say that those women were in situations of violence.[35]

Given the limitations of the "juridical-rational model," in the early 1990s feminists increasingly redefined the issue of violence against women as a public health issue and further developed a medical-therapeutic model to deal with violence against women (see Casa Eliane de Grammont n.d.; D'Oliveira n.d.). Coletivo Sexualidade e Saúde, for example, began to focus their efforts on the training or *capacitação* on gender mostly aimed at health care providers. As noted in chapter 2, by the mid-1990s feminists had abandoned the *conscientização* approach to end violence and replaced it with the gender *capacitação* approach. Under the guidance of Coletivo Sexualidade e Saúde, service providers and clients would gain a critical and technical knowledge about gender relations and gender violence through *capacitação* rather than *conscientização*. In 1994 and 1995, Coletivo Feminista Sexualidade e Saúde offered three courses of *capacitação para atendimento a mulheres em situação de violência* (*capacitação* for attending women in situation of violence). These courses focused primarily on the health care system, covering topics such as domestic violence, sexual abuse, incest, rape, mental health and gender violence, and health care services.[36] União de Mulheres de São Paulo also began to address violence against women from a public health perspective and worked on a project to establish a service within the Pérola Byington Hospital for women in situation of domestic violence (see União de Mulheres de São Paulo 2000).

Feminist NGO Pró-Mulher, Família e Cidadania (Pro-Woman, Family and Citizenship, formerly named Casa da Mulher do Centro) also embraced

Figure 3.2   Book about *Saúde das Mulheres* (Women's Health) and the practice of Coletivo Feminista Sexualidade e Saúde, on display at the desk of Delegada Maria Christina A. Mazzarello at the third women's police station in the city of São Paulo, July 2001. (*Photo by the author.*)

a therapeutic model, but this organization absorbed the gender violence and anti-victimization discourse by focusing on "intra-family violence," assisting, through conflict mediation, both men and women from a lower-class background. Coordinator of the family mediation program of Pró-Mulher, psychoanalyst Malvina Muskat, justifies the shift from "women" to "family" as follows: "When Pró Mulher was created in 1977, women had few rights recognized and our objective was to defend them. In 1992, when we decided to act as mediators, this situation changed: the dichotomy between woman-victim and man-aggressor was not as clearly defined. In today's conjugal fights it's difficult to say that one is only the victim or the aggressor" (quoted in Arruda 2002).

Considering the family as the major "agent of socialization" and promoter of violence in society, Pró-Mulher has developed since 1993 an alternative approach to family dispute resolutions through the method of "family mediation," a method Pró-Mulher borrowed from nonprofit organizations in France, Spain, and the United States. Pró-Mulher's mediation service is conducted by a psychologist or lawyer and seeks to facilitate communication between the parties. It also seeks to improve women's self-esteem, raise their consciousness, and promote their autonomy and empowerment. The organization further connects its mediation service to citizenship by claiming that clients learn from the mediators not only how to negotiate but also about their rights. Pró-Mulher refers clients to public attorneys and offers courses of *capacitação* on mediation for human rights organizations, as well as lawyers, psychologists, and social workers. In 1998, Pró-Mulher contributed to the first course of *capacatição* for policewomen working in women's police stations, which was coordinated by the CECF, as mentioned in chapter 2. The following year, Pró-Mulher organized a course of *capacitação* that specifically targeted policewomen (see the 2002 report of activities of Pró-Mulher, Família e Cidadania).

Adding Sexual Harassment to Conjugal and Family Violence
In addition to changing their focus from victimization to empowerment and from criminalization to therapeutic and mediation services addressing situations of conjugal and intra-family violence, in the early 1990s feminists influenced by the new gender discourse began to broaden the meaning of violence against women to also include *assédio sexual* (a translation of the English term "sexual harassment"). As defined by feminist anthropologist Maria Luíza Heilborn: "Sexual harassment is one form of violent relations towards one of the sexes [female] in Brazilian society" (quoted in Conselho Estadual da Condição Feminina de São Paulo 1994a, 23). For Heilborn, "[t]his theme is extremely important because it shows that violence also occurs in the public domain, at the workplace" (quoted in Conselho Estadual da Condição Feminina de São Paulo 1994a, 23).

In Brazil, *cantadas* (sexual proposals, flirting) at the workplace have generated complaints by women workers since the late 1970s. Feminist and women's NGOs also mobilized over this issue during the 1980s.[37] But not until the 1990s did *assédio sexual* become a visible and unquestioned issue within the women's movement and in society at large. In Rio de Janeiro, a law was enacted in 1991 establishing the civil responsibility of businesses when male employers tried to take sexual advantage of female employees through threat of firing them (Law n. 1,886/91). Extensive coverage by the Brazilian media of the 1992 U.S. congressional hearings on Anita Hill's sexual harassment allegations against Supreme Court nominee Clarence Thomas further propelled *assédio sexual* into the public discourse in Brazil. In the mid-1990s, although the dominant culture did not regard sexual harassment as a behavior that should be socially condemned, the media extensively reported debates on the gravity, especially for women, of sexual harassment at the workplace. The Union of Metalworkers from the industrial region of São Paulo included in its collective contract that sexual harassment practiced by someone in a superior position would result in civil responsibility on the part of the management, for physical and moral harm (Minc 2001). In 1995, women workers in São Paulo complained about sexual harassment on trains and demanded separate train cars for women. Their demand was actually met temporarily, but no law was passed to establish separate train cars for women and the practice soon lapsed. Echoing the position of the feminist movement, then feminist congresswomen Marta Suplicy and Maura Laura (PT) proposed before the Brazilian National Congress a bill to criminalize sexual harassment.[38]

It is worth noting that, although going beyond the domestic sphere, this new form of violence against women still rested on a binary oppositional framework that took into account only gender relations. As used by Brazilian feminist scholars and activists, the concept of gender violence replaced violence against women but continued to legitimate forms of violence related only to male-versus-female conflicts. This notion of gender violence assumed a hierarchical and dichotomous perspective that did not take into account intersections of gender with race, class, sexual orientation, or other socially constructed categories that position women differently and inform diverse forms of violence against women. According to feminist sociologist Heleieth Saffioti, "[w]hen you think of gender violence, you automatically think of man as the perpetrator, because the sexual grammar suggests this."[39] As Maria Aparecida Schumaher, former member of SOS-Mulher and of the CECF, explains: "Gender is the only thing that makes us different. Violence against women, by virtue of our gender, is the violence perpetrated by a man against a woman, such as domestic violence and sexual harassment."[40]

In the 1990s, feminist and women's NGOs were unanimous in recognizing sexual harassment as a form of gender violence, and therefore as a crime that should be registered and investigated in women's police stations. This discourse was clearly articulated by the CECF. One of its brochures on sexual harassment even expanded Heilborn's definition by stating: "Sexual harassment comprises all forms of undesirable approaches with sexual connotation, provoking uneasiness at the workplace or jeopardizing our job" (Conselho Estadual da Condição Feminina de São Paulo n.d.).[41] This brochure also advises victims of sexual harassment to initiate their complaints through the women's police stations, characterizing the issue under the crime of *constrangimento ilegal* (illegal constraint).[42]

However, while there was feminist consensus on sexual harassment as a form of gender violence and as a crime, feminist and women's NGOs debated whether racial discrimination and discrimination against lesbians constituted forms of violence against women. The same controversy was also visible in the way the CECF represented these issues.

Discrimination against Black Women
Racism and racial inequalities in Brazilian society are hard to deny. Analyzing the Human Development Index (HDI) of the United Nations Development Program from a racial perspective, Wania Sant'Anna (2001)

shows a significant difference between the positions of blacks and whites in Brazilian society. Without considering race, Brazil occupied the 63rd position among the 143 countries included in the 2000 ranking. Using race as another variable to measure the IDH, Brazil's Afro-descendent population dropped to the 91st position, whereas Brazil's white population occupied a higher position in the rank (48th). Despite these inequalities, until the late 1980s the Brazilian government, scholars, and the society at large claimed that, contrary to the United States and South Africa, Brazil was a "racial democracy" because Brazil never formally enforced segregation laws: race was not a category in Brazilian society; color was an ambiguous marker of identity; the population was racially mixed; and inequalities in Brazil were due to social class, not race or color.[43]

The thesis of "racial democracy," formulated by well-known scholars such as Gilberto Freyre in the early 1930s, has been challenged by the black community since its inception.[44] In 1951, the Lei Afonso Arinos (Afonso Arinos Law) legally defined racial discrimination as a misdemeanor, but this law did not have much impact on society. Afonso Arinos, the proponent of the bill, at the time argued against the formation of autonomous black organizations, which he believed would promote "black racism" or reverse racism (quoted in Nascimento and Nascimento 2000, 213). The expansion of the black liberation movement since the 1970s has increasingly politicized the issue of racism and has effectively challenged what the movement called the "myth of racial democracy."[45] Thanks to pressure by this movement, the Brazilian Constitution of 1988 redefined racism in its Article 5, XLII, as a "serious crime" with no statute of limitation. The government has also adopted affirmative action programs for promoting equal opportunities for blacks and other socially disadvantaged groups (Figueiredo 2003).

Black women have strongly participated in the black liberation movement and have been important actors contributing to the social, cultural, political, and legal transformations regarding race relations in Brazil in the last two decades. In the mid-1980s, black women's NGOs flourished and the black women's movement arose as a new political actor (Carneiro 1993a; Ribeiro 1995; Alvarez 1990; Roland 2000). Since then, black women activists have combined the struggles against racism and sexism, framing the meaning of discrimination, violence, health, reproductive rights, and education from both a racial and a gender perspective.

In the state of São Paulo, black women's NGOs, such as Geledés-Instituto da Mulher Negra and Casa da Mulher Negra, have provided services for battered women and victims of racism, following up on complaints initiated in women's police stations and regular police stations, as well as in the specialized police station created in the early 1990s in the city of São Paulo to process complaints about racial crimes. In the 1990s, black women's organizations politicized the issue of racial discrimination against women as a form of violence against women. Sueli Carneiro, co-founder of the black women's organization Geledés-Instituto da Mulher Negra, explains: "Whereas white feminists want to abandon the concept of discrimination and oppression, I will continue speaking of discrimination, because this exists and is the instrument of racism and sexism. Yes, we continue to be victims, real victims, of processes of exclusion, repression and discrimination."[46]

Although feminist and women's NGOs in São Paulo agree that racism is a crime, they diverge on whether racial discrimination against women is a form of violence against women (or gender violence). For those who define the issue in relation not only to gender but also to class and race, such as Geledés, Casa da Mulher Negra, and União de Mulheres de São Paulo, racial discrimination against women is violence against women and should be investigated in women's police stations. But the hegemonic feminist discourse on violence has resisted the incorporation of this new conception. As Sueli Carneiro forcefully asserts:

> Geledés has been forcing the [women's] movement to accept the idea that racial violence is an aspect of violence against women as serious as domestic violence. But the issue of violence has had a restricted meaning: rape, battering, sexual violence. For the movement, violence against women basically means domestic violence. Black women are expanding this concept. This is a new debate and acceptance on the part of the movement is not easy, the conversation is difficult, but this is an important political issue for black women. Racial violence must be accepted as violence against women.[47]

The conversation on racial violence as a form of violence against women proved to be difficult during the National Seminar on Violence against Women organized by the CECF in 1994 in preparation for the United Nations Fourth World Conference on Women in Beijing. As mentioned earlier, feminist anthropologist Miriam Grossi presented a paper addressing various forms of violence politicized by feminists since the late 1970s, including ethnic violence against black and indigenous women. Grossi's paper would serve as the basis for the official report on violence against women by the Brazilian government. In her conclusion, Grossi recommended that feminists "denaturalize" the concept of violence against women and not focus only on a male-versus-female perspective (see Grossi 1994b). While panelists reacted to Grossi's ideas by restricting the meaning of violence against women to gender violence (e.g., conjugal violence and sexual harassment), black women in the audience intervened to emphasize that racial discrimination is violence against women. But most white activists were not persuaded. For instance, former member of SOS-Mulher and of the CECF Maria Aparecida Schumaher expressed in an interview her reservations in accepting Grossi's ideas:

> I had difficulty with that presentation and those comments from the floor bringing in black women, lesbians, indigenous women, disabled women, etc. to define violence against women. That is not the form of violence I'm talking about. I'm not suggesting that they are wrong. Perhaps I'm not up to date . . . but in my view that is racial violence, it is not violence against women. I have difficulty understanding and accepting that concept. That is not a form of violence specific to the female gender.[48]

Feminist sociologist Heleieth Saffioti also expressed in an interview that she believes that racial discrimination is not gender violence. According to Saffioti, because women's police stations were created to investigate cases of gender violence against women, complaints of racial discrimination and police violence should be registered in regular police stations or in the police station specializing in racial crimes.[49]

Although most feminists and women's NGOs embraced Schumaher's and Saffioti's reasoning, in the 1990s the CECF was more receptive to black women's conception of racial discrimination as violence against women—though it did not move completely away from an exclusive gender perspective. The absorption of aspects of black activists' approach to violence against women was in part due to the growing participation of black women activists in the feminist movement and in the CECF during the last decade. In the early 1990s, the Commission on Black Women's Issues merged with the Commission Fighting Violence against Women. At the time, the CECF drafted the Convenção Paulista sobre a Eliminação de todas as Formas de Discriminação contra a Mulher (São Paulo's Convention to Eliminate All Forms of Discrimination against Women) and expressed in its section on violence that "[v]iolence against women is the most tragic manifestation of sexual discrimination; Black women represent the group that suffers in the most perverse manner sexual, racial, social, and cultural discrimination" (Conselho Estadual da Condição Feminina de São Paulo 1992).[50] In 1994, black women activists fully participated in the Encontro Feminista (Feminist Encounter) in São Paulo. The 1994 CECF booklet on violence against women explicitly stated that "[r]acism is a crime and a form of violence against women" (Conselho Estadual da Condição Feminina de São Paulo 1994b, 5). This booklet also advised victims of racism to press charges in women's police stations and to demand of policewomen to register their complaints as a crime of "racism" rather than "verbal offense" because the latter obscures the practice of racism (see Conselho Estadual da Condição Feminina de São Paulo 1994b, 3).[51]

In 1995, the unprecedented nomination of a black woman, Maria Aparecida de Laia, for the presidency of the CECF received strong support from the feminist movement. Laia was president of the CECF from 1995 to 2003, during the two administrations of Governor Mário Covas (PSDB) and his successor Geraldo Alckmin (PSDB), who was Covas' vice-governor and took office because Covas died before the end of his second term. Laia's eight-year tenure in the CECF was largely influenced by the United Nations' conferences of the 1990s and early 2000s, especially the conference on women held in Beijing in 1995 and the conference against racism, racial discrimination, xenophobia, and other forms of intolerance held in Durban in 2001. The international context of feminist politics and the fact that Laia is a self-identified black woman assured more visibility to discrimination against black women and further propelled the incorporation of racism and other forms of discrimination against women into the feminist agenda. As Laia explained in an interview, "[o]ur focus is not only gender, there are many women who suffer racial discrimination. In Brazil, half of the population is black and data shows that the level of education of our black community is lower than that of the black community in South Africa during Apartheid. This is a serious problem, and the Counsel, that fights against all forms of discrimination and gender, must get involved with racial discrimination, because this is also affecting women."[52] The CECF devoted so much attention to racial discrimination that it even organized, along with the Conselho Estadual da Comunidade Negra (State Council of the Black Community), a conference against racism, racial discrimination, xenophobia, and other forms of intolerance, held in São Paulo in 2001 in preparation for the national and international conferences on the same topic.

Like the 1994 CECF booklet on violence against women, the 1998 CECF booklet on women's police stations also advised victims of racism to press charges in women's police stations (see Conselho Estadual da Condição Feminina de São Paulo 1998a). However, this booklet regressed from its 1994 inclusion of racism and defined violence against women solely from a gender perspective: " 'Violence against women' refers to any act of violence based on gender, causing physical, sexual or psychological harm, including threat, coercion or forced seclusion, inflicted on women in either public or private spheres" (Conselho Estadual da Condição Feminina de São Paulo 1998a, 1).

Despite the CECF's recognition in the mid-1990s that racism is a form of violence against women, the hegemonic feminist discourse on violence against women has continued to rely on an exclusive gender framework, not considering racial discrimination against women as gender violence. After the Beijing conference, for example, the CECF established protocols of cooperation with several state secretaries to design public policies in accordance with the recommendations of the Beijing's Platform for Action. In the area of violence, the CECF and the Secretary of Public Security addressed violence against women from a human rights perspective, but referred only to domestic violence, intra-family violence, and sexual violence against women (see Conselho Estadual da Condição Feminina de São Paulo n.d.). Even in 1994, former member of the CECF's Commission Fighting Violence against Women, Lígia Santos, who identifies herself as black, revealed in an interview that the main focus of this commission was to address "domestic and sexual violence." Santos' explanation for this priority was vague, stating that, "[s]exual violence happens in the domestic sphere. Rape, sexual harassment. . . . It is more difficult for the victim to denounce. I think that's why we prioritize these issues. Besides, we wouldn't be able to deal with everything at once."[53] Certainly, the resistance of the CECF and most feminist NGOs to expand the meaning of violence against women beyond gender violence in the family contributes to the hegemony of conjugal violence as the paradigmatic case of violence against women.

Discrimination against Lesbians
Lesbian activists, like black activists, have faced limitations and resistance from feminists to include discrimination against lesbians as a form of violence against women. The feminist movement has focused mainly on heterosexual conjugal violence and has paid little attention to sexual orientation.

Homosexuality has never been criminalized in Brazil.[54] In fact, discrimination on the basis of sexual orientation has been legally condemned by new municipal and state constitutions enacted in the 1990s.[55] Nevertheless, the practice of discrimination on the basis of sexual orientation has not been punished or socially condemned. Culturally, although Brazil is known for sexual liberty, cross-dressing, and non-fixed sexual roles, especially during Carnival, scholars and activists report that Brazilians cannot safely identify themselves as non-heterosexual without running the risk of being ostracized by their families, losing their jobs, or even being physically harmed. Gay men are particularly subject to police violence in the streets and lesbians are subject to violence perpetrated by parents or ex-husbands. Gay and lesbian activists have mobilized against this kind of violence and other forms of discrimination since the late 1970s.[56]

Similar to black women's organizations, Brazilian lesbian organizations evolved out of two movements in the late 1970s: the gay movement and the women's movement. But unlike black women's organizations, lesbian organizations did not begin to grow significantly until the 1990s.[57] The high visibility of lesbians attending the 1994 Feminist Encounter of São Paulo, the preparatory meetings for the United Nations World Conference on Women, as well as in the International Association of Gays and Lesbians-ILGA's International Conference held in Rio de Janeiro in 1995 all contributed to the growth and visibility of gay and lesbian activism in Brazil.

Among other things, these local and international events prompted the increasing politicization of discrimination against lesbians as a form of violence against women. During the 1995 Feminist Encounter of São Paulo, the lesbian collective Coletivo de Feministas Lésbicas presented a document stating that "[c]ompulsory heterosexuality imposed on women through the family, school and the media, as well as physical and psychological harm, all constitute violence against all women" (Coletivo de Feministas Lésbicas 1994, 21). This document also asserts that: "Every form of discrimination is a crime, and therefore discrimination is violence. Thus, in order to address the specific form of violence against lesbians, we take into account all forms of discrimination against us, exerted through legislation, society, the market, and culture."[58]

While participating in debates and meetings on violence against women organized by feminist and women's NGOs and the CECF in 1994 and 1995, I observed members of Coletivo de Feministas Lésbicas raising the issue of discrimination against lesbians as a form of violence against women. According to Marisa Fernandes, one of this organization's founders, lesbian activists have politicized the issue of discrimination since the late 1970s, framing their discourse in the context of sexuality.[59] In the 1990s, however, Coletivo de Feministas Lésbicas began to focus on discrimination as violence and broadened their perspective on violence against lesbians as a human rights issue.[60] During the National Seminar on Violence against Women organized in Sao Paulo in 1994, Fernandes reiterated this perspective, urging feminists to include in their final report on violence that discrimination against lesbians is a form of violence against women and a violation of human rights.

The appropriation of the human rights framework by lesbian groups was influenced by the national and international context of feminist politics at the time. In preparation for the United Nations Conference on Human Rights, held in Vienna in June 1993, Brazilian feminists met in São Paulo in May of 1993 and wrote the "Letter of Brazilian Women to the World Conference on Human Rights." In this letter, they stated that acts against human rights comprised, among others, "the imposition of heterosexuality and the stigma attached to the person who dares to defy this norm" ("Letter of Brazilian Women to the World Conference on Human

Rights, May 1993"). During the Vienna conference, feminist activists from all over the world successfully framed violence against women as a violation of human rights and launched the now internationally acclaimed slogan, "women's rights are human rights." Since then, Brazilian feminist activists and the government have framed the issue of violence against women as a violation of human rights (see, e.g., CLADEM Brasil 1993, 1995; Conselho Estadual dos Direitos da Mulher do Rio de Janeiro 1993; Themis-Assessoria Jurídica e Estudos de Gênero 1997; Secretaria de Estado dos Direitos da Mulher–SEDIM and AGENDE–Ações em Gênero, Cidadania e Desenvolvimento 2002). In 1995, Brazil ratified the Inter-American Convention to Prevent, Sanction and Eradicate Violence against Women, also known as the Belém do Pará Convention. This convention related violence to discrimination and, among other things, asserted that any type of discrimination based on gender is a violation of the human rights of women.

Nevertheless, rarely have Brazilian feminist organizations and the government dedicated their attention to sexual orientation and discrimination against lesbians. Feminist NGOs working on the issue of violence against women in São Paulo (e.g., Pró-Mulher, União de Mulheres de São Paulo, Geledés, Coletivo Feminista Sexualidade e Saúde, and Casa da Mulher Negra) do not refer to discrimination against lesbians as a form of violence against women. Within the gender studies centers, feminist academics dedicating their attention to the problem of violence against women have not examined discrimination against lesbians either. In part, this is due to the fact that, in contrast with black women, lesbian activists are not as organized and represented in the feminist movement and in academia. But the lack of attention to sexual orientation is also a sign of homophobia within not only the feminist movement but in Brazil.

The CNDM and the CECF, as well, have virtually ignored sexual orientation and discrimination against lesbians. The 1992 São Paulo Convention on the Elimination of All Forms of Violence against Women, for example, does not mention discrimination on the basis of sexual orientation. The protocols of cooperation established by the CECF and various state secretaries do not refer to sexual orientation and the human rights of lesbians either. Only recently did the CECF publish a booklet about different forms of discrimination against women, including lesbians among other groups of women (Conselho Estadual da Condição Feminina de São Paulo 2001). Despite this minor inclusion, all brochures and booklets on violence against women published by the CECF have not explored sexual orientation and specific forms of violence against lesbians. As explained by Lígia Santos, member of the CECF's Commission Fighting Violence against Women in 1994: "Domestic violence and sexual harassment are the CECF's priority."[61] In short, the hegemonic feminist discourse on violence against women considers gender as the only social category legitimizing the experience of violence against women. Therefore, it excludes "other" forms of violence that have been politicized by women's organizations inside and outside of the feminist movement.

Conclusion

This chapter examined the progression of feminist discourse on violence against women since the 1970s, showing that, despite shifts in the 1980s and 1990s, the hegemonic discourse on women (or wives) and gender has excluded forms of violence related to other social categories such as race and sexual orientation. In the mid-1970s, given the context of political repression, political violence against women was the first form of violence politicized by the emerging Brazilian second-wave women's movement. By the late 1970s, the new context of *Abertura Política* (Political Opening), coupled with the expanding European and North American movements on domestic violence, contributed to the emergence of a hegemonic feminist discourse on domestic violence adapted to the Brazilian context of wife-murder cases. Police violence against prostitutes, homosexuals, and blacks was also politicized in São Paulo, but was not included in the hegemonic discourse on domestic violence.

In the 1980s, the redemocratization process and the work experience of feminists providing services to battered women favored the hegemony of a women/wives-*conscientização* (consciousness-raising) approach. This approach was based on a universalist and essentialist vision of women's oppression, serving to mask class and racial differences among women. It claimed to include all women in the same position of oppression, independent of their varying racial, class, and cultural backgrounds. Violence against women was equated with conjugal violence, and was conceived as the quintessential expression of male domination and women's victimization. From this perspective, conjugal violence would end with ideological feminist practices, such as women's *conscientização*.

In the 1990s, the women and wives approach was replaced by a hegemonic gender-*capacitação* approach that is based on a constructionist vision of the relations between the sexes. This approach criticizes essentialism and victimization. It also goes beyond the conjugal domain by strongly politicizing sexual harassment at the workplace. Although the gender approach introduces important questions that challenge essentialism, it is still based on a dichotomous and oppositional gender framework (male-versus-female) that ends up universalizing women's interests and identities. Consequently, it excludes other social categories—such as race and sexual orientation—as legitimate basis to define violence against women. Criminalization and *conscientização* are not viewed as effective ways to transform gender relations. In response, feminists have shifted to an emphasis on therapeutic models, along with the replacement of political or ideological knowledge (feminist *conscientização*) by critical or scientific knowledge (gender *capacitação*) as tools to understand and eradicate violence against women.

The increasing professionalization, transnationalization, and diversification of the women's movement (Alvarez 1997, 1998), as well as the therapeutic work experience of feminists dealing with both women and men in situations of violence, have led to a crisis in the women/wives-*conscientização* approach of the 1980s. Professionalization has replaced practices of *conscientização* with practices of technical and critical training (*capacitação*). On the other hand, transnationalization of women's activism has also fostered diversification at the local level. New political actors, such as black women and lesbians, have become stronger within the movement, challenging the universalist conception of women's oppression. As a consequence, other forms of violence against women (e.g., discrimination against black women and lesbians) have been politicized, competing with the hegemonic discourse on gender violence (e.g., conjugal violence and sexual harassment). This hegemonic discourse, in turn, though questioning essentialism, has delegitimized these new forms of violence, thus reproducing the 1980s universalizing approach to women and wives.

It would be simplistic to claim that the hegemonic feminist discourse on gender violence does not incorporate discrimination on the basis of race and sexual orientation due to the fact that feminists are white, heterosexual, middle-class, educated women. Being white and heterosexual might play a role in the supremacy of an exclusive gender discourse, but many feminists are lesbians and still do not mobilize over sexual orientation. Many lesbians do not identify themselves as black, but embraced struggles against racism in the 1990s. In other words, it is not adequate to explain the selective feminist politicization of social problems over time on the basis of an essentialist conception of identity politics.

The dominant cultural, social, and political institutions that produce and reproduce racism and homophobia in Brazil are barriers for the development of an identity politics in itself. The strength of the black movement, coupled with an emphasis on race by international development agencies and the recognition of racism as a crime on the part of the Brazilian government, has played an important role in breaking the feminist resistance to politicizing racial issues. This may explain why racial discrimination as a form of violence has been more readily incorporated than discrimination against lesbians into the hegemonic discourse on violence against women in the 1990s.

In short, the hegemonic feminist discourse on violence against women is both inclusive and exclusive of women's experiences of violence. On the one hand, given the high number of complaints of conjugal violence presented to women's police stations, the feminist politicization of conjugal and intra-family violence has been extremely important for the expansion of women's citizenship rights. As examined in the next chapter, conjugal violence constitutes the large majority of cases in women's police stations. Since policewomen are not necessarily advocates of the feminist discourse on violence against women, it is necessary that feminist organizations continue to politicize conjugal and intra-family violence.

On the other hand, by centering their attention primarily on the family and on violence from a binary gender perspective, the hegemonic feminist discourse on violence against women silences the struggles of groups of women who are also subject to forms of violence, such as racism and homophobia, but who are excluded from the exercise of citizenship rights due both to gender and other social structures, such as race and sexual orientation. Although cases of sexual harassment at the workplace have rarely been reported to women's police stations, feminist activists have unanimously defined this issue as a "new" form of gender violence, eligible to be investigated by women's police stations. This further suggests that, though politicizing violence against women in both private and public spheres, the feminist movement has not truly embraced a multicultural perspective on women's rights.

4

Constructing Crimes and Engendering a Contradictory Citizenship

Beautiful they are, as every woman is, because their harmed faces reveal a gesture of courage! Their stories, their fears and their revolt unveil a crime: *Violence against women.* Last time *Globo Repórter* focused on this issue, four years ago, there was only one police station specializing in crimes against women. Today, there are 64: 36 in São Paulo and 28 in other states. This week, our journalists followed the activities of the women's police stations and noticed that violence against women is escalating. But it is also growing the number of women breaking their silence and pressing charges against their violent male partners. As we will see in this show, they [male perpetrators] have been punished according to the law. That is the only way to end the profound distortion in Brazilian society, where so many men still think that they own their female partners.

—*Globo Repórter* (Rede Globo, July 1990)

This is how the evening television show *Globo Repórter*, produced by the Brazilian television network Rede Globo, introduced the issue of "violence against women" in 1990. Among other things, this show illustrated that by July of 1990—just a decade after feminists began mobilizing over the criminalization of violence against women, and only five years after the launching of the first women's police station—violence against women had become publicly recognized as a crime committed by men against women. This recognition represented an unprecedented cultural transformation regarding the public perception of violence against women in Brazilian society, where "so many men," as *Globo Repórter* stated, "still think that they own their female partners."

On the other hand, the show disseminated propaganda about the efficiency of women's police stations by stating that male perpetrators "have been punished according to the law." Yet, feminists claimed—and still claim—that despite the creation of women's police stations, the criminal justice system remained sexist. Both the women's police stations and the courts, feminists claimed, were not enforcing the laws, therefore not truly criminalizing violence against women. In 1990, for example, the first women's police station located in downtown São Paulo registered 5,631 Boletins de Ocorrência (Bulletins of Occurrence or B.O.s). Of these, only 19.55 percent (1,101) resulted in a full investigation with the completion of Inquéritos Policiais (Police Reports) sent to the courts.[1] This state of virtual impunity, combined with new cases of wife-murders where the accused were acquitted or not imprisoned even after being condemned by the juries, led feminist activists to revive, though altered, the old SOS-Mulher's campaign, "Silence as Accomplice to Violence" (O Silêncio É Cúmplice da Violência). In March of 1993, 75 women's organizations participating in the I Encontro Nacional de Entidades Populares contra a Violência à Mulher (First Meeting of Popular Organizations against Violence toward Women) launched the campaign "Impunity as Accomplice to Violence."[2]

While *Globo Repórter* did not accurately portray the reality of the criminal justice system, the show did illustrate the feminist discourse on gender violence, a discourse that was and continues to be based on a binary oppositional perspective of male-versus-female conflicts. The show therefore contributed to the reinforcement of the hegemony of this discourse, which does not give room, as noted in chapter 3, for the representation of forms of violence against women related both to gender and other social categories such as social class, race, and sexual orientation.

Like the feminist movement and the media, women's police stations play an important role in the construction of what constitutes "violence against women" in Brazilian society. But just as feminists, policewomen are not a homogenous group. As noted in chapter 2, some do not see violence against women as a "real" crime and may even dispute the need for the women's police stations. Divergence among policewomen (and among feminists) actually indicates that the meaning of "violence against women" is not as stable as *Globo Repórter* indicates; instead the meaning fluctuates and is constructed by social, political, and legal forces. As the women's police stations—and regular police stations as well—represent the gateway to the criminal justice system, the way in which policewomen give meaning to and process complaints takes on particular importance in the criminalization of violence against women through the state—and consequently, in the recognition of the women's citizenship right of having access to justice.

This chapter examines what policewomen consider to be a crime of violence against women, the cases they select to register, the legal typologies they apply to the selected cases, and how their interpretation contrasts the feminist definitions of crimes of violence against women. I argue that policewomen's responses to complainants—like the other steps in the processing of cases in the judiciary system—is a discursive practice that constitutes legitimate (or illegitimate) social categories within which women may (or may not) claim their rights through the state. In the case of the women's police stations, "gender" is constructed as the only legitimate social category that validates a complaint of violence against women. Thus, the criminalization of violence against women ends up both including and excluding women from having access to justice. In this sense, the women's police stations contribute to the construction of a contradictory form of gendered citizenship—contradictory because in theory this form of citizenship constitutes *all* women as potential subjects of rights, but in practice it entitles only *certain* women to claim their rights through the state.

The construction of gendered crimes and a contradictory citizenship is illustrated by the ways in which policewomen respond to the following cases: conjugal violence, police violence, racial discrimination, and sexual harassment. I have selected these types of cases for three reasons. First, they have been politicized by the women's movements, as discussed in chapter 3; second, complaints concerning each of these cases, although in different proportions, have been reported to the women's police stations; third, policewomen have responded to each of these cases in very different ways.

Jurisdiction of the Women's Police Stations

The jurisdiction of the women's police stations in the state of São Paulo has expanded in significant ways since the creation of the first women's police station. From 1985 to 1988, their jurisdiction basically covered the investigation of crimes defined in the Special Part of the Brazilian Penal Code under Title I (Chapter II and Section I of Chapter VI) and Title VI (Decree No. 23,769/85). These crimes included, among others, *lesão corporal* (actual bodily harm), *constrangimento ilegal* (illegal constraint), *ameça* (death threat or threat of battery), *estupro* (rape), and *atentado violento ao pudor* (violent sexual molestation). Although the code does not specify the sex of the victim, it was understood that the new police station would investigate these crimes as long as the victims were women. In 1989, under the administration of São Paulo state governor Orestes Quércia, the jurisdiction of the women's police stations was extended to include "crimes against honor" such as *calúnia* (calumny), *difamação* (defamation), and *injúria* (verbal injury), as well as the crime of *abandono material* (material neglect) (Decree No. 29,981/89).

The greatest change in the jurisdiction of the women's police stations took place in 1996, under the administration of Governor Mário Covas. Decree No. 40,693/96 not only extended such jurisdiction, but also gave a new character to the women's police stations. Beyond the crimes against women, the women's police stations were granted the power to investigate and file charges in cases of crimes against children and adolescents, according to provisos in the Estatuto da Criança e do Adolescente (Statute of the Child and the Adolescent). Other types of crimes against women, such as *homicídio de autoria desconhecida praticado no domicílio* (domestic homicide of known authorship), were also included into the jurisdiction of the women's police stations. The new legislation also included crimes such as *aborto* (abortion) and *infanticídio* (infanticide)—cases in which the women are "perpetrators" rather than "victims."

These major changes occurred as a result of broader transformations in the administration of the criminal justice system. On September 25, 1995, Law No. 9,099/95 created civil and criminal small claims courts with the objective of making the justice system move more quickly and efficiently. The criminal small claims courts were designed to deal with alternative penalties for cases of "infractions of minor potential offense." These penalties have included pecuniary compensations (fines and/or restitution), community services, and court-mediated conciliation. The law defined "infractions of minor potential offense" as crimes and violations with sentences of less than one year of detention. In these situations, the *inquérito policial* (police inquiry) ought to be replaced with a Termo Circunstanciado (Term of Circumstances or T.C.), a simplified inquiry with a summary of the occurrence, followed by a medical report, when necessary. Instead of proceeding to criminal investigations, police officers send the Termo Circunstanciado directly to criminal small-claims courts, thus reducing a significant amount of work in police stations.

The creation of the criminal small claims courts greatly affected the work of police officers and sparked a redistribution of powers amongst different types of police stations. Since the majority of the cases in the women's police stations—actual bodily injury and threat—carry sentences of less than one year, the new criminal courts had a special impact on the amount of work performed in the women's police stations. Hence, in 1996, policewomen successfully lobbied for the expansion of the jurisdiction of these stations (see Table 4.2 for crimes listed in the statistics of women's police stations since 1997). Soon after, Decree No. 42,082/97 conferred to the women's police stations the power to arrest individuals for breaching a judge's order to pay alimony. This mandate increased the work of women's police investigators and attracted male police officers to these positions. The impact of these legal changes will be discussed later in this chapter.[3]

The Police Stations Selected for Observation

My analysis of the ways in which policewomen process different types of complaints draws on extensive interviews with policewomen, police records, and participant-observation research in the first women's police station created in 1985, over a period of ten months in 1994, six months in 1995, one month in 1996, and one month in 2001.[4] During three months in 1995, I also regularly observed policewomen's work in another police station located in the neighborhood of Butantã. There were nine women's police stations in the city of São Paulo, all of which I visited.[5] This number has not changed since then. To update my data and confirm my arguments, I returned to São Paulo in 2001 to observe the work of policewomen in both the first women's police station and the Butantã's women's police station. I also conducted additional interviews with police officers, including the newly assigned male police investigators working for both stations. Although there had been important legal changes in 1996 redesigning the powers and jurisdiction of the women's police stations, the structure of these stations and the ways in which policewomen interacted with their clients had not changed.

I chose to spend most of my time in the first women's police station for different reasons. Since its inauguration, this women's police station has attracted enormous attention from both national and international media.[6] Furthermore, this police station has been more accessible than the others. Located in downtown São Paulo, near a subway station, since its inception this station has been the only one that functions 24-hours-a-day, including weekends and holidays. The other women's police stations operate in the same building as the regular district police, and only work a day shift, from 8:00 A.M. to 6:00 P.M. Unlike other police stations, the first women's police station displays a plaque that reads: Delegacia de Polícia de Defesa da Mulher (Police Station in Defense of Women), which can be seen from the street. When I first visited this women's police station, I stopped at a bar nearby to ask for directions. Everybody in the bar seemed familiar with its location.

Given its popularity and location, the first women's police station has always attracted more complainants than the others. In 1994, this was also the only women's police station with a psychologist and two social workers providing services within the police precinct, though such services were discontinued in 1995. Due to its large volume of cases, the first women's police station also has more police officers than the others. The women's police station in Butantã, for example, has only one *delegada* (police delegate), five *escrivãs* (police clerks), and two *investigadoras* (police investigators). In contrast, the first women's police station operates in a three-floor building run by seven *delegadas*, including the head, nine *escrivãs*, four *investigadores*, two *carcereiras* (guardians), one *agente de telecomunicações* (telecommunication police officer), and four military policewomen. Every 12 hours a team of one *delegada*, one *escrivã*, and one military police alternate shifts of twelve hours with a twenty-four-hour break in between each shift.

While the first women's police station stands out as the most accessible to clients and with more cases to process than the others, the way in which policewomen deal with their clients does not differ from the other women's police stations. The cases processed, both in type and proportion of incidence, have been basically the same in all women's police stations in the city of São Paulo. Data on clients' social class and racial backgrounds has not been consistently collected in the women's police stations. In fact, since 1995 policewomen have stopped to ask questions about clients' color and economic background. According to police officers, most clients in women's police stations come from a working-class background and, depending on the location of the police station, many are migrant working-class workers from the Northeast of Brazil. In terms of color, data available from the first women's police station during the month of September 1994 indicates that the majority of the victims were identified by the police officer as white (7,645), followed by *parda* (brown) (3,668), black (2,036),

Figure 4.1 First women's police station (in the evening), downtown São Paulo, July 2001. (*Photo by the author.*)

and yellow (70).[7] It is important to note that, regardless of having the color asked or identified by the officer, color in Brazil is a rather ambiguous category.

Law Enforcement and the Construction of Crimes

> The definition of a crime and the punishment of the person who commits the crime are a juridical creation and have changed throughout history according to the political demands of the moment.
>
> —Mariza Corrêa, *Os Crimes da Paixão* (1981, 20)

According to the dominant legal discourse in Brazil, the task of the judiciary police, as noted in chapter 1, is to investigate crimes based on the principle of legality, meaning that the characterization of a behavior as a crime is a matter of comparing the behavior with the legislation. The dominant legal discourse assumes that such a comparison (i.e., police officers' decisions to register or not to register complaints as a crime) is objective and neutral. The legal discourse also assumes that by enforcing the law, police officers are representing the interests of society and are not biased. In this sense, the role of policewomen in women's police stations is to enforce the law by applying substantive and procedural rules neutrally and objectively. It is not relevant that varying types of crimes are directly related to varying social facts. Likewise, the sex of victims should not be relevant to police officers' approach to complainants.

As mentioned in chapter 2, feminists have questioned the assumption of neutrality of the legal discourse, calling for the training of police officers from either a feminist or gender perspective in order to eliminate sexism in the criminal justice system. However, feminists do not question the principle of legality. They agree that the role of policewomen is to enforce the law, though policewomen need to be trained from a gender perspective. The feminist politicization of conjugal violence and sexual harassment, for example, seeks to enforce and redraft the legislation, rather than abolish legality. The campaign "Impunity as Accomplice to Violence" calls for the application of the law not the abolition or writing of law.

Yet "law enforcement" always depends on the interpretation of facts and laws, that is, on power and discursive struggles over the definition of social facts as legal matters. In other words, the registering of women's complaints in the women's police stations is a selective interpretation of social facts as crimes. The legislation on women's police stations does not mention the term "violence against women." It establishes only that the victim must be someone of the "female sex," listing varying types of crimes described in the Brazilian Penal Code. The lack of legal reference to violence against women makes it even more evident that the criminalization of this issue is the result of a process that involves power and discursive struggles both within the women's movement and within the women's police stations. Policewomen, like other police officers, do not simply apply the law to particular cases brought to the women's police stations. Instead, they *mediate* conflicts and *construct* crimes (see also Muniz, 1994; Vianna et al., 1995). Moreover, they *legitimize* social categories within which individuals and groups may (or may not) claim their rights through the criminal justice system, as illustrated by the cases that follow.

Conjugal Violence: The Paradigmatic Case

The defense of women, of the family, has always been our major concern.

—Rosmary Corrêa's booklet for electoral campaign (1994, 2)

As noted in the previous chapters, throughout the 1980s and 1990s, thanks to the women's and feminist movements, conjugal violence gained high levels of visibility in Brazilian society and was recognized as a serious social problem of public concern. With the creation of the women's police stations, this issue has grown to be the most commonly politicized—and reported—form of violence against women. Since 1985, feminist activists have attempted to shape the practices of policewomen so that the women's police stations do not reproduce the sexist practices of regular police stations. Feminists have urged policewomen to register the cases of conjugal violence as a crime without blaming female complainants for staying in their violent relationship. Although the feminist approach to gender violence in the 1990s became increasingly therapeutic-oriented, feminists still considered criminalization an important venue to address the problem. In this sense, from a feminist perspective, the male perpetrator must be treated in women's police stations as a "real" criminal, regardless of his value as breadwinner and parent. Perpetrators of violence against women must be punished as any other criminal.

Like feminists, policewomen consider conjugal violence the paradigmatic form of violence against women. In fact, most cases reported to the women's police stations concern conjugal violence. The first study of cases registered by women's police stations in São Paulo, conducted by Fundação Sistema Estadual de Análises de Dados de São Paulo (SEADE) and the Conselho Estadual da Condição Feminina (CECF) in 1987, revealed that 70 percent of 2,000 cases registered in the first women's police station from August to December 1985 concerned domestic violence (see Fundação Sistema Estadual de Análise de Dados de São Paulo-SEADE and Conselho Estadual da Condição Feminina de São Paulo 1987). Subsequent studies of the women's police stations, government reports, and data provided by the Serviço Técnico de Apoio às Delegacias de Defesa da Mulher de São Paulo all confirm that since 1985 most cases registered in women's police stations have systematically concerned conjugal violence in the form of actual bodily injuries or threats (see Vianna et al. 1995; Congresso Nacional 1993; Assembléia Legislativa do Estado de São Paulo 1994; Conselho Nacional dos Direitos da Mulher 2001). As discussed in chapter 2, the large number of battered women reporting these crimes has had an impact on policewomen's practices. Some policewomen begin to value their work in the women's police stations after "discovering" that conjugal violence is a pervasive problem in Brazilin society.

However, unlike feminists, policewomen are primarily concerned with the defense or preservation of the family, as expressed in the booklet of Corrêa's 1994 electoral campaign for the state assembly. The consequences of this strong concern about the defense or preservation of the family are twofold. First, forms of violence not related to the family structure or to gender relations are not likely to be taken seriously even by policewomen who "embrace the cause," in other words, those policewomen who make alliances with feminists. Second, policewomen's approach to conjugal violence is contradictory. While most policewomen I interviewed consider conjugal violence to be a "real" crime (with the exception of those who oppose contact with feminists), they do not take it as seriously as other crimes processed through regular police stations, such as robbery, homicide, drug trafficking, and kidnapping. Despite the fact that policewomen are likely to register complaints of conjugal violence, they do not view male perpetrators of conjugal violence as "real" criminals. Even policewomen who "embrace the cause" see the violent husband as an "honest" man, that is, a father and a worker who supports the family (see also Vianna et al. 1995, 11). For instance, at the same time that Delegada Rosmary Corrêa criticizes policewomen who "only reconcile couples," she describes her conception of male perpetrators of conjugal violence as follows:

> He was treated with respect [in the first women's police station], because he was not a marginal, an alcoholic, or a drug-addict. He was a worker, a citizen who didn't miss a day of work, who had a job and labor rights. The difference, the great difference [between the worker and a marginal] is that he is a citizen, he is not a bandit, a robber, a burglar, or a murderer. He is a citizen who needs to understand that violence against his wife is a crime. But he thinks he has the right to do it. So we register the crime, but treat him with respect.[8]

At the same time that the husband is not perceived as a "criminal," policewomen who embrace the cause understand the causes of conjugal violence from a feminist perspective. They define violence against women (meaning conjugal violence) as a manifestation of male domination. As Delegada Izilda Ferreira explains, the criminalization of conjugal violence is not a threat to the institution of marriage, "because the marriage is actually over once he beats her up for the first time. He is typically reacting as a *macho* [male] who thinks he owns his wife."[9] Police clerk Helena Siqueira adds to Ferreira's explanation by adding, "[a]lcoholism is not an excuse [to justify aggressions]."[10] In other words, policewomen who "embrace the cause" view conjugal violence not as a "deviant" behavior, but rather as an expression of unequal power relations between men and women. These policewomen also register complaints about conjugal violence even when complainants do not present visible bodily injuries. As Delegada Rosmary Corrêa explained:

> For us, it was difficult to deal with women who didn't present any bodily injuries. But many women had been beaten up for many years. How could we tell them to go back home? We used to discuss when we should prepare a Bulletin of Occurrence, what kind of Bulletin of Occurrence we should prepare, how to prepare a Bulletin of Occurrence, which ways would be the best, etc.[11]

Figure 4.2 *Delegada* registering a client's complaint at the first women's police station, July 2001. (*Photo by the author.*)

Policewomen opposing an alliance with feminists are also strongly concerned about the preservation of the family. Accordingly, they make a clear distinction between "honest" men and "criminals." As police clerk Mila Duarte explains: "Those criminals in the streets, those minors, kill very easily, because for them someone's life is not important. They are very different from a couple, people who work, who may be poor and even *favelados* [living in shanty-towns], but are not criminals."[12] But, unlike policewomen who embrace the cause, policewomen like Duarte do not view conjugal violence as a "real" crime. "Problems between a husband and wife must be resolved at home," says Duarte.[13] Policewomen like Duarte believe that the role of the women's police station is to "reconcile couples." They perform this role by providing clients with *aconselhamentos* (advice), rather than registering complaints of conjugal violence. "When the case concerns a neighbor, I don't give advice," explains Duarte. "I only do so when it's a couple or a member of the family. I'm very concerned about the family. I may regret the registering of the case later, because this may cause damage to the family."[14] Duarte's attempt to "reconcile couples" is not uncommon. According to a study conducted by the CNDM in 2001 that included 267 women's police stations throughout the country, 93.63 percent of police delegates reported that they provide "*aconselhamento*" (advice) and 42.7 percent said that the role of the women's police stations is to "promote reconciliation and mediation between the parts in conflict" (Conselho Nacional dos Direitos da Mulher 2001, 11).

For policewomen like Duarte, conjugal violence is not conceived as a manifestation of either power relations or alcoholism. Instead, they blame women for being "weak" and for raising *machistas* (sexist men). In Duarte's words, "[m]any women are beaten up because they ask for it. I think she should take responsibility and defend herself. She was strong enough to speak up when she was provoking it. So she should fight back."[15] When complainants are hesitant or ask to close their cases, policewomen like Duarte feel angry and insulted, interpreting clients' behavior as a sign of devaluation of the police's work.

The following interaction took place in the first women's police station and serves to illustrate this type of reaction by a female police officer. A complainant filed a case but neglected to appear for the deposition on two occasions. When she finally arrived to talk to the police clerk in charge of her case, the police clerk asked why she had neglected her previous appointments. The complainant explained that the first time her husband had threatened her. The second time she was scared and wanted to have her case closed. However, she was finally ready to have her case investigated. The police clerk seemed very upset: "You come here to demand your rights, and once things get better you disappear from the women's police station without a word. Now that the situation is bad again, you come back claiming your rights. You deserve a prize! Your case was closed." The complainant replied: "But I didn't receive any notice." The police clerk reacted: "I work here and scheduled your deposition a couple of months ago. I don't recognize the handwriting of the police clerk who sent you this new order of deposition." Then she grabbed the order of deposition from the complainant's hand, crumpled it and threw it in the garbage. "Only come back the next time he beats you up," said the police clerk. The complainant left the women's police station without trying to argue.

Policewomen who absorb the gender discourse without making explicit alliances with feminists are also concerned about the defense of the family. As Delegada Maria Tereza Gonçalves Rosa explains: "I tell her [the female complainant] to think about it [registering the complaint] and to make a decision. She must know whether she wants to either initiate an investigation against him or continue to live with him."[16] At the same time, Rosa is not angry at complainants who ask to close their cases, and she has no doubt that "beating is a crime." Rosa does not blame the victim for her situation either. Yet, she does not consider that the problem of conjugal violence is an expression of power relations. In her viewpoint, alcoholism is the source of the problem. "When he drinks, the problem begins," Rosa explains.[17]

Conceived as "deviance," the problem of conjugal violence is not related to the larger social and cultural structure. Complainants' choices are perceived from an individualistic perspective. That is why Rosa leaves the decision to pursue a police investigation to complainants, even when the closing of the case is against the law. But if the case involves a "serious" bodily injury, Rosa does not close the police investigation. "He attacked her with a scythe, it was extreme, and I didn't close the investigation," she explained when recalling a case that a female complainant had asked to be closed.[18]

The visibility of the bodily injury is an important factor influencing policewomen's decisions to register complaints of conjugal violence. As Delegada Rosmary Corrêa says:

> It's hard to register the case when she [the complainant] has no physical harm. But we couldn't tell her to go back home without doing anything. So we would register the case as *desinteligência*. This is not a crime, it isn't defined in the Penal Code. But judges have recognized it as a legitimate proof that the marriage is not well, that the female complainant has the right to ask for the divorce.[19]

Desinteligência(fights, misunderstandings) means that the couple argued and insulted each other, but did not come to grips. This kind of Bulletin of Occurrence is rarely followed by a police inquiry. During the first half of 1994, for example, all women's police stations in the state of São Paulo registered 5,675 Bulletins of Occurrence concerning *desinteligência* (see Table 4.1). Of those, only 57 (1 percent) were followed by police inquiries. This is a very small number compared to the number of police inquiries that followed the total number of Bulletins of Occurrence during the same period, 16,219 (28.14 percent). The registering of a case as *desinteligência* serves to calm down the complainant and helps her in case she files a divorce lawsuit against her husband.

It is important to note that cases registered as *desinteligência* represent the third highest percentage of Bulletins of Occurrence. As Table 4.1 indicates, during the first six months of 1994, all women's police stations in the state of São Paulo registered a total of 57,628 Bulletins of Occurrence. Of these, 19,284 (33.4 percent) concerned *lesão corporal* (actual bodily injury), 15,303 (26.5 percent) referred to *ameaça* (threat), and 5,675 (9.8 percent) concerned *desinteligência* (fights, misunderstandings). Table 4.2 indicates that the total of crimes registered dramatically increased from 1994 to 2000—jumping from 114,832 to 310,085. This increase cannot be explained as a result of an increase in the number of women's police stations in the state, since most of them (116) were created from 1985 to 1994, with the creation of only nine from 1995 to 2000. The expansion in the jurisdiction of the women's police stations in 1996 and 1997 to include crimes against children and other crimes such as homicide and abortion also does not account for the increase in number of cases reported and registered, since these crimes are rarely reported and registered in the women's police stations. Table 4.2 shows that *lesão corporal* (actual bodily injury), *ameaça* (threat), and *desinteligência* (fights, misunderstandings) continued to be the large majority of cases registered, confirming that conjugal violence is the most visible form of violence and constitutes the large majority of the cases processed in the women's police stations.

Lesão corporal is defined in Article 129 of the Brazilian Penal Code as an offense "to someone's physical integrity or health." The sentence for this crime varies according to the seriousness of the injury inflicted, which is determined by a physician working for the Medical–Legal Institute (IML), who examines the victim for physical abuse. The IML's criteria to classify injuries as either minor or serious range, among other things, from the victim's incapacity to work for more than 30 days, the existence of a major bodily injury resulting in threat of death, terminal disease, or permanent deformity. Minor actual bodily injuries carry a prison sentence of three months to one year, which can be replaced by fines. Serious actual bodily injuries carry a prison sentence of one to eight years, not replaceable by fines. And both are "public-action crimes," which do not depend, for their prosecution, on the victim's consent.

In contrast, there are crimes classified as "public-action crimes conditioned to representation" and "private-action crimes." In the first case, the crimes depend on the victim's initiative to report. In the second case, the crimes depend on the victim's consent to be prosecuted after six months of being reported. Threat is an example of a public-action crime conditioned to the consent of the victim, meaning that a woman who reports a complaint of threat must return to the women's police station six months after her case is registered to authorize the police officer to continue the

Table 4.1 Number of crime reports registered in Boletins de Ocorrência (Bulletins of Occurrence) and followed by Inquéritos Policiais (Police Inquiries) in all women's police stations in the state of São Paulo during the first six months of 1994

Crimes	Boletins de Ocorrência	Inquéritos Policiais
Lesão corporal (Actual bodily injury)	19,284	11,583
Calúnia (Calumny)	902	70
Difamação (Defamation)	1,151	98
Injúria (Verbal offense)	3,160	145
Constrangimento ilegal (Illegal constraint)	170	75
Ameaça (Threat to someone's life or physical integrity)	15,309	1,311
Estupro (Rape)	818	398
Tentativa de estupro (Attempted rape)	332	115
Atentado violento ao pudor (Violent sexual molestation)	620	363
Prática sexual mediante fraude (Sexual practice through fraud)	17	16
Sedução (Seduction)	261	81
Corrupção de menores (Corruption of minors)	92	38
Rapto (Kidnapping)	210	30
Favorecimento da prostituição (Supporting prostitution)	21	13
Rufianismo (Ruffianism)	1	1
Abandono material (Material neglect)	428	153
Maus tratos (Maltreatment)	495	257
Desinteligência (Fights, misunderstanding)	5,675	57
Outros (Others)	8,526	1,415
Total	**57,472**	**16,219**

Source: Serviço Técnico de Apoio às Delegacias de Polícia de Defesa da Mulher do Estado de São Paulo (Technical Service in Support of the Police Stations in Defense of Women in the State of São Paulo).

investigation. Threat is defined in Article 147 of the Brazilian Penal Code as "a verbal, written or physical threat of causing unfair and serious injury to someone." This crime carries a prison sentence of one to six months, replaceable by fines. Unlike threat, actual bodily injury is visible and leaves its traces on the body of the victim. Policewomen often tell complainants that it is easier to prove a crime of actual bodily injury than a crime of threat. This may explain the fact that only 8.5 percent of the Bulletins of Occurrence concerning threat in the first six months of 1994 led to police inquiries as opposed to 60 percent of Bulletins of Occurrence concerning actual bodily injury (see Table 4.1).

After the creation of the criminal small-claims courts in 1996, *lesão corporal* (actual bodily injury) and *ameaça* (threat) continued to appear as the crimes most registered in Bulletins of Occurrences and Terms of Circumstances, as Table 4.2 indicates. Given that actual bodily injury of minor harm and threat carry a prison sentence of less than one year, both types of crimes are supposed to be registered in Terms of Circumstances to be sent directly to the criminal small-claims courts. Unfortunately, data available since 1996 does not give a detailed breakdown of the number of inquiries and terms of circumstances. The data also does not indicate whether the occurrences of actual bodily injury are of "minor" or "serious" nature. Policewomen and feminists I interviewed in 2001 estimated that most of these cases had been sent to the criminal small-claims courts. Usually, these crimes are less likely to be prosecuted and punished than are public-action crimes. This especially applies to the criminal small-claims courts, where conciliation is the goal and alternative penalties (such as a small donation to charity's associations) end up trivializing cases of conjugal violence. For this reason, feminist activists and researchers have criticized the new courts (see Pimentel de Oliveira 1995; Conselho Nacional dos Direitos da Mulher 2001; Campos 2001). Policewomen have also expressed discontent with these courts. As Delegada Maria Cristina Mazzarello explained in interview:

If someone commits a crime, this person must be punished accordingly. If a person inflicts physical harm on another but pays an irrelevant sum of R$ 50 (equivalent to US$ 18 dollars) to charity, this person is not going to reflect on that behavior. The proof is that the same case will be registered again several times, because the guy will beat her up again, even when the victim gives up the prosecution of the case in court.[20]

Although conjugal violence is likely to be registered by policewomen, it should be noted that complaints of threat are harder to prove and are not taken as seriously as complaints of actual bodily injury. "Those who

Table 4.2 Number of crime reports registered in Boletins de Ocorrência (Bulletins of Occurrence) and Termos Circunstanciados (Terms of Circumstances), as well as complaints registered as *desinteligência* (misunderstanding) or under other crimes or not registered (Others) in all women's police stations in the state of São Paulo in selected years

Crime/Year	1994	1996	1997	1998	1999	2000
Lesão corporal	38,873	41,003	51,940	57,246	58,940	78,982
Vias de fato (Coming to grips)	—	—	9,267	11,096	12,940	18,583
Calúnia, difamação, injúria	10,743	12,098	13,813	15,181	17,076	19,276
Constrangimento ilegal	360	1,046	813	575	774	926
Ameaça	30,731	22,853	32,871	36,653	42,173	62,035
Estupro	1,641	1,953	1,873	1,834	1,833	1,882
Tentativa de estupro	600	612	580	555	543	521
Atentado violento ao pudor	1,299	1,754	1,437	1,829	2,008	1,980
Ato obsceno (Obscene behavior)	—	480	—	—	—	—
Prática sexual mediante fraude	26	—	—	—	—	—
Sedução	534	441	—	—	—	—
Corrupção de menores	197	217	—	—	—	—
Rapto	413	456	—	—	—	—
Favorecimento da prostituição	42	57	—	—	—	—
Rufianismo	2	—	—	—	—	—

Abandono material	851	1,765	—	—	—	—
Maus tratos	968	1,266	1,978	2,026	2,280	2,905
Desinteligência	11,361	12,887	99,096	108,202	120,532	118,168
Outros	16,131	49,318	—	—	—	—
Crimes included after 1997						
Homicídio (Homicide)	—	—	35	52	44	41
Tentativa de homicídio (Attempted murder)	—	—	195	227	187	213
Participação em suicídio (Assiting suicide)	—	—	63	55	35	18
Infanticídio (Infanticide)	—	—	5	3	2	1
Aborto (Abortion)	—	—	111	112	124	114
Crime sexual sem violência (Sexual crime without violence)	—	—	1,963	1,740	2,052	2,266
Crimes contra a família (Crimes against the family)	—	—	1,787	1,962	2,159	2,147
Prisões (Arrests)	—	—	117	598	—	1,142
Total	**114,832**	**148,208**	**217,827**	**239,530**	**263,702**	**310,058**

Source: Serviço Técnico de Apoio às Delegacias de Polícia de Defesa da Mulher do Estado de São Paulo (Technical Service in Support of the Police Stations in Defense of Women in the State of São Paulo).

threaten, don't kill," assures police clerk Mila Duarte. If the victim's problem may be discredited even in case of conjugal violence, what happens in cases concerning other forms of violence against women?

Police Violence against Women: A Case not to be Registered

Are you sure the perpetrator was a policeman?

—Police Clerk Rosana Santos

Police have become notorious for killing marginalized Brazilians such as street children and landless peasants. Most victims are young, poor and black. The numbers are staggering. In 1992 police in relatively prosperous São Paulo, population 15 million, killed 1,190 people. The same year in New York, half São Paulo's size, police killed 25 people.

—*New York Times* (August 9, 1997)

The democratization process in the 1980s restored political rights to Brazilians in general, but police brutality against blacks, poor people, homosexuals, and prostitutes did not end. New social movements emerged to protest this brutality, emphasizing the civil component of the discourse on human rights and citizenship rights. Despite new legislation enacted in the 1980s and early 1990s that ensures new civil rights to excluded groups, police brutality has continued (see Adorno 1995b; Americas Watch Committee 1991b). This lack of law enforcement of the new progressive legislation became a barrier for the advancement of citizenship rights. Hence, Caldeira and Holston (1995) characterize the democratization of Brazil as "disjunctive," meaning that political rights have expanded while civil rights have retracted.

Yet from a gender perspective, the emergence of women's police stations has contributed to the expansion of women's citizenship civil rights, entitling women to file complaints of violence against them. But if we think of *all* women and do not separate gender from other social categories such as race and class, the expansion of women's citizenship civil rights through women's police stations becomes questionable. After all, who can actually file a complaint in women's police stations? Does police violence against women and girls living in the streets, black women, and prostitutes count as violence against women? Where can women subject to police violence report and have registered their complaints?

Police violence is a kind of complaint that policewomen are not likely to register. The first time I visited the first women's police station in March of 1994 I observed how a police clerk dealt with this kind of case. I had an appointment with Delegada Izilda Ferreira, then head of the first women's police station. While waiting in the entrance hall [to introduce myself to the female police clerk who was behind a balcony], I took a seat and observed the interaction between complainants and this police officer.[21] A young black woman arrived, crying and walking with difficulty. Another young black woman and a white man came in with her. They all approached the female police clerk. The girl who was crying explained that she had been selling *acarajé* (a kind of food from Bahia) on the sidewalk in front of a building in Praça da Sé, a famous square in downtown São Paulo. She claimed that a male police officer ordered her to vacate the sidewalk. He started beating her, kicking her, and calling her a "bitch."

"Was he really a policeman?" asked the police clerk, suggesting that "maybe he was a private guard." The girl assured her that he was a police officer and insisted to register the complaint against him. "I want to register this case in a Boletim de Ocorrência," she added. She knew what a Boletim de Ocorrência was. "Do you know his name?" asked the police clerk. "He was beating me up, how could I know his name?" replied the girl.

The police clerk argued that it would be very difficult to prosecute her complaint without having the name of the perpetrator. Moreover, she would have to be subject to a physical examination (*exame de corpo de delito*), which would be worthless because she did not know the name of the perpetrator. The police clerk repeated many times that registering this case would be a waste of time. The girl insisted that she wanted to have her complaint registered. She asked to see the police delegate. The white male accompanying her advised her to give up: "Police are all the same, they are corrupt." The girl continued arguing: "Police cannot beat us up just because they are the police."

Turning to the police clerk, the girl said that policewomen should go to Praça da Sé and check the name of the perpetrator. The police clerk explained that the women's police station's staff does not go to the place where the aggressions happen. "Why didn't you call 190 [the phone number of the police for emergency cases]?" inquired the police clerk. The girl said she was afraid of being beaten up even more. The police clerk replied: "*Quem não deve, não teme*" ["Those who are innocent, have nothing to fear," a popular proverb in Brazil].

"I want to talk to the police delegate, I want to register my complaint in a Boletim de Ocorrência," insisted the girl. The police clerk advised her to either go back to Praça da Sé and find out the name of the perpetrator, or call 190. There was a public telephone in the hall, close to the balcony. The girl asked the police clerk if she had a *ficha* (a coin used for public telephone in Brazil). "It is not necessary to use any *ficha* to call 190, it is free, but this phone is out of order," noted the police clerk. After some more arguing, the girl and her friends left the women's police station. The girl said that she would not give up, she would call 190 from a public telephone in the street. "I have the right to register this complaint in a Bulletin of Occurrence," she continued to argue.

As I watched this interaction, it was clear that the police clerk overtly avoided registering the complaint. The complainant not only had the right to talk to the police delegate but her case could have been registered in a Bulletin of Occurrence. However, not all kinds of crimes can be investigated in specialized police stations. In the case of women's police stations, there is an understanding among policewomen, feminists, and complainants that this kind of police station would process crimes of "violence against women," although the legislation on women's police stations does not make any specific reference to this term.

While conducting interviews with feminists in São Paulo, I asked them what they thought about this case of police violence. There was no consensus on whether the women's police stations should have processed it. Some, like feminist sociologist Heleieth Saffioti, felt it was not a case for the women's police stations. Expressing the feminist discourse on "gender violence," she argued that the kind of violence suffered by the girl was not a result of her gender. For members of the black women's NGO Geledés-Instituto da Mulher Negra and the feminist collective União de Mulheres de São Paulo, the case should have been registered and investigated in a women's police station. But, as noted in chapter 3, the hegemonic feminist discourse on violence against women equates the issue with conjugal violence, and more recently also with sexual harassment. The new language on "gender violence" does not leave room for forms of violence that relate to other social categories besides gender. The case of the girl selling *acarajé* at Praça da Sé cannot be expressed through this language, because it involves gender, race, class, and state authority.

When I asked policewomen to define violence against women, they always referred to conjugal and domestic violence. The issue of police violence was spontaneously raised only once. The exception was police investigator Helena Siqueira, who comes from a working-class background, defines herself as black, and had been involved with the Workers' Party (PT) and the black movement. After I told Siqueira the story of the girl in Praça da Sé, she suggested that perhaps the policewoman was trying to protect her colleague.

> People are afraid of registering complaints against both civil and military police officers, but especially against the military police. If you call the police, asking them to come to the place where the offense is happening, it can be dangerous. Sometimes, the victim ends up being beaten up again.

I don't know if the police clerk asked the girl who the perpetrator was either to obtain more information or to confuse her. In any case, the police clerk should have allowed the girl to talk to the police delegate.[22]

Police violence against prostitutes is a case even less likely to be registered. When I asked Siqueira about how policewomen would respond to complaints initiated by prostitutes, she replied:

> If a prostitute looks for a women's police station to file a complaint, I don't know. . . . This is a kind of profession that is not respected. It depends on the police officer. But the police is the police. It is tough. It is the power of authority. The case will only be registered if a group pressures the women's police station to do so.[23]

According to Delegada Rosmary Corrêa, prostitutes do not go to the women's police stations despite the fact that the doors of this kind of police station are legally open for them. As she explains:

> During the five years I worked in the first women's police station, I counted with my fingers the number of prostitutes that appeared there. Since the beginning, journalists would ask me: "What about the prostitute? Does she go to the women's police station?" She suffers a lot of violence. Although we would always say that it is not right to beat her up or rape her for the fact that she is a prostitute, we would hardly see prostitutes in the women's police station. We repeated this message endlessly during meetings, on television shows, and so on. Prostitutes are also victims of rape, they are victims of battering, and the doors of the women's police station are open for them.[24]

Police investigator Ivete Ramos, on the other hand, assured me that the women's police stations process many complaints concerning police violence. Without being asked about prostitutes, she immediately added that "[e]specially prostitutes go to women's police stations to file a complaint. This kind of complaint is registered, as everything else in the women's police station, and the investigation is not closed."[25] Ramos is mostly concerned, however, about the violence perpetrated by male military police officers against their female partners. As she says: "Nowadays, we are also witnessing violence perpetrated by civil police officers against their wives. This is a serious problem. I think we should do research on the subject to find out why there is so much violence especially in the home."[26] Delegada Izilda Ferreira also told me that she had processed cases of violence against prostitutes when she was working in the women's police stations. But she had never faced a case of police violence against prostitutes, and she doubted there had been any. According to Ferreira, this kind of case is not taken to the women's police stations,

> [b]ecause the perpetrator is usually caught in the act. In the first women's police station, it is more common to see prostitutes complaining about violence in motels. I've never seen any case involving the police. Besides, the first women's police station is very close to the *corregedoria* [the police sector in charge of monitoring the work of police officers]. So, if prostitutes have had any complaints against the civil police, they probably have gone to the *corregedoria*.[27]

Prostitutes do go to the first women's police station late at night, though not to file a complaint: they are generally taken there by male police officers to be searched by female police officers.[28] Rosana Silva, a military police officer who was working in the entrance hall of the first women's police station in 1994, explained to me in detail how and why prostitutes are searched there. Early one evening, I was about to leave the women's police station when Silva asked me to stay and watch how different and "exciting" their work is late at night. She told me that female complainants who go there are "really" harmed, because they arrive in the women's police station right after the aggression has happened. But the most "exciting" thing is when policewomen *revistam* (search) prostitutes taken to the first women's police station by male police officers. She described these *revistas* (searches) as follows: "Prostitutes are unclothed in the women's police station, and the female police officer, wearing gloves, examines their vaginas and anus. Sometimes they [prostitutes] hide in their uterus a weapon, money or drugs. Everything must be done in the presence of witnesses, because the police is not allowed to keep the money of the prostitutes, only the weapon and drugs." Silva recalled that, a week before our conversation, she had *revistado* (searched) a teenager who was carrying drugs in her vagina. The girl also carried US$ 300.00. "She was crying a lot, not because she had been caught by the police, but rather because she feared that drug dealers would think she had disappeared with the drug and the money."

Silva explained that police must conduct *revistas* whenever someone is considered *suspeito* (a suspect). As she pointed out, a "suspect" is "someone who runs from the police, changes his or her way in the streets when he or she sees the police. Sometimes the person is a vagrant and looks at the police with fear. Sometimes, the person throws out something in the street when the police are passing by. There have been cases of prostitutes who left little packets of marijuana in the police car before arriving in the women's police station to be searched."

According to Silva, "suspects" are subject to two kinds of *revista*. The first one is called *busca pessoal preliminar* (preliminary personal searching). It is usually done in the streets. In this case, the searched person is not unclothed. The police touches parts of his or her body to make sure that the person does not carry any weapon. "This kind of *revista* is necessary," says Silva, "when we accost someone in the street, or when we take someone to jail in a regular police station." Although Silva does not say directly that race, class, and sexuality influence police officers' perceptions of who must be "accosted" in the streets, prostitutes, blacks, and gays have been especially subject to this type of *busca pessoal preliminar*.

The second kind of police search is called *revista minuciosa* (detailed searching). The searching of prostitutes in the first women's police station is an example of *revista minuciosa*. The person is unclothed and the police officer examines her vagina and anus. "This kind of *revista* is often done to individuals who we suspect are carrying drugs, a gun or stolen goods," explained Silva. "Prostitutes usually carry these things and I always wear gloves while examining their vagina. When they have their period it's awful!"

According to Silva, "Most people don't know about these *revistas* in the first women's police station. One evening, the psychologist came in to pick up something she had forgotten here and she was surprised by seeing me examining a naked woman. She found it 'interesting.' " Delegada Izilda Ferreira, coordinator of all women's police stations in 1994, was not surprised when I asked if this "detailed search" was a common practice in the first women's police station. She did not think that it was a distortion of the women's police stations' role to serve all women.

As I listened to Silva's and Ferreira's descriptions of this police search in the first women's police station, I was constantly asking myself how a police station *in defense of women* could serve the purpose of harassing women who are struggling to survive in the streets. Although by law, prostitutes are not criminals, both male and female police officers treat them as such. No wonder Delegada Rosmary Corrêa could count with her fingers the number of prostitutes who initiated complaints of violence throughout the five years she headed the first women's police station. The silencing of police violence is in large part due to policewomen's interests in protecting the legitimacy of their institutional base. Furthermore, the hegemonic feminist discourse on violence against women does not call attention to this problem. Without pressure from organized sectors of civil society, policewomen are even more likely to dismiss this kind of complaint. Do they also tend to silence or minimize the criminal consequences of complaints concerning racial discrimination?

Racial Discrimination against Women: Is it Violence against Women?

Racism here is the famous *injúria* [verbal offense].

—Delegada Maria Inês Valenti

As noted in chapter 3, in 1951 the Lei Afonso Arinos (Law Afonso Arinos, Law No. 1,390/51) declared for the first time in Brazil that discrimination on the basis of color, sex, or marital status was a *contravenção penal* (misdemeanor), carrying criminal penalties of 15 days to one year in prison and fines.[29] But only in the late 1980s, due to the growth of the black liberation movement, did racism become part of the public discourse and was recognized as a *crime* (felony). As defined in Article 5, XLII, of the Brazilian Constitution, enacted in 1988 during the democratization process, racism is a felony. According to the Constitution, the crime of racism has no statute of limitations, and fines cannot replace prison sentences for the crime of racism. In addition, Law No. 7,716/89 and Law No. 8,081/90 define racism as a public-action crime. Thus, by law, racism is a serious crime and does not depend on the victim's initiative to be prosecuted.

Along the lines of the women's police stations, specialized police stations dealing specifically with racial crimes, known as Delegacias de Crimes Raciais (Police Stations of Racial Crimes), were created in the state of São Paulo in the early 1990s, without excluding other regular and specialized police stations from registering this type of crime. But, contrary to the women's police stations, the Delegacias de Crimes Raciais did not last long and were closed in 1999 (Decree No. 44,448/99). The following year, the Secretary of Public Security created a working group, GRADI-Grupo de Repressão e Análise aos Delitos de Intolerância (Group of Repression and Analysis of Crimes of Intolerance), composed of police delegates and military police officers, to study and prevent crimes of intolerance on the basis of social, religious, sexual, sports team follower, or other identity differences (Secretary of Public Security's Resolution No. 42, March 13, 2000). To this end, GRADI was in charge of creating a database including information about police inquiries and court cases, but complaints of racial crimes would no longer be investigated by a specialized police station anymore. Thus, as noted by Debert and Gregori, "in São Paulo, the political preoccupation with forms of racial violence did not receive the same institutional representation as did violence against women" (2002, 16).

The legislation on women's police stations has ignored racial crimes against women. Yet, as policewomen revealed to me in interviews, a few complaints of racial discrimination against women have been reported to the women's police stations. But do policewomen view racial discrimination and racism as a crime? Do they consider that racial discrimination against women is "violence against women?" In their view, should women's police stations register and investigate this kind of complaint?

As pointed out in chapter 3, there is a consensus among feminists and within the women's movement that racism and racial discrimination is a crime. However, they differ on whether racial discrimination against women should be processed through either the women's police stations or the police station specializing in racial crimes. In other words, they differ on whether racial discrimination against women constitutes "violence against women." For those who define this issue in relation not only to gender, but also to class and race (such as members of Geledés-Instituto da Mulher Negra and União de Mulheres de São Paulo), racial discrimination against women is "violence against women" and should be processed in the women's police stations. For those who define violence against women solely as a consequence of gender relations, that is, as a result of male-versus-female power relations, racial discrimination against women is not "violence against women" (or "gender violence") and should not be processed in the women's police stations.

Police officers in general tend to either dismiss complaints about racial crimes or register these cases as *injúria* (verbal offense). Article 140 of the Brazilian Penal Code defines *injúria* as "an offense to the dignity of a person." It is a private-action crime that carries penalties of one to six months in prison, or fines. By registering complaints of racism as *injúria*, a crime that carries less severe penalties than the crime of racism, police officers minimize the criminal consequences of the racial offense and characterize it as a "non-serious" crime. That is why the 1994 CECF booklet on violence against women advised victims of racism to demand that policewomen register complaints of racial crimes under the criminal type of racism or racial discrimination, rather than *injúria* (see Conselho Estadual da Condição Feminina de São Paulo 1994b).

Police officers' practice of registering racism as a crime of *injúria* was common even in the police station specializing in racial crimes. Police officers' motivation might be related to the fact that the penalty of imprisonment, assigned to the crime of racism, is disproportionate to a verbal offense. To correct this disproportion, a new law was passed in May 1997, creating the crime of *injúria racial* (verbal offense to someone's dignity on the basis of his or her race), which carries penalties less severe than the crime of racism, but more severe penalties than the crime of *injúria*.[30]

On the other hand, it is important to situate police officers' resistance to register crimes of racism within the broader context of racial politics in

Brazil. The Brazilian population is certainly marked by miscegenation, which leads to difficulties in establishing clear-cut racial identities. But racial discrimination is a widely accepted practice in Brazil; those with lighter skin have privileges and more access to social, political, and economic power. Historically, the state and the dominant culture have denied the existence of racism, constructing a myth of a "racial democracy," an ideology that serves to maintain white supremacy in the country. Due to miscegenation and racism, even darker-skinned Brazilians have a tendency to identify themselves, and each other, as white or, at best, *pardas* (brown), not blacks—a practice known as *embranquecimento* (the act or effect of whitening).[31]

Accordingly, policewomen I met in the women's police stations tended to deny the existence of racism. Policewomen also "saw" most clients' color as white, as indicated by the available data on the color of clients. But not all policewomen shared the same conception of racism and racial discrimination. For instance, policewomen in alliance with feminists (such as Rosmary Corrêa, Izilda Ferreira, Ivete Ramos, and Helena Siqueira) viewed racial discrimination and racism as a crime and did not oppose registering this crime in the women's police stations. However, these policewomen diverged on the criminal classification of complaints about racism and racial discrimination: Those who identified themselves as black, such as Ramos and Siqueira, classified this type of complaint as a crime of "racism;" those who did not identify themselves as black, such as Corrêa and Ferreira, classified this crime as *injúria* (verbal offense).

Investigator Helena Siqueira, for example, recalled being subject to racism many times. In 1993, she took the initiative to file a complaint of racial prejudice for being insulted by virtue of her color. She filed the case in a regular police station, rather than in a women's police station, because the former was closer to the place where the offense had happened. She had been shopping at Ceasa (a large food market) when a seller called her *negona* (big Niger)—a derogatory term.

> I immediately reported to the guards of Ceasa, who tried to persuade me not to register the case. I replied that he was responsible, he was not drunk, and people around were laughing at me. We both went with the guards to the regular police station nearby. The police delegate prepared the Bulletin of Occurrence under the criminal type of "investigation of racial prejudice" and sent the case to the police station specializing in racial crimes. The delegate did not register that the perpetrator was caught in the act.[32]

A year later, the investigation of this case had not been completed. Another case of racial discrimination she recalled had been registered in the women's police station, but the investigation had been closed.

Police investigator Ivete Ramos also told me about her experience with racism. She was working in a regular police station in the early 1980s when a complainant insulted her by virtue of her color, calling her *negrinha* (little Niger). She reacted slapping the complainant on the face. The police delegate registered the case against Ramos under the criminal type of *vias de fato* (coming to grips). Ramos believed that he was unfair, because she had been the victim of an offense as well, however she did not take any initiative to also register her case at the time. As she explained:

> I was conscious about violence against blacks. At the time, I was involved with neighborhood groups fighting against racism. But I didn't know my possibilities and limits as a police officer. Today, I would have registered the case by myself. Although we know that law enforcement in this country is a privilege, I would have typed the whole thing preparing a B.O. of racial crime.[33]

Ramos contends that racial discrimination against women could be processed through either the women's police stations or other police stations. A few cases of racism were taken to the women's police station where she used to work. She recalled one of them as follows: a complainant responding to a help-wanted ad in a newspaper called the hiring company's manager, who interviewed her over the phone. Impressed by the candidate's work experience, he asked her to come to the office. When she arrived there, the secretary made her wait for a moment and came back saying that the position had already been taken by someone else. Quietly she added: "Unfortunately, you are black." This case was registered in a Bulletin of Occurrence. However, "[a]s there was no witness, it would be hard to prove, and it ended up being closed."[34]

Delegada Rosmary Corrêa also believed that the women's police stations should register complaints about racial discrimination and racism, but she classified these cases under the criminal type of *injúria*. Corrêa recounted that, while working in the first women's police station from 1985 to 1989,

> [t]his issue [racial violence] was already viewed as a problem, but it was not common. I personally registered one or two complaints. One, for example, concerned a domestic worker who had been barred from using the elevator because she was black. I think this was not exactly racial violence, but discrimination against her due to the fact that she was a domestic worker and a black person.[35]

Policewomen opposing feminism, such as Carlinda de Almeida and Iraci Medeiros, did not view racial discrimination and racism as a crime.

Delegada Iraci Medeiros recalled a complaint concerning racial discrimination, but she did not even accept the complainant's identity. As she explained, "Someone called her a *negra*. But she wasn't even black. Besides, there was no crime."[36]

Policewomen who absorbed aspects of the gender discourse but did not make an explicit alliance with feminists also did not consider that racial discrimination and racism should be registered in the women's police stations, since, for them this issue is not a "serious" crime. Delegada Maria Inês Valenti, for example, who was not a feminist ally in the mid-1990s, expressed in an interview conducted in 1995 that "[r]acism isn't and shouldn't be included in the women's police stations' jurisdiction." Valenti argued that "[r]acism here [as opposed to in the United States] is very limited. What exists here is the famous *injúria*, when you call someone a *negro*."[37] In her view, insulting someone on the basis of color was not a crime. In 1995, when she became head of the Assessoria das Delegacias de Polícia de Defesa da Mulher do Estado de São Paulo (now called Serviço Técnico de Apoio às Delegacias de Polícia de Defesa da Mulher do Estado de São Paulo), Valenti planned to erase from the registration book in the entrance hall of every women's police station the question concerning color. The CECF, at the time headed by Maria Aparecida de Laia, a black woman, tried to prevent Valenti from putting this idea into practice, arguing that society should have access to statistics on the color of women who report to the women's police stations.

Policewomen's varying responses to racial discrimination and racism should not be interpreted as an individual choice or as a result of their personality. Social and political factors shape their legal culture, such as the myth of a "racial democracy" and the hegemonic feminist discourse on violence against women. The growth of the black liberation movement in the 1980s challenged the myth of racial democracy. The black women's movement also expanded in the 1980s, as noted in chapter 3, fighting against racism and sexism. Thanks to black women's mobilizations, racial discrimination against women and racism have become an important issue for both the CECF and the feminist movement. Yet the hegemonic discourse on violence against women has not incorporated race as another category, besides gender, informing women's experiences of violence. Given the little work experience of policewomen in dealing with cases of racism in women's police stations, they have not "discovered" the existence of this problem, as they have for cases of conjugal violence. However, such work experience may not be necessary for policewomen who identify themselves as blacks, who have named their experiences facing racism, and who have been involved with black organizations, as in the situation of Siqueira and Ramos.

Sexual Harassment: Felony or Misdemeanor?

Sometimes, sexual harassment is characterized as a felony of violent sexual molestation; sometimes it is seen as verbal offense; and sometimes it is characterized as sexual molestation, that is, a misdemeanor.

—Delegada Maria Cristina Santos[38]

Although not referred to as *assédio sexual*, the issue of sexual harassment began to be denounced by female workers in Brazil in the late 1970s. The women's movement in São Paulo also addressed sexual harassment throughout the 1980s. But only in the 1990s did feminists strongly mobilize over this issue and name it *assédio sexual*. Feminists framed *assédio sexual* as a form of violence against women. They considered this issue important because it showed that violence against women occurred not only in the domestic sphere but also in the public sphere, at the workplace. The intensive coverage of the 1992 U.S. congressional hearings on Anita Hill's sexual harassment allegations against Supreme Court nominee Clarence Thomas further helped to raise the visibility of sexual harassment in the women's movements and in society at large.

Like racism and racial discrimination, the conception of sexual harassment as a crime is not universally held in Brazilian society. However, while racism has been legally proscribed since 1951, until 2001 there was no legislation in Brazil defining sexual harassment as a crime. In the early 1990s, feminists fought for the creation of new labor and criminal laws to punish perpetrators. At the time, then feminist congresswomen Marta Suplicy and Maura Laura (PT) introduced to Congress a bill that would criminalize sexual harassment, as pointed out in chapter 3. This bill was not approved. In its place, Congress approved, in 2001, a bill proposed by congresswoman Iara Bernardi (PT) that became Law No. 10,224/01 and added Article 216-A to the Brazilian Penal Code, defining the crime of *assédio sexual* as an act of constraining or threatening a worker in an inferior position at the workplace to obtain sexual advantage from this employee. According to this new law, *assédio sexual* carries a penalty of one to two years of detention.

Even before the passing of this law in 2001, feminists were in agreement that, as a form of "gender violence," *assédio sexual* should be criminalized, registered, and investigated through the women's police stations. Incorporating *assédio sexual* into the hegemonic feminist discourse on violence against women since the early 1990s, the CECF published in 1993 a pamphlet defining this issue as "all forms of undesirable approaches with sexual connotation, provoking uneasiness in the workplace of jeopardizing our job" (Conselho Estadual da Condição Feminina de São Paulo 1993). The CECF classified these "undesirable approaches" under the criminal type of *constrangimento ilegal* (illegal constraint), a public-action crime (i.e., a felony, not a misdemeanor) defined in Article 146 of the Brazilian Penal Code as "the action of forcing someone, through the use of violence or threat, to do what is forbidden by law, or not to do what is allowed by law." *Constrangimento ilegal* carries a prison sentence of three months to one year, not replaceable by fines.

Despite the absence of specific legislation addressing sexual harassment, the women's police stations did receive some complaints concerning this issue already in the 1980s, though complainants would not use the term *assédio sexual*, since it did not enter the public discourse until the 1990s. "Ten years ago complainants would report cases of sexual harassment, but would not name the crime as such," said Delegada Rosmary Corrêa in 1994.[39] Policewomen have registered these cases, though under varying criminal types not necessarily matching the feminist classification of the issue as *constrangimento ilegal*.

The fact that complaints about sexual harassment were registered, even when there was no legislation criminalizing it, shows that policewomen indeed reconstruct social facts and selectively translate them into crimes when they apply the law. The very registering of any case results in the reconstruction of women's complaints. The enforcement of law always constructs crimes. But when there is no legislation naming what complainants call a crime, and police officers still register the issue as a crime, such registering is further proof that legislation is just one among other reference texts, and that law enforcement is a process of signification not as neutral and objective as the dominant legal discourse often claims. This does not mean that police officers give meaning to social facts and legal texts according to their individual will. Social and political processes shape their decisions to register (or not to register) complaints and to classify them in criminal terms. Both the registering of sexual harassment and the ways in which it was registered can be attributed to the visibility this issue gained in the early 1990s.

Most policewomen recalled in interviews the case of "the American judge" when describing how they processed complaints concerning sexual harassment. Indeed, some of them heard about the issue for the first time once the media covered the *Hill vs. Thomas* case. Policewomen in alliance with feminists such as Corrêa, Ferreira, Ramos and Siqueira viewed sexual harassment as a felony and articulated a discourse akin to the feminist discourse on the issue. According to Corrêa, "*assédio* [sexual harassment] is hard to prove, but women come to the women's police stations with the support of their unions. While working in the first women's police station we used to register these cases to help complainants to file a labor rights lawsuit against their employers."[40] Corrêa used to register these cases under the criminal type of *constrangimento ilegal* (illegal constraint), as recommended by feminists.

Like Corrêa, Ferreira justified registering sexual harassment as a felony in order to protect complainants' labor rights. Ramos added that, depending on the story told by complainants, policewomen adapted the legislation to the case by registering it under the criminal types of "either violent sexual molestation, verbal offense, threat, or illegal constraint."[41] She recalled during our interview a case that had been registered as *atentado violento ao pudor* (violent sexual molestation), leading to the prosecution and conviction of the perpetrator. *Atentado violento ao pudor* is a felony defined in Article 214 of the Brazilian Penal Code as the act of "coercing someone, through the use of violence or serious threat, to practice with him or to allow him to practice a libidinous action that is different from intercourse." It carries a prison sentence of six to ten years, not replaceable by fines. "But this was not a crime of *assédio*," explained Ramos, "because there is no legislation criminalizing *assédio*; it was a 'violent sexual molestation'. We must take advantage of little lacunas in the law until sexual harassment is legally encoded as a crime."[42] Ramos was aware that "lacunas in the law" could be filled in different ways. She pointed to an example of the CECF's pamphlet on *assédio sexual* that was on her desk and said: "This kind of material is very important for policewomen, and we are sending them to all women's police stations; some policewomen have never heard about *assédio*."[43]

Delegada Márcia Salgado further expressed that, "[t]here are some people connected to these movements [the women's movements] trying to criminalize *assédio*. They characterize it as *constrangimento ilegal* [illegal constraint]. And because the first complaint about the issue [brought to the women's police station] was registered as illegal constraint, this characterization became more accepted among policewomen."[44] Based on my interviews, however, Salgado's comments applied only to policewomen in alliance with feminists. In fact, some of these policewomen were even harder on the perpetrator of *assédio*, registering the complaint under the criminal type of *atentado violento ao pudor* (violent sexual molestation), which is a "serious" felony, almost as serious as rape. It is a public-action felony that carries a prison sentence of six to ten years, not replaceable by fines.[45] On the other hand, some policewomen in alliance with feminists also approached sexual harassment in a much softer way than feminists. Some policewomen registered this kind of case as either *injúria* (verbal offense) or *ameaça* (threat), both of which are felonies that carry a prison sentence of one to six months, replaceable by fines.

Policewomen who opposed any relationship with feminists did not view sexual harassment as a crime. Delegada Iraci Medeiros, for example, said that "[t]here is no crime of *assédio*. It doesn't exist."[46] Following the legality principle, Medeiros emphatically argued that a crime is only what the legislation defines as such. Medeiros also believes that she applies the law neutrally and objectively. She mentioned two cases that she had registered *against* a woman who complained about *assédio*. "She was lying," explained Medeiros. "[S]he was accusing her boyfriend of forcing her to have sex with him. But she went to the motel with him because she wanted [to], there was no crime, there was no injury. She forged the existence of a crime committed against her, and by doing that she committed a crime herself."[47]

Police clerk Mila Duarte agreed with Medeiros that *assédio* was not a crime and that complainants forged stories of *assédio*. She believed that complainants reported cases of *assédio* because the issue had become more popular. "Women take advantage of this situation just to make money. She [the complainant] comes here saying that she was a victim of *assédio*. But she knows that she can get an *indenização muito gorda* [large sum corresponding to reparation]."[48] Duarte only registered cases of *assédio* when the *delegada* advised her to do so. But she registered these cases not as a felony, but rather as a misdemeanor, such as *importunação ofensiva ao pudor* (sexual molestation). Sexual molestation is defined in Article 61 of the Lei das Contravenções Penais (Law of Misdemeanors, *Decreto-lei* No. 3,688/41) as the act of "molesting someone, either in a public or accessible place, in ways that are offensive to the honor of the person." As a misdemeanor, the practice of a sexual molestation does not carry a sentence as severe as other sexual crimes defined in the Brazilian Penal Code. The perpetrator of a sexual molestation is simply subject to fines.

Policewomen who absorbed aspects of the gender discourse without making explicit alliances with feminists also followed the legality principle. They affirmed that *assédio* was not a crime, because there was no legislation criminalizing it. But, unlike those who opposed alliances with feminists, these policewomen were in favor of registering complaints of *assédio* in a Bulletin of Occurrence. Thus, they "adapted" the legislation to the social reality, though they did not register this kind of case as a felony. Instead, they registered *assédio* under the misdemeanor of *importunação ofensiva ao pudor* (sexual molestation). Furthermore, unlike those who opposed alliances with feminists, policewomen who absorbed aspects of the gender discourse favored the criminalization of *assédio* through the enactment of a specific legislation. As Delegada Maria Tereza Rosa explained:

> In the case of *assédio*, I tell complainants that this is not a crime, although there has been much propaganda about it. I think it should be criminalized.

But *assédio* is not a crime yet, because there is no law defining such issue as a crime. The only thing I've heard about is a law establishing a sort of reparation for moral injuries. Thus, I try to fit the case into *importunação ofensiva ao pudor* [sexual molestation]. But I explain that this is a misdemeanor. In fact, it is not completely right to register *assédio* as *importunação ofensiva ao pudor*, because the law defines this misdemeanor as an action that takes place in public, whereas *assédio* usually occurs in privacy. But I have no other choice. Some people register *assédio* as illegal constraint, but this felony doesn't correspond to the case at all.[49]

As my observations and interviews with policewomen illustrate, complaints about *assédio* were more likely to be registered in Bulletins of Occurrence than complaints about police violence and racial violence. Even policewomen who did not make alliances with feminists (such as Duarte) registered complaints of *assédio*—though not as a felony. Thus, in the case of *assédio*, the dominant legal discourse—based on principles of legality, neutrality, and universality—was transformed by the practices of policewomen.

It is important to note that, in contrast to police violence, complaints about *assédio* do not pose a threat to the legitimacy of police authority—in this case, the perpetrator is not a police officer. Moreover, compared to racial discrimination and racism, *assédio* has gained more visibility in the media. Finally, the feminist and women's movements have strongly incorporated the issue of sexual harassment into their hegemonic discourse on gender violence.

Despite the increasing feminist politicization of sexual harassment as a form of gender violence, coupled with its growing visibility in the media and its ultimate recognition as a crime in 2001, the dominant conception of violence against women in Brazilian society—and among policewomen—still corresponds to conjugal violence. Indeed, the data on the disposition of cases processed in the women's police stations shows that the large majority of the complaints concern *briga entre marido e mulher* (fights between husband and wife).

Conclusion

The multiple and contradictory ways in which policewomen register complaints in the women's police stations show that "gender," as a legitimate social category, is constructed not only when state managers enact legislation creating a unique institution to "defend" women. The actual work of state agents in the judiciary system, such as female police officers who process women's complaints, also contributes to the construction of gender as a social category. Legislation on women's police stations does not indicate that this kind of police station must process cases of violence caused only by virtue of women's *gender*. The legislation does not define the term "violence against women" either. Therefore, rather than focusing on the legislation, to uncover the legal meaning of violence against women it is necessary to examine the ways in which policewomen register complaints in the women's police stations. This is also important to see the connections between the construction of social categories and the construction of citizenship rights—in the case of women's police stations, the right to have access to the criminal justice system.

The multiple ways in which policewomen give meaning to violence against women illuminate the contradictory form of gendered citizenship that is constructed by policewomen in the women's police stations. On the one hand, state agents have their own interests, as illustrated by the way in which policewomen address police violence. The silencing of this type of violence leads to the repression of complainants' rights, not simply because the state is "essentially male," but rather because state agents are protective of their institutional base and wish to legitimize their authority. On the other hand, state agents' interests are also shaped by the discourse of civil society actors, particularly by NGOs. As the cases of conjugal violence, racial discrimination, and sexual harassment show, policewomen may absorb aspects of feminist discourses and may foster both social control and social change through either the repression or advancement of women's rights.

As a result of policewomen's absorption of aspects of the hegemonic feminist discourse on gender violence, policewomen's discursive practices in the women's police stations contribute to the hegemony of this feminist discourse in society at large, as well as to the construction of a form of gendered citizenship. Once we bring gender into the analysis of citizenship civil rights, the case of the women's police stations suggests that feminists have succeeded in showing that the "house" (where conjugal violence takes place) is an important social space where women have not been fully recognized as citizens in Brazilian society. Thus, Roberto DaMatta's (1985) allusion to the "house" as the social space of citizens and the "street" as the social space of "others" becomes problematic when we bring gender and the issue of conjugal violence into the discussion of citizenship rights. Indeed, the establishment of women's police stations all over the country, and the large number of cases of conjugal violence reported, indicates that battered women are becoming subjects of civil rights for the first time in Brazilian history. These gendered police stations contribute to the formation of a gendered citizenship that benefits married women or women in heterosexual love relationships.

Yet, the construction of gendered citizenship is *contradictory*, because it is also accompanied by the exclusion of women whose rights are curtailed by their membership in other groups not defined by gender only. This is well illustrated by the ways in which policewomen deal with racial discrimination, police violence, and prostitution. The exclusion of blacks, women living in the streets, and prostitutes from the exercising of rights before the judiciary police is a good illustration of Caldeira's and Holston's (1995) characterization of Brazilian democracy as "disjunctive." DaMatta's (1985) account of the "street" as the social space of "others" (i.e., of non-citizens) applies perfectly to such an exclusion. For policewomen, the (heterosexual and white) house and workplace are the only realms where women's civil rights deserve protection. From the perspective of police-women, "citizens" are workers and those who own and/or remain in their houses, not "polluting" the streets or causing "trouble" to citizens.

However, even from a gender perspective, the construction of gendered citizenship is also *contradictory*, because policewomen are mainly concerned about the preservation of the family. They may resist register-ing cases of conjugal violence and do not view male perpetrators as "real" criminals. The fact that policewomen see male perpetrators as "citizens" in opposition to "criminals" suggests both that they do not believe these male perpetrators are "real" criminals and that "criminals" are not citizens. Thus, while policewomen challenge gender relations of power in the family, they also reinforce a dominant sexist ideology in Brazilian society.

Despite their contradictions and limitations, the women's police stations have been an important achievement of the feminist movement and have greatly benefited women in situations of violence, especially conjugal violence. That is why the following and last chapter will examine battered women's experiences in the first women's police station.

5

Engendering Battered Women's Sense of Rights

In the past battered women had two choices: either to silence violence against them, fearing more harm at home; or to look for any police station in the city, running the risk of being subjected to prejudice and humiliation. When the *delegacia da mulher* [women's police station] was created, this situation changed altogether. Women have gained a place that not only guarantees their protection, but also provides them with advice.

—*Globo Repórter* (Rede Globo, July 1990)

She [the policewoman] told me that it isn't right to harm women. My husband said he would hire an attorney and nothing would happen to him. When I told her about this, she replied: "Don't worry, in the *delegacia da mulher* [women's police station], he can't do anything." I felt more confident and asked myself: "Without the *delegacia da mulher*, what could we do?" We must hold hands and press charges. We must help each other. It isn't right to be beaten up.

—Rosenete Campos (Interview, São Paulo, May 23, 1994)[1]

In the beginning of my field research, I focused my attention on how feminists and policewomen were "constructing" violence against women and gendered citizenship, not taking seriously the complainants' perspectives on the women's police stations. It was only after conducting my first interview with a woman who had complained about conjugal violence that I "discovered" how I was underestimating the importance of the women's police stations in complainants' lives. The quotes above illustrate some of the effects these stations have on battered women who take the initiative to break from enduring situations of conjugal violence and go to the women's police stations. As noted in the previous chapter, the majority of the cases reported to the women's police stations have continually concerned (heterosexual) conjugal violence. Moreover, the number of complaints has dramatically increased over the years, indicating that the establishment of hundreds of women's police stations in São Paulo and throughout Brazil has contributed to the expansion of women's rights and has encouraged women in violent heterosexual love relationships to report the violence they had been suffering in silence.

My interviews and interactions with clients in the first women's police station revealed, among other things, that I was not taking into account the complainants' interests and agency.[2] By complainants' "agency" I mean their ability to use the women's police stations according to their needs and interests, which are re-constructed in the women's police stations, in their homes, and in society at large.[3] In other words, clients are not passive recipients of state reforms in the criminal justice system. Neither are they "passive victims" or "accomplices" to violence, as Brazilian feminist scholars have observed (Heilborn 1993; Brandão 1998; Saffiotti 1994). They are not "heroes" either. Their interests and social practices are shaped by the social, cultural, political, and economic context in which they live. They live in a hierarchical society, marked by drastic levels of inequalities shaped by race, class, gender, and sexuality structures and ideologies. Since their needs and interests are different from those of feminists and policewomen, an examination of clients' perspectives is necessary to our understanding of the importance and contradictions of creating an all-female space within the repressive arm of the state to address the issue of violence against women.

Yet, like feminists and policewomen, clients do not constitute a homogenous group. Women in situation of conjugal violence do not have the same needs and interests of women who are sexually harassed in the workplace, or who are discriminated against due to their skin color or sexual orientation. By focusing exclusively on the perspectives of battered women, this chapter serves as an illustration of how a specific group of women approach and utilize the women's police stations according to their needs and interests, thereby contributing to the construction of gendered citizenship in ways that contrast with both the feminist and police approaches to gendered citizenship. The following questions will guide the discussion: When and how do battered women decide to go to the women's police stations? Why do they go to the women's police stations? What are their interests and how do they contrast with the interests of feminists and policewomen? What do they expect from the women's police stations? How do they use the women's police stations and what do they learn from going there?

Drawing on interviews with battered women as well as existing research in Brazil on how battered women use the women's police stations

(Muniz 1996; Vianna et al. 1995; Soares 1996; Brandão 1998), this chapter shows that battered women do not necessarily seek the criminalization of their male perpetrators and approach the women's police stations according to their needs and interests. In addition, complainants are also influenced by their interactions with policewomen. In contact with policewomen, including those who are not necessarily in alliance with feminists, battered women learn to articulate a distinct gender identity and sense of rights (see also Brandão 1998). Within this perspective, not only collective actors of civil society, such as feminist activists, en*gender* the state (Alvarez 1990), but the state also en*genders* other actors in civil society, such as battered women.

Most complainants come from a working-class background, some are poor and migrant women from the impoverished northeast region of the country, and most only have a few years of education. While cultural and economic forces shape battered women's hesitation about criminalization, social class limits their alternatives to solve or negotiate domestic conflicts outside of the criminal justice system. Migrant women also face isolation and do not have access to family members to help and "protect" them from the perpetrators. Yet, other reasons encourage battered women to overcome their fears about involving the police, such as the specificity of the women's police station as an institution to "defend" women, the need to protect their children from witnessing or being subject to violence, and the encouragement of the media, employers, or friends who have "successfully" used the women's police stations (see also Brandão 1998).

Given the interactions between class and gender, battered women approach the women's police stations in ways that contrast with the feminist goal of criminalizing domestic violence as well as the legal definition of the function of the police as enforcer of the law. Like other members of the working class who look for the police to mediate intra-class disputes, they approach these stations as an arena of "mediation" and "alternative dispute resolution" to redraw the conjugal contract (see Muniz 1996; Vianna et al. 1995).[4] Brandão (1998) shows, however, that battered women use these stations as a weapon to "protect" their physical integrity and to "threaten" or "scare" the perpetrators in order to end violence as well as to redraw the conjugal contract.

Drawing on Brandão's study, Sorj (2002) pointedly explains that battered women take advantage of the hierarchical values and ideologies that inform the dominant political culture in Brazilian society and ally themselves with the women's police stations to both challenge and reinforce the dominant culture. Feminist values and ideologies that inspired the establishment of the women's police stations are appropriated in complex ways not only by state agents but also by clients of the state. To "scare" their partners, battered women play with the ambiguous role of the police in Brazil. By law, the police must investigate crimes according to legal procedures and norms established by a constitutional state based on principles of a liberal democracy. In practice, however, the police and society view this institution not simply as a representative of public power to investigate crimes and to provide security. The police are corrupt, violent, and arbitrary, and thereby do not fulfill their legal responsibility. The population in turn often expects the police to exercise "vengeance" on behalf of victims of violence. Therefore, both the police and the population often ignore legal procedures and norms regardless of whether the population knows them.

In line with Brandão and Sorj, this chapter shows that in the contradictory terrain of legality and arbitrariness, feminist and masculinist values, which characterize the women's police stations, battered women learn to articulate a sense of women's rights that both draws and departs from the liberal feminist and criminal approaches to violence against women. They request the public authority of the police to use force but not to enforce the law, in order to "scare" the perpetrators and neutralize power differences within the private sphere. They appropriate the liberal legal and feminist ideologies of individual rights to gain "autonomy" in their own terms, that is, to defend their right to have a family free from private and public violence. But they are not necessarily interested in separating from the perpetrators and do not intend to use the public authority of the state to further punish their male partners and their communities. In this sense, they try to negotiate with both public and private gendered authorities when they go to the women's police stations. They try to rely on the power of policewomen and feel frustrated when the police do not "scare" their male partners and do not "solve" their problem quickly. Yet, they also fear criminalization, which for them must serve as a threat but not a reality. In sum, like policewomen, though for different reasons, they both challenge and reinforce the dominant hierarchical gender relations and the masculinist police culture.

Looking for "Protection" in the Women's Police Stations

There's a women's police station, let's go there!

—Aparecida Andrade (Interview, São Paulo, September 22, 1994)

It's a day like any other in the newly-created women's police station in São Paulo. At 7:45 am, ten women are already in line in front of the police station's closed doors. Some women show visible wounds, especially on their faces, caused by their husbands, fathers, brothers. . . . They do not know what exactly they can achieve there, but the name of the women's police stations says *Defesa* da Mulher [in *Defense* of Women]. Indeed they need defense.

—*Tribuna Operária* (July 9–15, 1985)

Since the late 1970s, Brazilian feminists have emphasized the importance of criminalizing conjugal violence, along with other measures such as the provision of psychological and social services to address the multifaceted needs of victims of violence. They claim that criminalization gives visibility to an issue that has been culturally and legally constructed as "normal." Criminalization expands women's rights and helps to liberate women from male domination. As noted in chapter 3, feminist scholars and activists conceive of conjugal violence as a structural problem within Brazilian society. Contrary to most policewomen and battered women, feminists do not approach this problem as a consequence of "deviant behavior" caused by alcoholism or jealousy. For feminists, the root causes of conjugal violence rest on the gender inequalities created and reinforced by social, economic, and cultural structures, ideologies and institutions that maintain male domination. Criminalization is just one among other means to help end gender inequalities. The women's police stations are important because they begin with the premise that women need protection. Criminal law is used to change the culture, to provide women with security, and to help them gaining autonomy as individual subjects of rights.

As noted in chapter 1, the establishment of women's police stations has made public and largely visible in Brazil the issue of conjugal violence as a crime.[5] On August 6, 1985, the day after the inauguration of the first women's police station, there was a line of 500 women waiting to talk to Rosmary Corrêa, the first head of this station, and to file their complaints. The popularity of this women's police station prompted the creation of similar stations all over the country, and encouraged hundreds of thousands of women to take their complaints of conjugal violence to the women's police stations.

Yet, filing a complaint of conjugal violence (or other forms of violence against women) in police stations is a difficult decision. Battered women are concerned with the preservation of their family and are hesitant about criminalizing and stigmatizing the father of their children. Besides fearing revenge from the perpetrators and not exactly knowing what kind of "punishment" will be meted out to perpetrators, there is also the fear of being ridiculed, harassed, or abused by police officers, especially by male police officers. Furthermore, the involvement of perpetrators in organized crime in the *favelas* (shantytowns) where many complainants live may contribute to their fear of incriminating the perpetrators. Black women's organizations, such as Geledés-Instituto da Mulher Negra, further argue that black women fear both regular and women's police stations, because they are afraid of racism against them and their partners.[6] That is why it is important for complainants to know that there is an institution where women from all racial and class backgrounds can report complaints of violence and be treated with respect.

Among the fourteen complainants I interviewed in 1994 and 2001, thirteen of them complained about conjugal violence and one complained about sexual abuse of her daughter by a family member. Their ages ranged from 21 to 48 years. Twelve of them came from poor families and only two from low-middle-class families. Half of the women identified themselves as *brancas* (white) and the other half as *pardas* or *morenas* (brown). One of them also identified herself as *negra* (black). At first she said hesitantly that *"eu sou, é, parda, né? Meu registro está escrito parda"* (I am, hum, *parda*, you know. My birth certificate says I'm *parda*). I asked what she thinks her skin color is and she said, *"eu acho que eu sou da raça negra, you know. Sou da raça negra"* (I am from the black race. I'm from the black race).[7] Ten of the women worked outside home. Five were migrants from the northeast region of the country. Their employment ranged from domestic work, to shop assistance, to insurance selling, and to coordination of a child care center. None had completed high school. Except for having a higher proportion of *pardas* (brown) women, the social and economic background of these complainants is representative of the background of the majority of women who press charges in the women's police stations throughout the country.[8]

However, this should not imply that conjugal violence only occurs among low-income people. Cases reported to the women's police stations do not reflect the totality of occurrences in society. As documented by Brazilian studies of police stations, low-income women and men lack access to the court system and often go to police stations, including the women's police stations, to solve their civil and criminal grievances. Consequently, they resort to police stations to help them "solve" or "mediate" intra-class conflicts (Oliveira 1994; Kant de Lima 1994; Muniz 1994; Vianna et al. 1995). In contrast with the middle and upper classes, low-income couples cannot afford marriage counseling, for example (Brandão 1998). Upper- and middle-class women may be equally subject to conjugal violence, but they have more resources to deal with their problems outside of the criminal justice system. Thus, despite having access to this system, they prefer not to publicly expose their families in women's police stations or in the courts.

The complainants I interviewed revealed that they had been beaten up by their male partners for many years. Some had gone several times to regular police stations and to women's police stations. A few of them were in the women's police stations for the first time. Most interviewees had heard about the women's police stations through television or radio and described going there as a "courageous" action. They felt "protected" while talking to the police delegate in the women's police stations, but not necessarily afterward. They all considered that the women's police stations were better than regular police stations, although they did not see all policewomen as necessarily better than policemen.

Aparecida Andrade, for example, went to the women's police station for the first time in 1990, after watching the episode of *Globo Repórter*, produced by the television network Rede Globo, which had focused on the issue of violence against women and women's police stations. Andrade's friend had just been beaten up by her husband, and Andrade suggested: "There is a women's police station, let's go there!"[9] Her friend replied, "No, I don't know where it is." Andrade insisted: "Let's look for it."[10] Andrade served as witness in her friend's case. Just a few years later, she ended up going to regular police stations and to women's police stations a couple of times—not because of her friend, but for herself. In 1994, when we met in the first women's police station, she was 32 years old, divorced from her first husband, separated from her second partner, and raising three children by herself. She had worked as a shop assistant but at the time was unemployed, sometimes managing to sell products on consignment for the Avon company. She was receiving US $70.00 per month from her first husband to support two children (4 and 5 years old, respectively), and nothing from her second partner to raise a six-month-old child. Andrade had only attended school until the 6th grade. Born in the impoverished northeast region of Brazil, and identifying herself as *branca* (white), she migrated alone to São Paulo when she was 18 years old in search of better life conditions but she planned to return to the northeast by the end of 1994.

The first time that Andrade filed her complaint of *lesão corporal* (actual bodily injury) in the women's police stations was in 1992. She went by herself, after being beaten up a couple of times. "He used to come back home drunk. One day he bought bus tickets for us to go to the beach. Because I wanted to wear a bikini, he beat me up and pushed me down the stairs. I fainted and woke up later in a hospital."[11] Andrade did not take the case to the women's police stations at the time, but threatened her partner to do so if he abused her again. "He had already beaten me up four times, but I was afraid of coming here. I didn't have the courage, because in the case of my friend her husband continued beating her up."[12] A month later he harmed her again. She decided then to file a complaint against him in the women's police station. After pressing charges for the first time, she felt "courageous." As she says, "Not every woman has the courage to face it. My friend wanted to close her case. She didn't do it because I didn't allow her to do it. The *delegada* (female police delegate) also advised her not to close the case. In my case, he implored me to give up. I didn't give up."[13] The *delegada* registered Andrade's case and sent an order of service to her partner. Andrade and her husband returned to the women's police station together. "Then, he started to insult me, and she [the policewoman] ordered him to shut up. He behaved very well in front of her, quietly, not saying a word. But when we left, he forced me to take the same bus and harmed me in the street close to my house. Some men saw the scene and almost lynched him."[14]

Before going to the women's police station, Andrade tried to register her case in regular police stations. She went there five times, but male police officers did not take her case seriously. "They told me that, 'Here we have a lot of crimes to solve. Our cases concern criminal and serious matters. Little fights between husband and wife must be dealt with at home, you can solve these problems in the women's police stations,' they said, laughing at me."[15] Andrade believes that the women's police station is better than a regular police station, "because here we talk to women, we trust them more than men. Usually, men take men's side."[16]

Rosenete Campos' experience of going to the women's police stations and to one regular police station was similar to Andrade's. Campos had been beaten up by her husband for eight years. In silence for so long, she "was afraid of scandal" and had some hope that the situation could change: "Neighbors could hear in the night and used to ask the day after: 'What happened?' And I used not to say anything, I was hiding for shame, because of my children, too. Sometimes they didn't even know I had been beaten up. I used to cry and the day after everything was normal. But the last time, he threatened to kill me and put a gun on my face. Only now I see that there is no remedy, it's enough."[17]

Campos had heard about the women's police stations through television and radio, but was feeling completely helpless and isolated: "I was feeling horrible, not knowing what to do. I was raised in a cloister, so I had no place to go."[18] In May 1994, after being beaten up again, her 19-year-old daughter took her to the regular police station near their house. Male police officers did not take her case seriously, telling her to go to the women's police stations: "They were laughing at me. I was already wounded, more than now, and they made fun of me. I took a taxi to come here, but the taxi driver discouraged me, saying that I would be humiliated again. It seems that men defend each other, as if women should be beaten up in silence. I was so scared that I didn't come here."[19]

Two months later, after being beaten up again, she looked for the help of her only friend, who advised her to go to the women's police station. At first, Campos resisted: "It's not going to make any difference," she told her friend, who insisted and accompanied her to the women's police station. It was Campos' first time at the women's police station. I followed up her case. It was registered in a Bulletin of Occurrence as *lesão corporal* (actual bodily injury). She was immediately referred to the Instituto de Medicina Legal (Legal Medical Institute) close to the women's police station. There the physician prepared the *exame de corpo de delito* (bodily exam). A few days later, she returned to the women's police station with her husband for further questioning. She then gave me an interview in one of the police-women's rooms, while her husband stayed in the entrance hall.

Campos was 43 years old at the time. Born in the northeast region of Brazil, identifying herself as *parda* (brown), she moved to São Paulo with her family when she was a baby, but was not raised by her parents, who had divorced and left her and her two sisters at an orphanage. Six years later, she was sent to a cloister by her aunt. She worked hard for the nuns, cleaning and cooking. Thanks to her aunt, she also studied, though only finishing the 5th grade. "Can you believe that I had my birth certificate only when I became an adult? I didn't even have a name. Isn't that absurd?" she reflected in shock.[20] When she was 17 years old, she married "to escape and know the world outside the cloister," as she interprets it.[21] Her husband, who owns small hotels, did not allow her to keep in touch with her family. They have four children and since the marriage Campos has never worked outside her home.

Campos was surprised by the women's police station. She expected to be treated like male police officers had treated her in a regular police station, making her wait for a long time and not paying attention to her case. But in contrast, at the women's police station, "I felt very protected," she says, "they treated me well and I felt more confident. She [the police-woman] said that a man cannot beat up a woman. When he came here, he was reduced to a little thing. So I felt more secure."[22] Just as Andrade, Campos considers that the women's police station is a much better environment for women than regular police stations. As she explains: "Here, everybody treated me well, I don't even know who the police delegate is. It's not like having that authority, like men."[23] She went even further saying that, "[w]omen are always women, I think we have more capacity than men. I'm not putting down men, but they seem to be *machistas* [sexist]."[24]

Contrary to Campos, Marta Silva was not excited about the treatment received from a female police delegate. Born in São Paulo, identifying herself as *branca* (white), a shop assistant, and divorced with two children, she was 27 years old when we met in the first women's police station. Silva had already been to a regular police station and two different women's police stations to file a complaint against her male partner. In one of these women's police stations, the female police delegate made her feel "more nervous and upset." As she recalled, the police officer nastily affronted her by saying: "You will go back to him. This was just a misunderstanding, it was not important. He didn't break your nose."[25] Silva was upset because she was in pain and the policewoman was treating her like a "beast," she explained. Besides, she had been well treated in the other two women's police stations. In her view, the female police delegate was acting exactly like male police officers. She believes that male and female police officers should be less pretentious and more careful, because "the victim arrives in the women's police station in panic, in despair, and she may lose her mind afterwards."[26]

Lucinda Barbosa had a better experience with policewomen and preferred the women's police stations than regular police stations. But she did not hold an essentialist perspective on male and female police officers. As she explained, "Here [in the women's police station], it's different. They pay more attention than in the other places [such as regular police stations]."[27] Once she accompanied a friend to a regular police station and "the *delegado* [male police delegate] turned to her and said that she liked [to be beaten up] otherwise she wouldn't be with him. So it's a waste of time to go to a regular police station, because the *delegado* doesn't solve anything, unless you find a nice *delegado* who can understand you. This makes a difference. If you find someone who understands you, he will prepare the Bulletin of Occurrence. But if you find someone like our husband[s], it will be a waste of time!"[28] Yet, in the women's police station, although receiving better service, Barbosa also had to persuade the female police delegate that she was right: "She asked whether I thought that I was also wrong and I said that I was not guilty of anything, because he had no reason to harm me, he was wrong."[29]

I met Barbosa at the first women's police station on July 7, 2001. She was 33 years old, single, had three children, and identified herself as belonging to the "*raça negra*" (black race). Barbosa attended school until the 7th grade and had worked until 1995 printing serigraphy for a soccer club. She had developed repetitive stress injury in both arms due to this work and had become incapable of continuing her work. Born in the northeastern state of Bahia, she migrated to São Paulo in 1979. Each of her children, ages 17, 14, and 12 respectively, had a different father. The youngest is the son of the man she reported to the women's police station for having physically harmed her.

Barbosa looked for the first women's police station for the first time in December of 2000, when her partner injured her foot with a screw-driver after an argument about sharing the cost of a medical exam she had to take. She felt he should contribute because he "always spends my money, he drinks, he gambles, and he smokes."[30] Her partner had beaten her up several times throughout the 11 years they were living together. "Once he hit my shoulder with the gate and I had my right arm swaddled for three days. He was like that, and he would come and go, come and go."[31] When I met Barbosa she was living with her family in a board hut in a *favela* (shantytown) in São Paulo. She had decided to go to the women's police station because her children had witnessed the last fight in December and she feared for their security. "My daughter protested and when I saw that he was going to hit her, I decided to do something. My 14-year-old son also protested. I was afraid he was going to harm them. A friend who had already come here helped me."[32]

In the women's police station, Barbosa had her case registered in a Bulletin of Occurrence for *lesão corporal*. She was immediately referred to the Instituto de Medicina Legal (Legal Medical Institute) for an exam of the bodily injury. Later, her case was sent to the criminal small-claims court, where the judge asked whether she was still living with her partner and whether she wanted to pursue a criminal lawsuit. She did not want to close the case because she felt this was necessary to "protect" her children. The judge sent the file back to the women's police station to get the deposition of the perpetrator. That is when Barbosa told me that she was very pleased with the women's police station. "It helped me. They registered my case and advised me, this helped a lot! Now it's my decision to continue or not with him."[33]

Not all policewomen treat complainants respectfully, but the testimony of these complainants suggests that they feel much better in women's police stations than in regular police stations, trusting female police officers more than male police officers. They articulate a gender discourse by comparing male with female police officers, and they feel protected by female authorities, finding in the (female) state the protection that they cannot find from men at home. Indeed, in the presence of female police officers, men "behave." More than "protected," complainants feel "confident." The testimony of these complainants also indicates that they go to the women's police stations with higher expectations than when they go to regular police stations. I will turn now to these expectations, examining how they think the women's police stations can help them and how they use the women's police stations.

"Scaring" Men to End Violence and Redraw the Conjugal Contract

At least three months in prison, to scare him.

—Aparecida Andrade (Interview, São Paulo, September 22, 1994)

Right now, I feel sorry for him. That's how women are.

—Rosenete Campos (Interview, São Paulo, May 23, 1994)

In the early 1980s, Brazilian feminists attempted to make visible the issue of domestic violence by creating NGOs, such as SOS-Mulher, which would provide legal and psychological services for battered women. At the time, feminists believed that battered women's autonomy required, among other things, separation from male perpetrators. However, feminists soon realized that victims were not always willing to separate from their male perpetrators and that not all women were seeking "autonomy." On the contrary, most of them continued living with their partners or engaged in new violent relationships.

When the women's police stations were established, the problem of conflicting expectations between those who provide services and those who look for help did not disappear. Although not all policewomen share the feminist goal of "autonomy" and may resist registering different types of complaints of violence against women, they are likely to take cases of conjugal violence seriously. Before registering these cases, they tell complainants that the perpetrator may be imprisoned, though only the judge can make this decision. By law, police officers cannot incarcerate perpetrators, unless they are caught in action. But in contrast to regular police stations, the women's police stations do not even have cells.

Policewomen are careful in advising complainants about the consequences of registering the cases, because they either want to discourage complainants from having the case registered, or they want to alert complainants that the police investigation cannot be closed, particularly when the case concerns a public-action crime, such as serious actual bodily injury. By law, the investigation of public-action crimes cannot be closed under the request of the victim. Once policewomen register these cases, they expect complainants to collaborate with their work, to not give up, and to not ask them to close the investigation later on. Despite their advice, most women who complain about conjugal violence ask policewomen to close the police investigation.[34] Policewomen, like feminists in the SOS-Mulher, feel frustrated with complainants' ambivalence in continuing a police investigation that may lead to imprisonment or criminalization of their partners. Yet, as discussed in chapter 4, whereas feminists attempt to understand the reasons why complainants do not leave their perpetrators, policewomen feel upset with complainants. They feel insulted, saying that complainants are not "recognizing" their work, making them "waste their time." They also feel angry at complainants, echoing a popular Brazilian proverb that says: *Mulher gosta de apanhar* ("Women like to be beaten up").

Complainants also feel frustrated. They expect policewomen to solve all their problems, and to do it immediately. As Delegada Izilda Ferreira points out, "They want us to change their lives in one day."[35] In fact, complainants have different expectations when they go to regular and women's police stations. These expectations range from imprisonment of their male partners to scaring them and fixing up their marriage, so that they will not be beaten up anymore. Complainants try to threaten their violent partners, saying that they will press charges in the women's police stations. They use the women's police stations as a weapon to scare their partners and neutralize unequal relations of power in the home (see also Brandão 1998). If they are treated well in the women's police stations, they go back there as many times as they are beaten up, until they discover that the women's police stations can only partially and temporarily "scare" their partners but cannot "solve" their problems. Besides fearing revenge from their partners after registering the case, they also fear the imprisonment and criminal stigmatization of their partners. After all, if the judge finds the male perpetrator guilty, he becomes a "criminal" under the law, even if he is not sent to prison. As a consequence, he is not only stigmatized but this is grounds for not hiring him for any job. Complainants who are actually separated from their perpetrators and do not depend on them, either emotionally or economically, do not fear this consequence. On the contrary, they want policewomen to put perpetrators in prison.

Aparecida Andrade, for example, was already separated from her partner when she went to regular police stations and women's police stations. As Andrade recalled, during her first visit to the women's police station, the female police officer registered her case in a Bulletin of Occurrence and threatened the perpetrator by saying: "If you harm her again, you will be in jail."[36] He had been sentenced to prison or to pay a fine, which he paid. As the beating continued on, Andrade pressed charges again in the women's police station. Once again, the female police officer registered the case and threatened him saying that, "If you just touch her hair, you will be ordered to come back and will be in jail," recalled Andrade.[37] In her view, "[t]his is wrong. I think the women's police stations should not simply threaten the guy. They should put him in jail, at least for three months, to scare him, to let him know that he will be imprisoned for months if he harms someone."[38] Andrade believes that he will stop looking for her and abusing her only when he is imprisoned for a while. "The first time I came here, he was really scared of being imprisoned. Now, he is not scared anymore. He knows that he can pay a fine and nothing else will happen to him."[39] Despite her frustration with the women's police station, she said that she would go there again whenever necessary: "I have already told him that I will come to the women's police station each time he harms me. Let's see if he will have enough money to pay fines. At some point, he will be in jail. He must be imprisoned."[40]

Like Andrade, Lindalva Macedo also believes that the women's police stations should be harder on perpetrators. Born in São Paulo, identifying herself as *parda*, divorced from her first husband and separated from her second partner, Macedo was 25 years old in 1994. Then she was raising two children and working as a shop assistant. It was her second time in the women's police station. Two years before, her first partner had harmed her and she took the case to a regular police station, where male police officers laughed at her, shouted at her, and told her to go to the women's police stations. Although at the time her complaint was registered in the women's police station, she gave up later and asked female police officers to close the investigation. "I felt sorry for him," she explained, somewhat regretting not having continued on at the time.[41] In 1994, her second partner also harmed her. She separated from him and went to the women's police station. This time, she expected policewomen to be "tough." Based on the experiences of friends who have been in women's police stations many times, she thinks that the women's police stations are not helping enough. "Policewomen should chew the guy out instead of simply counseling. Just talking doesn't change anything," she explained.[42] Beyond "chewing out," "policewomen should keep the guy in jail for a while," she added. "He will then learn not to harm a woman and to fight only with men," explained Macedo.[43] In her view, "[t]here should be more justice. Women do not have the same force as men. Women go to the women's police stations and things do not change. This makes me feel angry."[44]

Unlike Andrade and Macedo, Hortência Santana went to the women's police stations expecting not to put her husband in jail, but rather to "scare" him and not be harmed again. Born in São Paulo, identifying herself as *branca* (white), she worked outside the home as the coordinator of a childcare center. Her husband was a van driver. They had one son. Santana was 29 years old in 1994, when she went for the first time to the women's police station. She decided to go there because her husband had slapped her and slightly harmed her hand during a fight. At first, she looked for the help of her father, who worked as a police delegate in a regular police station. He advised her to consult with the family's lawyer and to go to the women's police station. She separated from her husband and, under the guidance of the lawyer, went to the women's police station. "I came here to get advice," she explained, "because I was scared by his attitude, he was drunk and we had a fight. Many women feel ashamed and do not look for the police. I don't have this problem, probably because I am well informed about the police."[45] She believed that the women's police stations helped her, because her husband was "in panic" when she filed the complaint, which contributed to fixing their marriage. She just wanted to "scare" him and show that she would not stand to be harmed anymore. As she said, "[i]t's not because I'm a woman that he can do whatever he wants. I wanted him to be conscious of what he had done, in order not to repeat it. He saw that he can't harm me. It was good to come here because he learned a lot."[46] When we met in the women's police station, Santana was trying to close the investigation of her case. Her father and the lawyer had advised her that, once registered, the case could not be closed. She was aware of that, "but now, feeling calm, I think it was not so serious."[47]

Like Santana, Rosenete Campos also realized that the women's police stations could be used to "scare" her husband in order to change his behavior. As she pointed out, "[h]e never expected that I would come here. He was surprised, feeling devastated. At first, he threw away the order of service. Then he started to regret his attitude and asked me to forgive him. He is even talking about God now, saying that God is going to help us. He had lost his faith, he had no enthusiasm, not even to work. I had advised him to talk to me instead of beating me up. Things are much better now. I wish I had come here the first time he harmed me."[48] After Campos gave me an interview, she mentioned: "Right now, I feel sorry for him. That is how women are."[49]

Contrary to Campos, Lucinda Barbosa did not hesitate about the continuation of her case, but she was not interested in the criminalization of her male partner. At first she was asked by policewomen in the women's police station whether she wanted to continue the case. Then she was asked by the judge in the small-claims criminal court. On these two occasions, she decided to proceed with the criminal lawsuit because she fears for the life of her two children who are not his children. "He will not kill his son, but he can kill my other two children," she explained.[50] He failed to appear twice in the women's police station and once in the small-claims criminal court. Barbosa said that he had consulted with an attorney who works for drug dealers and he was advised that, "this will not have any consequence. It will be your word against hers."[51] Barbosa was also afraid of closing her criminal case because this was her way of preventing him from beating her up again. "He can beat me up again. The way he's threatened me up to now, next time he will do it. We see many cases like this. If I continue with the case, he will not touch me, he can argue with me, but he will not touch me, he's scared, he's conscious that if something happens to me, he can go to jail, so he's scared."[52]

Barbosa's brother and mother pressured her to close her case. They argued that, because they are evangelicals, she should look for an amicable solution. In response, Barbosa asked her mother why she had left her father. Her mother said that he was not beating her up, but he had

mistresses. Barbosa reasoned that it was more difficult to deal with violence than with betrayal, because in the situation of betrayal one could
move away. But in the situation of battery, he would have to change his
behavior. Barbosa did not have much hope that he could change, but that
was what she wished to happen.

Her decision to continue with her criminal case was also an attempt to
give an example to her children. As she explained,

> [i]f his son continues to see this, he can become just like his father. He
> drinks, he insults and harms me. Once, after spending several days out with-
> out any communication, he came home in the middle of the night and
> brought two girls and a man. The man ended up sleeping in my bed, next
> to me and my son; one of the girls was on a mattress by the side of the bed;
> and he and the other girl woke up later and went to the kitchen. It was a
> complete disrespect, and he ordered me to shut up, he wanted to beat me
> up, he said that I was wrong, that I was crazy, that he could go out at any
> time and come back the day he wanted.[53]

I asked Barbosa if she wanted him to go to jail. She replied that, "[n]o,
because in the beginning I asked whether the filing of the case would
imprison him, and they told me he wouldn't be arrested or imprisoned,
that he would be on parole, that he would have to come here once a
month."[54] She explained that "the jail is awful, my brother was arrested
without being guilty, and I know how the jail is horrible."[55]

Barbosa mentioned that many women in the *favela* (shantytown) fear
denouncing conjugal violence because their partners and sometimes the
women themselves are involved with drug trafficking and have committed
murder, like her brother-in-law. She thinks that even in these situations
women should denounce conjugal violence. But, according to Barbosa, if
the woman is a "*mulher errada*" (wrong, dishonest woman) as opposed to
a "*mulher direita*" (right and honest woman), that is, if she is involved in
those criminal activities she is unable to denounce the violence. Barbosa
had advised her sister to leave her partner and to disappear while he was
in jail, but her sister was afraid and also said that she loved him. Barbosa
was concerned that her two sons were going to get involved in drug trafficking. She struggled with taking herself and her family out of different
types of violence: domestic violence in the home, violence resulting from
drug trafficking in the community, and police violence in the jails of
regular police stations. Barbosa clearly used her criminal lawsuit to protect
herself and her children from these types of violence, even if such protection was precarious and temporary. She would like her partner to leave the
house and received advice from policewomen to look for a public attorney
to separate and divide their property. But until July 2001 she was still living

with him, her brother and the three children in a small board hut in a *favela* in São Paulo.

Eliene Souto went to the first women's police station in July of 2001 for the first time because her ex-partner had threatened to kill her with a gun. Born in an interior town in the northeastern state of Pernambuco, Souto was 26 years old and studied up to the 4th grade. She had migrated to São Paulo with her partner to find a job and better living conditions. Her partner was illiterate and worked as a driver. They lived together with their 7-year-old daughter for six years. He did not let her work and was constantly threatening to kill her because he suspected she had a boyfriend. Her neighbors would advise her to go to the women's police station, but she did not want to go. Her only extended family member in São Paulo was an aunt, who also helped her giving emotional support.

When we met at the first women's police station, Souto had been separated from her partner for a year, but he continued to threaten her. She was working as a live-in maid and he did not know where she lived. She was afraid of him. The last incident took place when she went to pick up her daughter at his house. She managed to leave the house with her daughter and run to a church nearby, where the minister helped her to call the police. The military police officers in charge of emergency calls referred her to the women's police stations; her employer's daughter, an attorney, had already advised her to go to the women's police station. She said she finally had the "courage" to go because "he cannot use a gun, I don't want my daughter, who is already totally scared, to see him with a gun. That is why I decided to do something, I don't want her to see this."[56] He had been threatening her for a long time and would tell her that if she looked for the police it would be worse for her. "Whenever I told him I was going to call the police, he would reply that it was a waste of time, because the police are male like him. And I would reply: 'Let's see.' Why is there Justice? I have thousands ways of proving that I don't have another man, as he says. Now he sees that I'm working, he doesn't pay alimony to my daughter. I'd like him to leave me alone, but he doesn't want. I work, I don't pay rent, I can take care of my daughter, I want to be alone and in peace!"[57] Souto had never been to a regular or women's police station. Her friends had told her to look for the latter, not the former, because in the regular police station she would have to wait for many hours, whereas in the women's police station she would receive a better treatment. Souto was not complaining about the service. She did not know what the women's police station could do to help her, but "I want that they help me and advise me."[58]

As these testimonies show, complainants are not necessarily seeking the criminalization of their perpetrators (see also Brandão 1998;

Vianna et al. 1995). They want to change their partner's behavior, using the women's police stations to scare men and redesign the power relations at home. The fact that some of them want to close the investigation of their cases, "feeling sorry" for their perpetrators, should not imply that they are not resisting and not reacting against the Brazilian proverb: *Em briga de marido e mulher, ninguém mete a colher* (Fights between husband and wife are nobody's business).

Although the interests of complainants are diverse and conflict with both feminists' and policewomen's interests, the fact that complainants go to the women's police stations makes public an issue that had been kept in secrecy for many years and accepted as "normal." Complainants are trying to change their lives, taking advantage of the women's police stations as much as they can to balance power relations with their partners. More importantly, they "discover" that they have rights as women. They challenge both their partners and state agents by taking complaints to regular police stations and women's police stations, even if they do not want their perpetrators to be punished with imprisonment. Although the women's police station, as any kind of police station, is an institution designed to investigate "crimes," complainants are not really using it for purposes of criminalization. None of my interviewees mentioned that they had been victims of a "crime." None of them articulated the feminist discourse on battering as crime, in fact none was familiar with feminism. None of them viewed perpetrators as "criminals." Yet, they did articulate a discourse on rights, more specifically a "negative" women's rights discourse, framed as "it isn't right" to be injured. That is one of the most important lessons they learned from policewomen, as the following section further illustrates.

Articulating a Gendered Identity and a Sense of Rights

It isn't right to be beaten up.

—Rosenete Campos (Interview, São Paulo, May 23, 1994)

I don't know if I am a feminist, I only want to have my rights.

—Anastácia Leite (Interview, São Paulo, October 10, 1994)

Complainants learn from their experiences in the women's police station not only to articulate a gender identity, but also a discourse on women's rights. They discover that they have the right not to be beaten up, and the women's police station opens a space for them to exercise the right to complain about conjugal violence. Yet their sense of women's rights is not connected to feminism, since most complainants are not familiar with feminism. Furthermore, in contrast with the feminist discourse, complainants' conception of conjugal violence is not associated with the larger structure of society. It is associated with alcoholism, jealousy, and *machismo*. In addition, their sense of women's rights is not the same as the liberal and individualistic feminist perspective on women's rights. They view their rights within the context of their families and communities. Not accidentally, most of them do not seek the women's police stations to criminalize their perpetrators, or to punish them through imprisonment.

Rosenete Campos, for example, who believes that the women's police stations can help a woman by "protecting" her, learned from policewomen that she "has rights." In the women's police station she was informed about the existence of public attorneys to serve those who cannot afford to pay a lawyer. She looked for these attorneys and learned about custody of children, alimony, and property rights. She also felt more confident in the women's police station because the female police officer assured that she has "the right not to be beaten up." As she recounted:

> She [the policewoman] told me that it isn't right to harm women. My husband said he would hire an attorney and nothing would happen to him. When I told her about this, she replied: "Don't worry, in the women's police stations, he can't do anything." I felt more confident and asked myself: "Without the women's police stations, what could we do?" We must hold hands and denounce battering. We must help each other. It isn't right to be beaten up.[59]

Campos's experience in the women's police station helped her not only to develop a sense of women's rights, but also the belief that reporting battering is necessary for women. She also developed a sense of collective action. Yet this was not accompanied by the feminist discourse on battering as crime. In fact, Campos had heard about feminism through television, but did not have anything to say about it. She did not associate battering with a criminal activity and did not speak of her husband as a criminal. She believes he beats her because he is jealous of her. In her view, he is "sick with jealousy," and as a result, "[h]e needs medical and psychological treatment." Not coincidentally, she felt "sorry for him" after registering her complaint.[60]

Like Campos, Marta Silva also learned about her rights by going to the women's police stations and did not frame her case in criminal terms. As she pointed out, "I was treated very well in the women's police stations. The female police officer gave me a lot of information, she advised me to look for a public attorney and initiate a lawsuit against him in order to receive alimony. The public attorney told me about the documents I needed in order to sue him."[61]

Silva went to the women's police station in search of "protection" and legal information. Like Campos, she did not really want to criminalize the perpetrator. When I asked about the meaning of the Bulletin of Occurrence that the female police officer had just prepared, Silva hesitated and said: "This is just a report, isn't it? It isn't conclusive, it's just a report of what I have told her, it's not going to discredit his name."[62] At the same time, she wanted him "to learn that women are not an object, men cannot beat them up. Women are human beings, they have a heart. Besides, I'm the mother of his son."[63]

Although Silva did not know of any feminist organization, she thought that feminists were middle-class women fighting only for those who already have some money. Yet she considered herself a feminist if this meant that women have the same capacity as men. Like Campos, she learned in the women's police station to articulate a gender discourse that puts women in the center. As she explained: "I think I am a feminist, why not? I can work, I can think. Women work like crazy in the home, then they work outside home and they also take care of children. So we are not the fragile sex. We are much stronger than men. We are the ones who give birth and feel the pain."[64]

Margarida Lapenda also learned about her rights in the women's police station, viewing conjugal violence as a psychological rather than criminal problem. In 1994, when we met in the first women's police station, she was 36 years old, married, with two children, working for Stanley as a seller of women's products. Lapenda, who identified herself as *branca* (white), went to the women's police station in search of psychological treatment for her husband, who verbally abused her and threatened to kill her. In her view, he is violent because of alcoholism. Just like Silva, Lapenda did not intend to "punish" her husband. Although she did not want to register her case in a Bulletin of Occurrence, the female police officer insisted, arguing that it was necessary to "preserve her rights" in case she decided to divorce. This would prevent her from being accused of "abandoning" her family. She had decided to leave her house to see if her husband would change his behavior. Lapenda heard about the women's police stations through television, when she watched an interview with Delegada Rosmary Corrêa. As Lapenda recalled: "*Doutora* Rose [as Corrêa is publicly known] said that women must look for their rights and this gave me incentive to come here."[65] She also heard about feminism through television, but she could not say much about it: "Usually, I don't understand it."[66]

Anastácia Leite, 21 years old in 1994, also learned about her rights in the women's police station, particularly the right "not to be beaten up." Her approach to conjugal violence was associated with alcoholism as well, although she expected the women's police station to process complaints. Like most interviewees, she was not familiar with feminism. Born in the northeast region of Brazil and identifying herself as *parda* (brown), Leite migrated to São Paulo when she was 15 years old, marrying soon after. She had four children and worked as a house cleaner when we met in the women's police station in 1994. She went to the women's police station because her husband had harmed her. "He was drunk," she said.[67] Leite heard about the women's police stations through friends who had filed complaints there. In her view, "[t]he women's police station was created to help women, to protect them. It is not because he is the husband that he has the right to harm me."[68] She believes that the women's police station can help women by registering and processing their complaints. Leite heard about feminism through television, but did not have much to say about it. By the end of the interview, she added: "I don't know if I am a feminist, I only want to have my rights."[69]

It is worth noting Barbosa's final words of advice to women, illustrating that, although not framing conjugal violence as crime, battered women develop a distinct gendered identity and sense of women's rights in the women's police stations, and use these stations not only to "protect" themselves and their children, but also to teach men that it is not right to beat women.

> If women have a problem with their husbands, partners or even any man in the streets, they must report and have the case registered, because if we don't do anything they will continue to harm us. Sometimes even a neighbor can beat you. That is why I think we have to denounce, at least to report the case; and if afterwards the woman wants to withdraw the complaint, at least she did her part, so they [men] know that they can't treat women in that manner, that women must be treated with care. I am sure that we, as women, give them love and care, because they don't accept anything else. That is why I think this must change.[70]

Conclusion

Throughout this book I have discussed the multiple and conflicting interests of diverse groups of women in the women's movement and in the women's police stations. I have discussed the social and political processes shaping the dynamics of the relationships between feminists and policewomen, all resulting in the construction of a contradictory gendered citizenship. As this chapter demonstrates, this discussion is further illuminated when we add the perspective of battered women who report cases of conjugal violence, that is, violence perpetrated by a husband, boyfriend, or ex–male lover. The experiences of battered women show the importance as well as the contradictions of creating an all-female space within the repressive arm of the state. The focus on battered women sheds light on the complexities of criminalizing the issue of conjugal violence.

The women's police stations are important for battered women, because they do feel more "protected" by these stations than by regular police stations, they learn about their rights as women, and they can make alliances with female police officers to better negotiate gender inequalities in the home. In regular police stations, battered women are often mistreated and do not feel as comfortable to disclose their pain to male police officers. The fact that the women's police stations of São Paulo are named *Delegacias de Polícia de* Defesa *da Mulher* (Women's Police Stations to *Defend* Women) is an indication of their distinct treatment of women clients, at least in principle. This name is an important symbol and message for women, especially women within conjugal and heterosexual violent relationships.

In theory and often in practice the women's police stations recognize battered women's right to live without conjugal violence. In this perspective, citizenship rights are not simply expanded by the women's police stations: Women's rights are en*gender*ed. The women's police stations, the media, and female friends or female employers who have heard of the women's police stations or have used them, all of these institutions and social actors encourage battered women to look for the women's police stations. Once they denounce their situation, a form of violence that was hidden and considered private becomes public. Reporting a complaint of conjugal violence and having it registered in a Bulletin of Occurrence is the social, cultural, political, and legal materialization of a private violence that otherwise would not become visible and would not gain public attention.

Reporting, however, is an extremely difficult action, especially when the case involves persons who know each other. According to a 2002 national research on victimization conducted by the University of São Paulo, an average of one third of victims of various types of crimes took the initiative to report such crimes to the police. However, while robbery as well as theft of cars and motorcycles had almost 100 percent report rate, crimes involving acquaintances and family members were underreported. According to this study, only 14 percent of sexual crimes were reported (Ilanud 2002). This trend was highlighted in similar studies conducted by the University of São Paulo in 1992 and 1997.

In light of this data, it is not surprising that battered women who look for the women's police stations feel "courageous" and yet ambivalent about the continuation of their cases. It is important, however, to further examine the reasons behind their hesitations and fears, because they can illuminate specific contradictions in the criminalization of conjugal violence. Both gender and social class contribute to the fact that mostly working-class women report cases of conjugal violence to the women's police stations. On the one hand, gender oppression shapes battered women's decision to go to the women's police stations and to forge an alliance with policewomen. On the other hand, social class shapes their reliance as well as distrust in the police and their ambivalence about criminalization. They suffer multiple forms of violence, private and public, at the same time. They use the women's police stations to reduce violence in the home and to prevent their children from getting involved in activities that will increase violence in their community, such as drug trafficking. But they also know that the police can harm their family and their community. So they report and withdraw the complaint to threaten their partners and to control the police, only collaborating with the investigation to a certain extent. They do not want to go as far as having the perpetrators incarcerated. They play with and against the authority of a police force that is often authoritarian.

Complainants learn to go to the women's police stations as many times as they are beaten up. But they end up replacing the lack of protection in the home with a precarious and temporary protection from the state. After a while, they realize that such a protection is fragile and limited, as the case of Aparecida Andrade illustrates. After all, the perpetrators also learn that policewomen will not imprison them.

Complainants become more aware of their rights as women when they go to the women's police station, but they still do not approach their "autonomy" from an individualistic perspective. Contrary to liberal notions of citizenship and women's rights, complainants' unit of analysis of the violence that affects them is the family and the community, not the individual. This is the case because the private, conjugal violence they experience is intertwined with the public violence exerted by the community and the police.

Policewomen in turn individualize the cases and are likely to register conjugal violence as a crime. From an individualistic perspective, they teach complainants a "negative" discourse on women's rights, framed as "it's not right to harm women." Thus, although the women's police stations provide space for complainants to see that many women go through similar experiences, as Rosenete Campos testifies, complainants' cases are not connected to social, cultural, and economic structures. The women's police stations are not well connected with other governmental and non-governmental services either. Although the women's police stations end up appropriating a liberal feminist approach to women's rights, complainants do not learn about feminist organizations when they go to the women's police stations because policewomen themselves are not familiar with feminism, since policewomen believe that feminists are "against men."

Feminist activists and scholars are aware of the contradictions in the practices of both complainants and policewomen. Since the early 1980s, when they opened SOS-Mulher groups and learned that the needs and interests of battered women are complex, feminists have demanded from the state the creation of integrated services to address the problem of conjugal violence from criminal as well as social and psychological perspectives. They are aware of the limitations of criminalization, especially in the case of conjugal violence. They are also aware of the specific needs of working-class women in situation of conjugal violence, although theoretically they have not emphasized the connections between private and public forms of violence against women.

Yet, like working-class battered women, feminist activists emphasize criminalization as a means to promote democracy and gender equality in Brazilian society. Although they would like to see the law enforced, especially in cases of wife-murders, they take advantage of the ambiguous role of the police and approach criminal law as a symbolic instrument to threaten and teach men to behave differently. The 2001 feminist bill proposed and passed by Congress to criminalize sexual harassment is a good example of the feminist use of criminal law as a symbolic tool to make cultural changes in Brazilian society. In the justification of the bill, feminist Congresswoman Iara Bernardi carefully explains that the perpetrator will be subject to up to two years of *detenção* (detention), which is different from *reclusão* (reclusion). While the latter means that the perpetrator will be incarcerated, the former type of punishment does not lead to imprisonment and can be replaced with alternative penalties, such as community service (Bernardi 2001).

As noted in chapter 1, while the number of women's police stations increased in the 1980s and in the 1990s, the state of São Paulo created only one shelter with the capacity to host no more than fifty people (fifteen battered women and their children). Women's NGOs, on the other hand, relied on the state to address the issue of violence against women once the first women's police station was created. Since the late 1980s, feminists have been critical of the women's police stations' performance, due both to the limitations of criminalization as well as the lack of feminist or gender-based training for policewomen. But feminists have not had enough resources to establish non-governmental services for battered women. They attempted to improve and create new city services outside of the criminal justice system for battered women by participating in the administration of leftist and female mayors of the city of São Paulo, such as Luiza Erundina in the early 1990s and Marta Suplicy more recently. During both administrations, feminists have successfully coordinated the Casa Eliane de Grammont, a governmental organization that provides psychological, legal, and social services for battered women. But Casa Eliane de Grammont has not had the same capacity to assist women as the women's police stations have. Without services outside the criminal justice system to complement the work of policewomen, complainants cannot move beyond the women's police stations, having few resources to empower themselves in their homes and in their communities and to continue claiming their rights through the state.

By creating women's police stations without meaningfully incorporating feminist claims into the state and without providing services outside the criminal justice system for complainants to deal with both private and public forms of violence, Brazilian state managers have "honored" feminists and women with a masterpiece that appears as a single and solitary birth in the eyes of Brazilian women. If, as Alvarez (1990) pointedly asserts, Brazilian feminists contributed to engendering democracy (and the state) during the transition from military to civilian ruling in the 1970s and 1980s, we faced in the 1990s an ironic reverse movement: the state, through the women's police stations, engendered society. But battered women have not been passively engendered by the state. Like feminists and policewomen, battered women have fought violence according to the resources available to them. Moreover, like feminists and policewomen, they have contributed to the construction of a contradictory gendered citizenship, both challenging and reinforcing a hierarchical society and dominant masculinist culture.

Conclusion

Toward a More Inclusive and Grounded Feminist Approach to the State and Gendered Citizenship

There is no doubt that the 1985 creation of the world's first women's police station in São Paulo was an important historical and political phenomenon with local, national and international repercussions. As of June 2003, there were 339 women's police stations throughout Brazil (AGENDE and CLADEM 2003). Although 125 of these stations have been established in the state of São Paulo alone and only 10 percent of the municipalities have women's police stations, every state throughout the country has at least one women's police station (see Conselho Nacional dos Direitos da Mulher 2001). Inspired by this Brazilian phenomenon, eight countries in Latin America—Argentina, Colombia, Costa Rica, El Salvador, Ecuador, Nicaragua, Peru, and Uruguay—have created women's police stations (Corral 1993; Feijóo and Nari 1994; Chinchilla 1994; Nelson 1996; Jubb and Izumino 2002; Santos 1999a). In the late 1980s, European countries, such as Spain and Portugal, established a space for women complainants within regular police stations or some version of women's police stations (Station 1989). Furthermore, since the early 1990s, hundreds of all-women's police stations have been created in the main metropolises of Pakistan and India (*San Francisco Chronicle* 1993; War against Rape 2003; Oherald.com 2003).

In Brazil, the establishment of women's police stations over the past 19 years has promoted significant changes in women's lives. Despite their limitations, these stations have largely contributed to the construction of gendered citizenship, a form of citizenship that recognizes the social differences and inequalities between women and men, granting both equality before the law as well as full access to political, economic, and civil citizenship rights.[1] In addition to opening up a job market for women on the police force, the women's police stations have expanded victims' citizenship rights, especially the right of access to justice for battered women, allowing them to denounce a violence that not too long ago remained an invisible crime that was considered a private and even "normal" practice accepted and condoned by society (Suárez and Bandeira 2002; Sorj 2002; Alvarez 1990). The women's police stations have encouraged hundreds of thousands of women, particularly battered women from the working class, to report the violence that they had been suffering in silence. The number of complaints has increased over the years even when the number of women's police stations has remained the same. In 2000, for example, 310,058 complaints of violence against women were registered in the 125 women's police stations in the state of São Paulo. In 2002, the same women's police stations registered 356,667 complaints.[2]

Nevertheless, the women's police stations are also fraught with contradictions that plague the police force and the administration of justice in general, as well as the female police force and the all-female police stations in particular. As this book and other studies of the women's police stations have shown, very few cases that originate in women's police stations go to trial; the São Paulo Police Department and other police departments throughout Brazil continue to discriminate against policewomen, and women's police stations; gender-based training for police officers in general and policewomen in particular has not been included in the curriculum of the police academies; policewomen do not necessarily perceive violence against women as serious and "real" crimes; and complainants generally do not seek the criminalization of their perpetrators (Conselho Nacional dos Direitos da Mulher 2001; Silva n.d.; Silva 1992; Machado n.d.; Brandão 1998; Muniz 1994; Nelson 1996; Santos 1999a, 1999b; Conselho Nacional dos Direitos da Mulher 2001; Jubb and Izumino 2002, 2004). Similar findings have also been reported by studies of women's police stations in other countries in Latin America (Jubb 2001; Jubb and Izumino 2002) and in South Asia (Research Centre for Women's Studies, SNDT Women's University 1999).

Existing research tends, however, to focus on micro-level analyses of the contradictions in the women's police stations, thereby neglecting to examine how political processes shape the social interactions between feminists, policewomen, and complainants. In addition, existing research tends to homogenize the interests and identities of each of these actors, failing to theorize the complex and often contradictory relationship between and among these different groups of women. Finally, existing research on the women's police stations has not further examined women's rights from a multicultural perspective on gendered citizenship, therefore overlooking the interconnections of race, class, gender, and/or sexual orientation as the basis for granting women the right to live without violence and to claim the enforcement of this right through the state (for exceptions, see Nelson 1996; Santos 1999a, 1999b, 2000).

Feminist analyses of the state in Latin America have examined the complex relationship between women and the state from both a political and historical perspective, illuminating some of the contradictions in the construction of gendered citizenship as illustrated by the case study of the women's police stations. Moving away from essentialism and structuralism, scholars conceptualize the state in Latin America as a "differentiated set of institutions" and a "site of struggle" both representing and reconstructing gender relations (Alvarez 1990; Alexander 1991; Waylen 1996; Rai 1996; Schild 1998; Alvarez 1999–2000; Santos 1999a, 2004; Molyneux 2000). Scholars also explain the relationship between the state and women as "evolving and dialectic," contingent upon the political conjuncture (Alvarez 1990; Waylen 1996; Rai 1996; Lievesley 1996; Metoyer 2000) and the political regime (Molyneux 2000).

Although showing that the state is not a monolith and does not have pre-established and essential intentions regarding women, this literature has not completely moved away from a macro-level analysis (for exceptions, see Santos 1999a, 2004).[3] It is certainly true that the contradictory relations between feminists, policewomen, and their clients in the women's police stations in São Paulo are situated within the context of changing state-society relations during the political transition to democracy in Brazil. However, as this book has demonstrated, even under governments controlled by the same party, policewomen have held conflicting interests and divergent positions with regard to feminists and complainants. Feminists have also diverged on their approaches to violence against women. And battered women have interacted with women's police stations according to their specific needs and interests, which are informed by inequalities of gender, race, and social class.

Therefore, by positing the relationship between the state and women solely as a function of the political conjuncture, the political regime, or the party in power, feminists theorizing the state in Latin America have overlooked the particular culture of the specific institutions within which women interact. In addition, they have ignored the micro-level changes in civil society and the day-to-day interactions between the state actors and their clients. Finally, like students of the women's police stations, feminist state theorists have not paid sufficient attention to the interconnections of gender, race, class, and sexual orientation and how these forces influence the practices and discourses of both state and civil society actors regarding the construction of gendered citizenship (for exceptions, see Alexander 1991; Schild 1998; Santos 1999a, 2001).

This book has contributed to feminist state theory and studies of women's police stations in Latin America by examining the political and social processes shaping the dynamics of the complex and often contradictory relationship between women and the state from both a macro and micro perspective, exploring the construction of gendered citizenship as a result of the interactions between specific social actors, such as feminists, policewomen and complainants. By looking at the interests and identities of these actors and how they relate to each other from both a macro and micro, as well as a political and historical perspective, this study has served as an example of how to uncover the interacting forces and processes shaping the contradictions and the changing dynamics of state-society relations, therefore contributing to our understanding of the possibilities and barriers for the full exercise of citizenship rights in Latin America today.

Drawing on extensive interviews as well as participant observation and archival research, this book has shown that, through the creation of the women's police stations, both the Brazilian state and society have engendered each other in complex and contradictory ways. Feminists, policewomen and women clients are heterogeneous groups, with multiple and often conflicting interests between and among themselves. The relationships between these groups of women continue to evolve not only because of the political conjuncture or the party in power. They have evolved due to interactions between the political conjuncture, the hegemonic masculinist police culture, developments in the feminist discourse on violence against women, and the impact of the contact policewomen sustain with women clients, all of which resulted in the construction of a contradictory gendered citizenship.

As chapter 1 has demonstrated, the process of creating and negotiating the world's first women's police station in São Paulo illustrates the complex interactions between politics and gender. In the early 1980s, during a period of political transition from a military dictatorship to a civilian and democratic regime, feminists were actively involved in the political transition and took advantage of the opportunity to bring their gender-based agenda to the newly democratizing state (Alvarez 1990). Violence against women was just one among many issues they had politicized in the late 1970s and early 1980s. Feminists approached this issue from social, economic, and cultural perspectives, and demanded that the state create "integrated services" including legal, criminal, social, and psychological assistance to women victims of violence. They also demanded the creation of shelters.

The state responded to these demands narrowly, providing only criminal services through the creation of the first all-women's police station in 1985.

Although not sharing the essentialist assumption that informed state offi-cials' "separatist strategy" of opening a women's police station, feminist activists and feminist academics embraced the idea of creating this new police station. However, they did demand specialized, feminist training for all police officers. They actively participated in the process of designing the new police station and were successful in securing some access to the São Paulo police department at the time. In alliance with the then-governor of São Paulo and the secretary of public security, feminists were able to over-come the resistance of the police force to the establishment of the first women's police station. Moreover, feminist activists—all of which had fought against the military dictatorship and some of whom had been in exile, imprisoned, and/or tortured by the police during the military regime—also overcame their reservations and fear of the police and began to learn to negotiate with them. Consequently, the political conjuncture, as Alvarez (1990) has observed, certainly contributed to the reciprocal transformation of state and society. In the process of creating the first women's police station, three actors—feminists, state officials, and police officers—had their interests reciprocally transformed to a certain degree.

In addition to the political conjuncture, other forces have contributed to the contradictions that emerged from the creation of a women's space run by policewomen (not feminists) within the repressive and masculinist arm of the state. Throughout the 1980s, the first women's police station gained popularity among the female population and attracted enormous attention from local, national, and even international media. Politicians saw women's police stations as a useful political tool and, despite the continued resistance on the part of male police officers, more women's police stations were immediately established in São Paulo and throughout Brazil. Nevertheless, as expected by feminist activists and scholars, police-women working for the women's police stations were not inherently in alliance with feminists and did not necessarily treat their female clients better than male police officers.

As chapter 2 has shown, not all policewomen view violence against women as serious and "real" crimes. Since the creation of the first women's police station, policewomen have assumed three different positions regarding feminists—explicit alliance, opposition, and ambiguous alliance. These three positions have coexisted within the Sao Paulo police department since 1985—with one position more dominant than the others at various times. Also, individual policewomen have held at least two of these positions over the course of their career.

The multiple and often conflicting interests of policewomen have been shaped not only by the political conjuncture, but also by the legal principle of neutrality and the masculinist culture of their concrete institutional base—the police department. But this culture has been challenged both by internal and external actors, such as policewomen and feminists, even under the influence of the same political regime. Policewomen's daily experience working with female victims of violence has transformed, to a lesser or greater extent, their conception of the criminal nature of violence against women. Their legal culture has also been transformed by their interaction with feminists in the CECF and by the changing feminist discourses on gender violence, *capacitação*, and women's human rights, all within the context of the professionalization and transnationalization of feminism. The growing number of women's police stations has also empowered policewomen as distinct gendered actors within the police department.

Chapter 2 further demonstrates that the state is not only a site of struggle and a set of differentiated and internally contradictory institutions, it is also "a complex of *concrete* institutions with which women interact in direct and immediate ways" (Haney 1996, 759; my emphasis). The relationship between the state and women is indeed evolving and dialectic, but it is more than a function of the political regime. It evolves due to multiple and interactive, macro and micro, local and global, processes.

The interests of feminist activists are not homogenous either, as discussed in chapter 3, and have been shaped by multiple, interactive forces that go beyond the political conjuncture. Chapter 3 examines the feminist debates over the meaning of violence against women for two reasons. First, the feminist and women's movement in Brazil has been a key organized actor of civil society in the struggles for democracy and gendered citizenship, contributing to the expansion of women's citizenship rights. Second, how feminists define issues concerning women (for example, violence against women) occasionally influences public policies as well as the discourses and practices of agents of the state, such as policewomen, who provide services to women.

Since the mid-1970s, different groups of feminist activists have politicized and mobilized over diverse forms of violence against women. However, not all feminist definitions of violence against women have been accepted by the state and by the dominant feminist groups within the movement as legitimate forms of violence against women. As discussed in chapter 3, since the late 1970s the hegemonic feminist discourse on violence has defined (heterosexual) conjugal violence as the privileged case of violence against women, therefore silencing other forms of violence against women, specifically violence against prostitutes, black women, and lesbians. Since the 1990s, sexual harassment has also been framed as a form of "gender violence" and has been incorporated into the hegemonic feminist discourse on violence against women. In 2001, sexual harassment was even legally recognized as a crime with the approval of a feminist bill introduced to Congress.

By focusing on a gender framework that does not consider the inter-connections of gender with other social categories such as class, race, and sexual orientation, the hegemonic feminist discourse on violence in Brazil has contributed to a contradictory gendered citizenship. This discourse is contradictory because it both includes and excludes different groups of women from claiming the right to live without violence and the right to defend that right through the women's police stations.[4]

Within the women's police stations, policewomen's processing of complaints also contributes to the construction of a contradictory gendered citizenship. Although policewomen's practices and discourses are not homogenous, overall they agree with the hegemonic feminist discourse on conjugal violence as the privileged form of violence against women to be registered in the women's police stations. In contact with hundreds of thousands of cases concerning conjugal violence, policewomen's interests and identities are gendered to a certain degree, as demonstrated in chapter 2. But policewomen's masculinist police culture also shapes their practices in the women's police stations. Not all policewomen view conjugal violence as a "real" crime. While some favor the criminaliza-tion of conjugal violence, others tend to focus their work on the preserva-tion of the family as the most important goal and focus their attention on reconciling couples rather than pursuing justice.

Complaints of police violence against women and racial violence against women, as discussed in chapter 4, are rarely recognized as legitimate cases of violence against women to be investigated by the women's police stations. Complaints of sexual harassment, also reported to the women's police stations, have a better chance to be registered, although policewomen consider the cases of conjugal violence more important than the cases of sexual harassment. In sum, the practices of policewomen in the women's police stations both include and exclude different groups of women from the exercise of their citizenship right of access to justice. Even in the cases of conjugal violence, which are more likely to be registered, policewomen's practices contribute to a contradictory gendered citizenship. Because policewomen do not constitute a homogenous group and their practices are shaped by both the hegemonic feminist discourse on violence and the masculinist police culture, they end up both legitimizing and undermining the feminist gender-based discourse on violence.

It is worth noting that the contradictory practices of policewomen in the women's police stations are also present in the criminal courts. A study following up on the cases sent by the women's police stations to the criminal courts in Rio de Janeiro revealed that the district attorneys and the judges characterized those cases as having more of a "social" rather than "criminal" nature (Carrara et al. 2002). Studies of small claims courts in Porto Alegre (Fields 2001) and in São Paulo (Melo 2000), where most cases are sent to by the women's police stations, have also highlighted the "trivialization" of cases of violence against women in these courts due to the innocuous nature of the "alternative penalties" (e.g., small fines and community services) established by the judges, as well as the emphasis of these courts on the reconciliation of couples rather than the safety of women and the pursuit of justice.

In November of 2001, feminist activists and legal professionals, who were critical of the way the small-claims courts were dealing with cases of violence against women, organized a campaign in São Paulo for the creation of a Juizado Especial para Crimes de Violência de Gênero (Special Court for Crimes of Gender Violence).[5] At the time, they sent a letter to the then-president of the São Paulo Tribunal of Justice, Márcio Martins Bonilha, to create a special court, but the president denied their request. In February of 2002, they renewed their demand by sending another letter to the newly appointed and current president of the São Paulo Tribunal of Justice, Sérgio Augusto Nigro Conceição. On November 25, 2003, the International Day of Non-Violence against Women, the president of the São Paulo Tribunal of Justice announced the creation of a Juizado Especial para Crimes de Violência de Gênero (Special Court for Crimes of Gender Violence). Based on the experience of the women's police stations and the small-claims criminal courts, it is anticipated that gender-based training, as well as attention to the specific class-, race-, and gender-based needs of complainants, will be of crucial importance for the functioning of this court if it is to fulfill the feminist values and goals that inspired its creation.

Although in a different context, some insights can be also drawn from a similar experience with a domestic violence court in the United States. Thanks to the battered women's movement to end violence against women, a domestic violence court was set up in January of 1984 within the Chicago court system (Wittner 1998). While considered a victory for the movement, the court also presented problems similar to those faced by the women's police stations and the small-claims courts in Brazil. As reported by Wittner (1998), the court was initiated with six feminist advocates, funded independently of the court. However, the court did not function as originally planned because attorneys, officers, clerks, and judges still blamed the women for their own victimization. Wittner explains, "[t]he marginalization of the women in court was not simply the consequence of procedures that elevated legal professionals to center stage in processing complaints, but reflected power inequalities of race, class, and gender. Because women, as well as working-class, poor, and less educated groups, regularly use the lower courts to settle problems and resolve conflicts over personal relationships, gender, class, and cultural differences between these groups and court workers are not uncommon" (1998, 23).

Wittner's observation resonates with the situation of battered women who take their complaints to the women's police stations. As discussed in chapter 5, most complainants come from poor or working-class backgrounds, many of whom are also migrant women from the impoverished northeast region of Brazil. An examination of the experience of these complainants adds to my analysis of gendered citizenship and further illuminates the contradictions in the women's police stations. Complaints of (heterosexual) conjugal violence constitute the majority of the cases processed in women's police stations. However, in contrast with the feminist discourse on the criminalization of gender violence and the established legal function of the women's police stations to prosecute perpetrators, complainants do not necessarily seek the criminalization of their abusers. The nature of their intimate and ongoing relationship with their abusers certainly plays a role in complainants' hesitations toward the criminalization of the abusers. But other factors, such as their class, racial, and cultural background, also contribute to their reluctance. The conjugal violence facing these complainants in the domestic sphere cannot be separated from public forms of violence they also suffer within their communities and when they interact with the police.

Therefore, complainants use the women's police stations both against and in alliance with policewomen. Rather than seeking criminalization, they attempt to use the force and authority of the police, not law enforcement, to "scare" their abusers and gain some power to renegotiate their conjugal contract and to end violence in the home and in the community. But they also undermine the power of the women's police stations in order to protect their community and their family from police violence.

In the process of reporting complaints of conjugal violence, complainants also learn from policewomen to articulate a distinct gender identity and a sense of women's rights, expressed as "it's not right to be beaten up." In this perspective, the state, through the women's police stations, engenders society. But due to existing inequalities of class, gender, race, and culture complainants construct a contradictory gendered citizenship in their own terms, according to their needs and interests, which do not necessarily follow the democratic principles governing the rule of law. In the end, complainants, like policewomen, both challenge and reinforce hierarchical values in Brazilian society and the dominant masculinist police culture.

Together the five chapters in this book point to the following recommendations for future research and public policies regarding violence against women and the construction of gendered citizenship in Brazil as well as in other countries in Latin America. First, it is necessary that researchers, activists, and policymakers pay attention to the specificity of different forms of violence against women. By disaggregating them, we will be able to offer solutions that are more compatible with the needs and interests of the victims. But our analyses of different forms of violence against women should not separate the private from the public spheres. Our approach to violence against women should also take into account the interconnections of gender, race, class, sexuality, and culture. In other words, we should approach gendered citizenship from a multicultural perspective, not only from a gender perspective. Within a multicultural framework, we should also examine how private and public forms of violence interact in the lives of different groups of women and men.

Second, in order to further uncover the social and political processes shaping the construction of gendered citizenship, we should develop a more grounded theory of the state. We need to examine the social construction of women's rights both from a macro and micro, as well as political and historical, perspective. To this end, it is necessary to conduct further ethnographic and comparative research on specific institutions within which women and feminists directly interact. Rather than assuming the interests and identities of state agents and civil society actors, we need to make their interests and identities the object of study. Ethnography can help us to concretely grasp how the interests, identities, and cultures of state agents and civil society actors are formed and transformed. Ethnography may also help us to uncover how the state "(*re*)*posiciona a los sujetos femininos a través de sistemas interpretativos institucionalizados*" ("repositions female subjects through institutionalized interpretative systems" (Alvarez 1990–2000, 62); my translation).

Comparative and cross-national research on different institutional sites of the state would also help us to better understand how the political might interact with and shape specific institutional cultures differently. Comparative research on state responses to violence against women within the criminal justice system and the health-care system, for example, would help us to better understand the contradictions in the women's police stations and in the criminal courts to address the problem of violence against women.

Finally, studies of the state and gender tend to focus on feminist politics with regard to legislative and governmental policy processes. Yet the justice system is crucial terrain for the advancement of democracy in Latin America (see also Caldeira 1996). In the past 15 years, progressive legislation has been enacted by newly democratic states in the region. Nevertheless, the lack of law enforcement continues to be a major barrier to the exercising of newly granted citizenship rights. As Macaulay (2002, 80) explains, this occurs because of "the lack of effective remedies and anti-remedies, and the structural flaws in the institutions of the justice system."

The context of new emerging democracies and neoliberal states in Latin America has posed new challenges to feminists and social movement actors. One of the major challenges they face is having their claims meaningfully incorporated into state structures and policies (Molyneux 2000, 67; Alvarez 1999–2000). Creating an institutional space for women, though important, is not sufficient to make meaningful change, as evidenced by contradictions in women's policy machineries run by feminists (Alvarez 1997; Schumaher and Vargas 1993; Friedman 1998; Schild 1998). The "separatist strategy" is even more contradictory when those occupying the all-female institutional space are policewomen (or legal professionals in the case of criminal courts) not receiving gender-based training and are not necessarily in alliance with feminists.

According to Alvarez, an effective feminist lobbying would require constant questioning of any "gender-based policy" adopted by a given state or the United Nations; a "re-translation" from inside and outside of the institutional lobbies (1999–2000, 63–4). The case of women's police stations shows that this re-translation is necessary in all sites of the state. The battle for gender-based training, for example, will continue within the new special court for crimes of gender violence in São Paulo. A multi-cultural approach to violence against women will be needed in this court as well. Attention to the relationship between public and private forms of violence facing the complainants who use this court will also remain necessary.

In sum, the primary lessons from this book are twofold. First, feminist state theorizing and research on women's police stations in Latin America will be more grounded if researchers pay attention to specific institutional cultures both from a macro and micro, historical and political, perspective, thereby grasping in concrete terms the dynamics of state-society relations and the construction of gendered citizenship. Second, gendered citizenship will be more inclusive if it rests on a broad and multicultural construction of women's interests and women's rights taking into account not only gender, but also race, class, sexuality, and culture.

References

Adorno, Sérgio. 1995a. Discriminação racial e justiça criminal em São Paulo. *Novos Estudos* 43: 45–63.

———. 1995b. A violência na sociedade brasileira: Um painel inconcluso em uma democracia não consolidada. *Sociedade e Estado* 10(2): 299–342.

Afinal. 1986. Novo quadro. April 8.

Ações em Gênero, Cidadania e Desenvolvimento (AGENDE) and Comitê Latino-Americano e do Caribe para a Defesa dos Direitos da Mulher (CLADEM Brasil). 2003. *O Brasil e a Convenção sobre a Eliminação de Todas as Formas de Discriminação contra a Mulher: Documento do movimento de mulheres para o cumprimento da Convenção sobre a Eliminação de Todas as Formas de Discriminação contra a Mulher—CEDAW, pelo Estado brasileiro: Propostas e recomendações.* Brasília.

Alexander, M. Jacqui. 1991. Redrafting morality: The postcolonial state and the Sexual Offences Bill of Trinidad and Tobago. In *Third world women and the politics of feminism*, eds. C. T. Mohanty, A. Russo, and L. Torres, 133–152. Bloomington and Indianapolis: Indiana University Press.

Alvarez, S. E., E. J. Friedman, E. Beckman, M. Blackwell, N. S. Chinchilla, N. Lebon, M. Navarro, and M. R. Tobar. 2002. Encountering Latin American and Caribbean feminisms. *Signs* 28(21): 537–579.

Alvarez, Sonia E. 1990. *Engendering democracy in Brazil: Women's movements in transition politics.* Princeton: Princeton University Press.

———. 1994. The (trans)formation of feminism(s) and gender politics in democratizing Brazil. In *The women's movement in Latin America: Participation and democracy*, ed. J. S. Jaquette, 13–64, 2nd ed. Boulder, CO.: Westview Press.

———. 1996. Concluding reflections: "Redrawing" the parameters of gender struggle. In *Emergences: Women's struggles for livelihood in Latin America*, eds. J. Freedman, R. Abers, and L. Autler, 137–151. Los Angeles: University of California, Los Angeles, Latin American Center Publications.

———. 1998. Latin American feminisms "go global": Trends of the 1990s and challenges for the new millennium. In *Cultures of politics/politics of culture: Re-visioning Latin American social movements*, eds. S. E. Alvarez, E. Dagnino, and A. Escobar, 293–324. Boulder, CO.: Westview Press.

———. 1999–2000. En qué *estado* está el feminismo? Reflexiones teóricas y perspectivas comparativas. *Estudios Latinoamericanos* 12–13: 47–66.

Alves, Branca Moreira, and Jacqueline Pitanguy. 1980. *O que é feminismo*. São Paulo: Brasiliense.

Alves, Maria Helena Moreira. 1987. *Estado e oposição no Brasil (1964–1984)*. Petrópolis: Vozes.

Amaral, Célia C. G. do, Ceclinda L. Letelier, Ivoneide L. Góis, and Sílvia de Aquino. 2001. *Dores invisíveis: Violência em delegacias da mulher no Nordeste*. Fortaleza: Edições Rede Feminista Norte e Nordeste de Estudos e Pesquisas sobre a Mulher e Relações de Gênero (REDOR), Núcleo de Estudos e Pesquisas sobre Gênero, Idade e Família (NEGIF), Universidade Federal do Ceará (UFC).

Americas Watch Committee. 1991a. *Criminal injustice: Violence against women in Brazil*. New York: Human Rights Watch.

———. 1991b. *Rural violence in Brazil*. New York: Human Rights Watch.

Ardaillon, Danielle. 1989. Estado e mulher: Conselhos dos direitos da mulher e delegacias de defesa da mulher. São Paulo: Fundação Carlos Chagas. Photocopied.

Ardaillon, Danielle, and Guita Grin Debert. 1987. *Quando a vítima é mulher: Análise de julgamentos de crimes de estupro, espancamento e homicídio*. Brasília, DF: Conselho Nacional dos Direitos da Mulher.

Arquidiocese de São Paulo. 1985. *Brasil: Nunca mais*. Petrópolis: Vozes.

Arruda, Roldão. 2002. Mediadores ajudam casais a superar conflitos. *Estado de S. Paulo*, March 31.

Assembléia Legislativa do Estado de São Paulo. 1994. *Relatório da Comissão Parlamentar de Inquérito constituída com a finalidade de apurar a violência e a discriminação contra a mulher no mercado de trabalho*. São Paulo: Assembléia Legislativa do Estado de São Paulo.

Avelar, Lúcia. 1996. *Mulheres na elite política brasileira: Canais de acesso ao poder*. São Paulo: Fundação Konrad-Adenauer-Stiftung.

Azerêdo, Sandra. 1994. Teorizando sobre gênero e relações raciais. *Estudos Feministas* 2 (Special Number): 203–216.

Babb, Florence E. 1996. After the revolution: Neoliberal policy and gender in Nicaragua. *Latin American Perspectives* 23(1): 27–48.

Barrig, Maruja. 1996. Women, collective kitchens, and the crisis of the state in Peru. In *Emergences: Women's struggles for livelihood in Latin America*, eds. J. Freedman, R. Abers, and L. Autler, 59–77. Los Angeles: University of California, Los Angeles, Latin American Center Publications.

Barsted, Leila de Andrade Linhares. 1994. Em busca do tempo perdido: Mulher e políticas públicas no Brasil 1983–1993. *Estudos Feministas* 2(Special Number): 38–54.

Benería, Lourdes. 1996. The foreign debt crisis and the social costs of adjustment in Latin America. In *Emergences: Women's struggles for livelihood in Latin America*, eds. J. Freedman, R. Abers, and L. Autler, 11–30. Los Angeles: University of California, Los Angeles, Latin American Center Publications.

Benjamin, Medea, and Maisa Mendonça. 1997. *Benedita da Silva: An Afro-Brazilian woman's story of politics and love*. Monroe: Food First Books.

Bernardi, Iara. 2001. *Assédio sexual: É crime e precisa ser punido*. Brasília: Câmara dos Deputados.

Brandão, Elaine Reis. 1998. Violência conjugal e o recurso feminino à polícia. In *Horizontes plurais: Novos estudos de gênero no Brasil*, eds. C. Bruschini, and H. B. de Holanda, 51–84. São Paulo: Editora 34.

Bruder, Silvana Rassi. 1992. Poder e proteção na delegacia da mulher de Florianópolis: Análise do discurso. Undergraduate thesis, Federal University of Santa Catarina, Florianópolis.

Bruschini, Cristina, and Sandra G. Unbehaum. 2002. Introduction. In *Gênero, democracia e sociedade brasileira*, eds. C. Bruschini and Sandra G. Unbehaum, 7–14. São Paulo: Editora 34 and Fundação Carlos Chagas.

———. 2002a. Os programas de pesquisa da Fundação Carlos Chagas e sua contribuição para os estudos de gênero no Brasil. In *Gênero, democracia e sociedade brasileira*, eds. C. Bruschini and Sandra G. Unbehaum, 18–58. São Paulo: Editora 34 and Fundação Carlos Chagas.

Cabral, Sérgio. n.d. *No tempo de Ari Barroso*. Rio de Janeiro: Lumiar Editora.

Caldeira, Teresa P. R., and James Holston. 1995. *Citizenship, justice, law: Limits and prospects of democratization in Brazil*. Paper presented at the XIX annual meeting of Associação Nacional de Pós-Graduação e Pesquisa em Ciências Sociais (ANPOCS), Caxambu.

Caldeira, Teresa P. R. 1996. Crime and individual rights: Reframing the question of violence in Latin America. In *Constructing democracy: Human rights, citizenship, and society in Latin America*, eds. E. Jelin and E. Hershberg, 197–214. Boulder CO.: Westview Press.

Camargo, Brígido Vizeu, Carla Giovana Dagostin, and Marisa Coutinho. 1991. Violência denunciada contra a mulher: A visibilidade via delegacia da mulher em Florianópolis. *Cadernos de Pesquisa de São Paulo* 78: 51–57.

Camargo, Márcia. 1998. Novas políticas públicas de combate à violência. In *Mulher e política: Gênero e feminismo no Partido dos Trabalhadores*, eds. A. Borba, Nalu Faria, and Tatau Godinho, 121–135. São Paulo: Editora Fundação Perseu Abramo.

Campos, Carmen H. de. 2001. Violência doméstica no espaço da lei. In *Tempos e lugares de gênero*, eds. Cristina Bruschini, and Céli Regina Pinto, 301–322. São Paulo: Editora 34 and Fundação Carlos Chagas.

Campilongo, Celso F. 1994. Os desafios do judiciário: Um enquadramento teórico. In *Direitos humanos, direitos sociais e justiça*, ed. J. E. Faria, 30–51. São Paulo: Malheiros Editores.

Carneiro, Sueli. 1993a. A organização nacional das mulheres negras e as perspectivas políticas. *Cadernos Geledés* 4: 8–14.

———. 1993b. Resposta da sociedade civil à violência racial e de gênero. *Cadernos Geledés* 4: 33–38.

———. 1997. Gênero, raça e ascensão social. *Estudos Feministas* 3(2): 544–552.

Carrara, Sérgio, Adriana R. Barreto Vianna, and Ana Lúcia Enne. 2002. "Crimes de bagatela": A violência contra a mulher na justiça do Rio de Janeiro. In *Gênero & cidadania*, ed. Mariza Corrêa, 70–106. Campinas, SP: Pagu/Núcleo de Estudos de Gênero-Unicamp.

Casa Eliane de Grammont. 1991. Distribuição dos atendimentos diretos durante o ano de 1991. São Paulo: Prefeitura Municipal de São Paulo. Photocopied.

Casa Eliane de Grammont. n.d. *Violência sexual: Uma questão de saúde e direitos humanos*. São Paulo: Prefeitura do Município de São Paulo.

———. n.d. *Violência no relacionamento amoroso*. São Paulo: Prefeitura Municipal de São Paulo.

Centro de Orientação Jurídica e Encaminhamento-COJE. 1984. Boletim do COJE. São Paulo: Governo do Estado de São Paulo. Photocopied.

Centro Feminista de Estudos e Assessoria-CFEMEA. 1993a. *As Mulheres no Congresso Revisor*. Brasília, DF: Centro Feminista de Estudos e Assessoria-CFEMEA.

———. 1993b. Manifesto das mulheres: Propostas de alteração do código penal brasileiro. *Estudos Feministas* 1(1): 159–161.

———. 1993c. *Pensando nossa cidadania: Propostas para uma legislação não discriminatória*. Brasília, DF: Centro Feminista de Estudos e Assessoria-CFEMEA.

———. 1994. *Guia dos direitos da mulher*. Brasília, DF: Centro Feminista de Estudos e Assessoria-CFEMEA.

Centro pela Justiça e o Direito Internacional-CEJIL, CLADEM Brasil-Comitê Latino Americano e do Caribe pela Defesa dos Direitos da Mulher, and AGENDE-Ações em Gênero, Cidadania e Desenvolvimento. 2003. *Document for CEDAW on the compliance by Brazil of shrunken obligations as State-party of the Convention concerning violence against women: The case of Maria da Penha*. Available at: http://www.cladem.org/english/national/brasil/penhacedawi.asp (accessed January 11, 2004).

Chauí, Marilena. 1985. Participando do debate sobre mulher e violência. *Perspectivas Antropológicas da Mulher* 4: 23–62.

Chinchilla, Norma. 1994. Feminism, revolution, and democratic transitions in Nicaragua. In *The women's movement in Latin America: Participation and democracy*, ed. J. S. Jaquette, 177–198, 2nd ed. Boulder, CO.: Westview Press.

Chuchryk, Patricia M. 1994. From dictatorship to democracy: The women's movement in Chile. In *The women's movement in Latin America: Participation and democracy*, ed. J. S. Jaquette, 65–108, 2nd ed. Boulder, CO.: Westview Press.

CLADEM Brasil-Comitê Latino-Americano e do Caribe para a Defesa dos Direitos da Mulher. 1993. *As mulheres e a construção dos direitos humanos*. São Paulo.

———. 1995. *Declaração dos direitos humanos desde uma perspectiva de gênero: Contribuições ao 50°. aniversário da Declaração Universal dos Direitos Humanos*. São Paulo.

———. 2003. *A condição feminina no novo milênio: 100% sem discriminação*. São Paulo: Governo do Estado de São Paulo.

———. 2003. *Conselho Estadual da Condição Feminina: Sua história, suas lutas, seu futuro, 1983–2003*. São Paulo: Governo do Estado de São Paulo.

———. n.d. *Protocolados de cooperação das Secretarias de Estado e o Conselho Estadual da Condição Feminina–SP: Beijing + 5*. São Paulo: Governo do Estado de São Paulo.

Cohen, Jean L., and Andrew Arato. 1997. *Civil society and political theory*. Cambridge and London: The MIT Press.

Coletivo de Feministas Lésbicas. 1994. *Lésbicas no Brasil: Contribuição para avaliação da década da mulher, 1985/1995.* São Paulo: Coletivo de Feministas Lésbicas.

Collins, Patricia Hill. 1991. *Black feminist thought: Knowledge, consciousness, and the politics of empowerment.* New York: Routledge.

Congresso Nacional, Brazil. 1993. *Relatório final da Comissão Parlamentar de Inquérito destinada a investigar a questão da violência contra a mulher.* Brasília, DF: Congresso Nacional.

Connell, R. W. 1987. *Gender and power.* Stanford, CT.: Stanford University Press.

Conselho Estadual da Condição Feminina de São Paulo. 1984. *Boletim informativo.* São Paulo: Governo do Estado de São Paulo.

————. 1985a. *Programa de ação para o biênio 85–87.* São Paulo: Governo do Estado de São Paulo.

————. 1985b. Delegacia especializada de proteção à mulher. São Paulo: Governo do Estado de São Paulo. Photocopied.

————. 1985c. Carta ao Secretário de Segurança Pública, Michel Temer, July 10. São Paulo: Governo do Estado de São Paulo. Photocopied.

————. 1986a. *Mulher negra: Dossiê sobre a discriminação racial.* São Paulo: Governo do Estado de São Paulo.

————. 1986b. *Violência sexual.* São Paulo: Governo do Estado de São Paulo.

————. 1986c. *Delegacia de defesa da mulher: O Que é e o que faz por você.* São Paulo: Governo do Estado de São Paulo.

————. 1986d. I encontro das delegacias de defesa da mulher de São Paulo. São Paulo: Governo do Estado de São Paulo. Photocopied.

————. 1991. *Respeito: Conquistamos na lei. Conquistaremos na prática.* São Paulo: Governo do Estado de São Paulo.

————. 1992. *A lei e a vida.* São Paulo: Governo do Estado de São Paulo.

————. 1993. *Assédio sexual no trabalho.* São Paulo: Governo do Estado de São Paulo.

————. 1994a. *Documentos fórum 2: Seminário nacional violência contra a mulher (síntese).* São Paulo: Governo do Estado de São Paulo.

————. 1994b. *Violência contra a mulher.* São Paulo: Governo do Estado de São Paulo.

————. 1998a. *Delegacias de polícia de defesa da mulher, ampliação das competências e suas alterações.* São Paulo: Governo do Estado de São Paulo.

————. 1998b. *Primeiro curso de capacitação para delegadas das delegacias de defesa da mulher: Violência de gênero.* São Paulo: Governo do Estado de São Paulo.

————. n.d. *Assédio sexual no trabalho.* São Paulo: Governo do Estado de São Paulo.

Conselho Estadual da Condição Feminina de São Paulo, and Instituto de Ação Cultural (IDAC). 1986. *Em briga de marido e mulher.* São Paulo: Governo do Estado de São Paulo. Photocopied.

Conselho Estadual dos Direitos da Mulher do Rio de Janeiro. 1993. *Direitos humanos da mulher.* Rio de Janeiro: Governo do Estado do Rio de Janeiro.

Conselho Municipal dos Direitos da Mulher de Belém and Conselho Estadual da Condição Feminina de São Paulo. 1994. *Seminário nacional prostituição e tráfico de mulheres: Documento final.* São Paulo: Conselho Estadual da Condição Feminina de São Paulo.

Conselho Nacional dos Direitos da Mulher. 1986. *Relatório do primeiro encontro nacional de delegadas lotadas em delegacias de defesa da mulher.* Brasília, DF: Ministéro da Justiça.

———. n.d. *Guia de defesa das mulheres contra a violência.* Brasília, DF: Ministério da Justiça.

———. 1999. *Memória: Gestão 95/99, Conselho Nacional dos Direitos da Mulher.* Brasília, DF: Ministério da Justiça.

———. 2001. *Pesquisa nacional sobre as condições de funcionamento das delegacias especializadas no atendimento às mulheres: Relatório final.* Brasília: Conselho Nacional dos Direitos da Mulher.

Contigo. 1985. São Paulo inaugura delegacia só para mulheres. August 5.

Corral, Thaís. 1993. Brazil's women-run police stations fight the odds. *Ms.* November/December: 18.

Corrêa, Mariza. 1981. *Os crimes da paixão.* São Paulo: Brasiliense.

Corrêa, Rosmary. 1994. *Uma mulher no combate à violência.* São Paulo: Rosmary Corrêa.

Correio Popular. 1991. Delegada quer ter abrigo para mulheres agredidas. April 5.

Costa, Albertina de Oliveira. 1994. Os estudos da mulher no Brasil ou a estratégia da corda bamba. *Estudos Feministas* 2(Special Number): 401–409.

Costa, Ana Alice, and Cecília Maria B. Sardenberg. 1994. Teoria e práxis feministas na academia: Os núcleos de estudos sobre a mulher nas universidades brasileiras. *Estudos Feministas* 2(Special Number): 387–407.

Couto e Silva, Golbery. 1981. *Conjuntura política nacional, o poder executivo e geopolítica do Brasil.* Rio de Janeiro: Livraria José Olympio Editora.

Cromberg, Renata Udler. 1994. A cena incestuosa: O problema da vitimização. In *Novos olhares: Mulheres e relações de gênero no Brasil,* eds. C. Bruschini and B. Sorj, 251–266. São Paulo: Editora Marco Zero.

D'Oliveira, Ana Flávia L. n.d. Violência nas relações de gênero como uma questão de saúde coletiva. In *I curso de capacitação para atendimento a mulheres em situação de violência,* eds. Coletivo Feminista Sexualidade e Saúde and Departamento de Medicina Preventiva (reader). São Paulo: Unpublished. Photocopied.

DaMatta, Roberto. 1985. *A casa e a rua: Espaço, cidadania, mulher e morte no Brasil.* São Paulo: Brasiliense.

Darcy de Oliveira, Rosiska, Leila Linhares Barsted, and Miguel Paiva. 1984. *A violência doméstica.* Rio de Janeiro: Editora Marco Zero.

De Barros, Fernando Rafael. 1988. Atrás das grades. *Veja,* December 7.

De Camargo, Regina C. E. 1995. In their own image: Video as an empowerment tool in Brazil. Masters thesis, San Francisco State University.

De Oliveira, Eleonora Menicucci, and Lucia Amaral Carneiro Vianna. 1993. Violência conjugal na gravidez. *Estudos Feministas* 1(1): 162–165.

Diário Popular. 1985. Secretário está satisfeito com a delegacia da mulher. August 16.

———. 1990. Alemanha deve adotar Delegacia da Mulher. December 8.

————. 1991. Casa da Mulher. May 11.

Dias, Erasmo. 1990. Solução gerou mais problemas. *Diário Popular*, March 28.

Dias, Lucy. 1985. Ao Abrigo da violência. *Cláudia*, August: 136–140.

Dos Santos, José Nunes. 1985. A polícia civil: Ligeiro escorço histórico. In *A instituição policial*, ed. Julita Lemgruber, 15–25. Rio de Janeiro: Departamento de Publicações da Ordem dos Advogados do Brasil—Rio de Janeiro (OAB-RJ).

Durhan, Eunice Ribeiro. 1984. Movimentos sociais: A construção da cidadania. *Novos Estudos* 10: 24–30.

Escandón, Carmen Ramos. 1994. Women's movements, feminism, and Mexican politics. In *The women's movement in Latin America: Participation and democracy*, ed. J. S. Jaquette, 199–222, 2nd ed. Boulder, CO.: Westview Press.

Escobar, Arturo. 1995. *Encountering development: The making and unmaking of the Third World*. Princeton: Princeton University Press.

Estado de São Paulo. 1985. Uma delegacia em defesa da mulher. August 8.

————. 1990b. Casa protege mulher em S. André. November 28.

————. 1991. Mulheres vítimas de violência terão abrigo. August 29.

Faria, José Eduardo. 1994. O judiciário e os direitos humanos e sociais: Notas para uma avaliação da justiça brasileira. In *Direitos humanos, direitos sociais e justiça*, ed. J. E. Faria, 94–112. São Paulo: Malheiros Editores.

Feijóo, María del Carmen, and Marcela María Alejandra Nari. 1994. Women and democracy in Argentina. In *The women's movement in Latin America: Participation and democracy*, ed. J. S. Jaquette, 109–129, 2nd ed. Boulder, CO.: Westview Press.

Figueiredo, Isabel S. de. 2003. *Ações afirmativas e transformação social: Uma abordagem constitucional*. Masters thesis, Law School at the Catholic University of São Paulo.

Filho, Daniel. 1988. *Antes que me esqueçam*. Rio de Janeiro: Editora Guanabara.

Folha da Tarde. 1985. A partir de hoje, uma nova delegacia só para a mulher. August 6.

————. 1991. Prefeitura acolhe mulheres ameaçadas de morte pelos maridos. August 28.

Folha de S. Paulo. 1983a. Proposta será debatida por seis entidades. March 9.

————. 1983b. Feministas vão a Montoro para pedir programa. March 9.

————. 1985a. Defesa da mulher. July 3.

————. 1985b. Delegacia de Defesa da Mulher será inaugurada hoje em S. Paulo. August 6.

————. 1985c. Mulheres policiais vencem a batalha contra o preconceito e chegam para ficar. August 25.

————. 1985d. No primeiro mês, Delegacia da Mulher atende 482 casos. September 7.

————. 1985e. Secretário propõe uma escrivã em cada delegacia. August 14.

————. 1986a. Delegacia da Mulher completa um ano com sete mil ocorrências. August 6.

————. 1986b. Defesa da mulher. August 7.

————. 1990a. Espancamentos lideram ocorrências nas delegacias da mulher de SP. May 12.

Folha de S. Paulo. 1994a. Novas/velhas violências contra a mulher no Brasil. *Estudos Feministas* 2(Special Number): 473–483.

―――. 1994b. Lutas feministas, violência conjugal e novas vilências contras as mulheres no Brasil. Paper presented at the Seminário Violência contra a Mulher Preparatório para IV Conferência Mundial sobre a Mulher, organized by Conselho Estadual da Condição Feminina, São Paulo, May 30–31.

―――. 1999. *Racismo e anti-racismo no Brasil.* São Paulo: Editora 34.

―――. 2003a. "Beijaço" gay reúne 2.000 em shopping center em SP. August 3. Available at: http://www1.folha.uol.com.br/folha/cotidiano/ult95u79567.shtml (accessed January 20, 2004).

―――. 2003b. Homossexuais realizam "beijaço" em frente à igreja no Rio. August 3. Available at: http://www1.folha.uol.com.br/folha/colidiano/ult95u79568. shtml (accessed January 20, 2004).

Franceschet, Susan. 2003. "State feminism" and women's movements: The impact of Chile's Servicio Nacional de la Mujer on women's activism. *Latin American Research Review* 38(1): 9–40.

Franchetto, Bruna, Maria Laura V. C. Cavalcanti, and Maria Luiza Heilborn. 1985. Introdução. *Perspectivas Antropológicas da Mulher* 4: 7–13.

Fraser, Nancy. 1991. Women, welfare, and the politics of need interpretation. In *Unruly practices: Power, discourse, and gender in contemporary social theory* 144–160. Minneapolis: University of Minnesota Press.

―――. 1997. *Justice interruptus: Critical reflections on the "postsocialist" condition.* New York: Routledge.

Friedman, Elizabeth. 1995. Women's human rights: The emergence of a movement. In *Women's rights, human rights: International feminist perspectives,* eds. J. Peters and A. Wolper, 18–35. New York: Routledge.

―――. 1997. *What Nairobi brought together, Beijing tore asunder: The effects of "transnationalism reversed."* Paper presented at the XX International Congress of the Latin American Studies Association, Guadalajara.

―――. 1998. Paradoxes of gendered political opportunity in the Venezuelan transition to democracy. *Latin American Research Review* 33(3): 87–135.

Fundação Sistema Estadual de Análise de Dados de São Paulo-SEADE, and Conselho Estadual da Condição Feminina de São Paulo. 1987. *Um retrato da violência contra a mulher (2038 boletins de ocorrência).* São Paulo: Fundação Sistema Estadual de Análise de Dados de São Paulo (SEADE).

Gazeta da Zona Norte. 1987. Apoio às mulheres e combate à violência, este é o lema da 4ª Delegacia da Mulher. March 7.

Góes, Marta. 1985a. Sob os punhos cerrados do marido. *Afinal,* July 23.

―――. 1985b. Mulher colecionando violência. *Afinal,* October 3.

Goldberg, Maria Amélia Azevedo. 1985a. *Mulheres espancadas: A violência denunciada.* São Paulo: Cortez Editora.

―――. 1985b. *Violência contra a mulher.* São Paulo: Comissão de Violência do Conselho Estadual da Condição Feminina.

Gonzalez, Lélia. 1991. The unified black movement: A new stage in black political mobilization. In *Race, class and power in Brazil,* ed. P. Fontaine, 120–134.

Los Angeles: Center for Afro-American Studies at the University of California, Los Angeles.

Gordon, Linda. 1990a. Family violence, feminism, and social control. In *Women, the state and welfare*, ed. L. Gordon, 178–198. Madison: University of Wisconsin Press.

———. 1990b. The new feminist scholarship on the welfare state. In *Women, the state and welfare*, ed. L. Gordon, 9–35. Madison: University of Wisconsin Press.

Green, James N. 1994. The emergence of the Brazilian gay liberation movement, 1977–1981. *Latin American Perspectives* 21(1): 38–55.

Gregori, Maria Filomena. 1993a. *Cenas e queixas: Um estudo sobre mulheres, relações violentas e a prática feminista*. São Paulo: Paz e Terra.

———. 1993b. As desventuras do vitimismo. *Estudos Feministas* 1(1): 143–149.

Grewal, Inderpal, and Caren Kaplan. 1994. Introduction: Transnational feminist practices and questions of postmodernity. In *Scattered hegemonies: Postmodernity and transnational feminist practices*, ed. I. Grewal, and C. Kaplan, 1–33. Minneapolis: University of Minnesota Press.

Grossi, Miriam Pillar. 1988. Discours sur les femmes battues: Représentations de la violence sur les femmes au Rio Grande do Sul. Ph.D. diss., University of Paris V. Paris.

———. 1993. De Ângela Diniz a Daniela Perez: A trajetória da impunidade. *Estudos Feministas* 1(1): 166–168.

———. 1994. Novas/velhas violências contra a mulher no Brasil. *Estudos Feministas* 2(Special Number): 473–483.

Guimarães, Antônio Sérgio Alfredo. 1995. Racismo e anti-racismo no Brasil. *Novos Estudos* 43: 26–44.

Guimarães, Antonio S. A., and Lynn Huntley. 2000. *Tirando a máscara: Ensaios sobre o racismo no Brasil*. São Paulo: Paz e Terra.

Haney, Lynne. 1996. Homeboys, babies, men in suits: The state and the reproduction of male dominance. *American Sociological Review* 61: 759–778.

Haraway, Donna J. 1991a. "Gender" for a Marxist dictionary: The sexual politics of a word. In *Simians, cyborgs, and women: The reinvention of nature*. New York: Routledge.

———. 1991b. Situated knowledges: The science question in feminism and the privilege of partial perspective. In *Simians, cyborgs, and women: The reinvention of nature*. New York: Routledge.

Harding, Sandra. 1987. Conclusion: Epistemological questions. In *Feminism and methodology*, ed. Sandra Harding, 181–190. Bloomington: Indiana University Press.

Hartsock, Nancy C. M. 1987. The feminist standpoint: Developing the ground for a specifically feminist historical materialism. In *Feminism and methodology*, ed. Sandra Harding, 157–180. Bloomington: Indiana University Press.

Hasenbalg, Carlos. 1996. Racial inequalities in Brazil and throughout Latin America: Timid responses to disguised racism. In *Constructing democracy: Human rights, citizenship, and society in Latin America*, eds. E. Jelin and E. Hershberg, 161–176. Boulder, CO.: Westview Press.

Hautzinger, Sarah. 1997. "Calling a state a state": Feminist politics and the policing of violence against women in Brazil. *Feminist Issues* 15(1–2): 3–28.

Heilborn, Maria Luiza. 1986. Mulher, cidadania e violência. Paper presented at the XXXVIII annual meeting of Sociedade Brasileira para o Progresso da Ciência, Curitiba.

———. 1987. Cidadania para as mulheres. *Ciência Hoje* 5(28): 13–15.

———. 1992. Fazendo gênero? A antropologia da mulher no Brasil. In *Uma questão de gênero*, eds. A. de O. Costa and C. Bruschini, 93–125. São Paulo: Rosa dos Ventos.

———. 1993. Gênero e hierarquia: A costela de Adão revisitada. *Estudos Feministas* 1(1): 50–82.

Hora do Povo. 1991. Casa abriga mulheres que fogem da violência. August 30.

Ilanud. 2002. Pesquisa de vitimização 2002 e avaliação do PIAPS. São Paulo: Ilanud, FIA–USP, Gabiente de Segurança Institutional. Photocopied.

Informativo MB. 1988. Violência sexual: defenda-se. January.

Isto É. 1986. Pancada fora de hora. February 5.

———. 1986. A coragem de falar. August 6.

Izumino, Wânia Pasinato. 1998. *Justiça e violência contra a mulher: O papel do sistema judiciário na solução dos conflitos de gênero*. São Paulo: Annablume.

Jornal da Tarde 1985. "Lotada, a Delegacia da Mulher Cresce," August 16.

Jaquette, Jane S. 1994. Introduction: From transition to participation—women's movements and democratic politics. In *The women's movement in Latin America: Participation and democracy*, ed. J. S. Jaquette, 1–12, 2nd ed. Boulder, Co.: Westview Press.

Jelin, Elizabeth, ed. 1990. *Women and social change in Latin America*. New York: Zed Books.

———. 1996. Women, gender, and human rights. In *Constructing democracy: Human rights, citizenship, and society in Latin America*, eds. E. Jelin and E. Hershberg, 177–196. Boulder, CO.: Westview Press.

Jornal da Tarde. 1985. Começa a funcionar a delegacia das mulheres. August 6.

———. 1985. Lotada, a Delegacia da Mulher cresce. August 16.

———. 1986. Delegadas, psicólogas e assistentes sociais reúnem-se para aperfeiçoar a Delegacia da Mulher. February 21.

Jornal de Pinheiros. 1986. Palestra sobre Delegacia da Mulher no *Jornal Pinheiros*. October 6.

Jornal de Santa Catarina. 1989. Nova delegacia gera conflitos. May 7.

Jornal do Brasil. 1985. Delegada é a única do Rio. September 4.

———. 1989. "Legalista" defende o fim das delegacias da mulher. May 12.

———. 1991. Mulheres indefesas. August 28.

Jubb, Nadine. 2001. Enforcing gendered meanings and social order: The participation of the National Police in the Nicaraguan women's and children's police stations. Paper presented at the International Congress of the Latin American Studies Association, Washington, D.C.

Jubb, Nadine, and Wânia Pasinato Izumino. 2002. Women and policing in Latin America: A revised background paper. Unpublished. Photocopied.

Junqueira, Eliane Botelho. 1998. A mulher juíza e a juíza mulher. In *Horizontes plurais: Novos estudos de gênero no Brasil*, eds. C. Bruschini and H. B. de Holanda, 135–162. São Paulo: Editora 34.

Kant de Lima, Roberto. 1989. Cultura jurídica e práticas policiais: A tradição inquisitorial. *Revista Brasileira de Ciências Sociais* 4(10): 65–84.

———. 1994. *A polícia da cidade do Rio de Janeiro: Seus dilemas e paradoxos*. Rio de Janeiro: Polícia do Estado do Rio de Janeiro.

———. 1995. Bureaucratic rationality in Brazil and in the United States: Criminal justice systems in comparative perspective. In *The Brazilian puzzle: Culture on the borderlands of the western world*, eds. D. J. Hess and R. A. DaMatta, 241–269. New York: Columbia University Press.

Keck, Margaret E. 1992. *The workers' party and democratization in Brazil*. New Haven and London: Yale University Press.

Keck, Margaret, and Kathryn Sikkink. 1998. *Activists beyond borders: Advocacy networks in international politics*. Ithaca: Cornell University Press.

Kehl, Maria Rita. 1995. Uma questão de classe. *Teoria & Debate* 8(29): 78–79.

Keller, Evelyn F. 1985. *Reflections on gender and science*. New Haven: Yale University Press.

Knabben, Júlia de Macedo. 1992. Mulher, vítima de violência atendida pela 6a. delegacia de polícia da capital—SC. Undergraduate thesis, Federal University of Santa Catarina, Florianópolis.

Kofes, Suely. 1993. Categorias analítica e empírica: Gênero e mulher: Disjunções, conjunções e mediações. *Cadernos Pagu* 1: 19–30.

Lamas, Marta, Alicia Martinez, Maria Luisa Tarrés, and Esperanza Tuñon. 1995. Building bridges: The growth of popular feminism in Mexico. In *The challenge of local feminisms: Women's movements in global perspective*, ed. A. Basu, 324–350. Boulder, CO.: Westview Press.

Lebon, Nathalie. 1996. Professionalization of women's health groups in São Paulo: The troublesome roads toward organizational diversity. *Organization* 3(4): 588–609.

Lemgruber, Julita. 1985. A polícia civil: Conflitos e contradições. In *A instituição policial*, ed. Julita Lemgruber, 207–236. Rio de Janeiro: Departamento de Publicações da Ordem dos Advogados do Brasil—Rio de Janeiro (OAB-RJ).

Lievesley, Geraldine. 1996. Stages of growth?—Women dealing with the state and each other in Peru. In *Women and the state: International perspectives*, ed. S. M. Rai, and G. Lievesley, 45–60. London: Taylor & Francis.

Lima Costa, Cláudia. 1997. *Being there and writing here: Gender and the politics of translation in a Brazilian landscape*. Paper presented at the 20th International Congress of the Latin American Studies Association, Guadalajara.

Lind, Amy Conger. 1992. Power, gender, and development: Popular women's organizations and the politics of needs in Ecuador. In *The making of social movements in Latin America: Identity, strategy, and democracy*, eds. A. Escobar and S. E. Alvarez, 134–149. Boulder, CO.: Westview Press.

Lopes, José Reinaldo. 1994. Crise da norma jurídica e a reforma do judiciário. In *Direitos humanos, direitos sociais e justiça*, ed. J. E. Faria, 68–93. São Paulo: Malheiros Editores.

Lovell, Peggy A., and Charles H. Wood. 1998. Skin color, racial identity, and life chances in Brazil. *Latin American Perspectives* 25(3): 90–109.

Macaulay, Fiona. 2002. Taking the law into their own hands: Women, legal reform and legal literacy in Brazil. In *Gender and the politics of rights and democracy in Latin America*, eds. Nikki Craske and Maxine Molyneux, 79–101. New York: Palgrave Macmillan.

Mac Dowell de Figueiredo, Samuel. 1995. Limites da intolerância. *Teoria & Debate* 8(29): 80–81.

Machado, Lia Zanotta. 1997. Confrontos políticos e desafios intelectuais. *Estudos Feministas* 3(2): 414–426.

———. n.d. Eficácia e desafios das delegacias especializadas no atendimento às mulheres: O futuro dos direitos à não violência. Unpublished. Photocopied.

Machado, Odete. 1991. Cidade ganha abrigo de mulheres. *Diário Popular*, March 4.

MacKinnon, Catherine A. 1989. *Toward a feminist theory of the state*. Cambridge: Harvard University Press.

———. 1987. Feminism, marxism, method, and the state: Toward feminist jurisprudence. In *Feminism and methodology*, ed. Sandra Harding, 135–156. Bloomington: Indiana University Press.

Mama, Amina. 1989. Black women and the police: A place where the law is not upheld. In *The hidden struggle: Statutory and voluntary sector responses to violence against black women in the home*. London: Race and Housing Research Unit.

Massuno, Elisabete. 2002. Violência contra a mulher: Delegacia de defesa da mulher, atribuições e problemas (1985–1998). In *Tratado Temático de Processo Penal*, ed. Marco Antonio Marques da Silva, 141–168. São Paulo: Juarez de Oliveira.

Melo, Mônica de. 2000. Juizado especial criminal e o acesso à justiça. São Paulo: Procuradoria Geral do Estado de São Paulo. Photocopied.

Metoyer, Cynthia Chavez. 2000. *Women and the state in post-sandinista Nicaragua*. Boulder, CO.: Lynne Rienner.

Minc, Carlos. 2001. Assédio sexual. In *Mulher, gênero e sociedade*, eds. R. M. Muraro, and A. Brandão Puppin, 64–72. Rio de Janeiro: Relume Dumará.

Mitchell, Michael. 1991. Blacks and the *abertura democrática*. In *Race, class and power in Brazil*, ed. P. M. Fontaine, 95–119. Los Angeles: Center for Afro-American Studies at the University of California, Los Angeles.

Mohanty, Chandra Talpade. 1991. Under western eyes: Feminist scholarship and colonial discourses. In *Third world women and the politics of feminism*, eds. C. T. Mohanty, A. Russo, and L. Torres, 51–80. Bloomington: Indiana University Press.

Molyneux, Maxine. 1986. Mobilization without emancipation? Women's interests, state, and revolution in Nicaragua. *Feminist Studies* 11(2): 227–253.

———. 2000. Twentieth-century state formations in Latin America. In *Hidden histories of gender and the state in Latin America*, eds. Elizabeth Dore and Maxine Molyneux, 33–81. Durham, NC: Duke University Press.

Moreira, Maria Ignez C., Sônia Fonseca Ribeiro, and Karine Ferreira Costa. 1992. Violência contra a mulher na esfera conjugal: Jogo de espelhos. In *Entre a virtude e o pecado*, eds. A. de O. Costa, and C. Bruschini, 169–189. Rio de Janeiro: Rosa dos Ventos and Fundação Carlos Chagas.

Mouffe, Chantal. 1992. Feminism, citizenship, and radical democratic politics. In *Feminists theorize the political*, eds. J. Butler, and J. W. Scott, 369–384. New York and London: Routledge.

Muniz, Jacqueline. 1994. O direito dos outros e outros direitos: Um estudo sobre negociação de conflitos nas DEAMs/RJ. Rio de Janeiro: Instituto de Estudos da Religião (ISER). Photocopied.

Nascimento, Abdias do, and Elisa Larkin Nascimento. 2000. Reflexões sobre o movimento negro no Brasil. In *Tirando a máscara: Ensaios sobre o racismo no Brasil*, eds. Antonio Sérgio Alfredo Guimarães and L. Huntley, 203–235. São Paulo: Paz e Terra.

Nash, June, and Safa, Helen, eds. 1986. *Women and change in Latin America*. New York: Bergin & Garvey.

Nelson, Sara. 1996. Constructing and negotiating gender in women's police stations in Brazil. *Latin American Perspectives* 23(1): 131–148.

Notícias de Itaquera. 1986. Delegacia da Mulher beneficia população. October 12–18.

Notícias de Itaquera. 1986. Delegacia da Mulher: um passo para reduzir a violência. January 10–16.

Oherald.com. 2003. All women police stations working in India. May 27. Available at: http://www.sameshield.com/news/awps.html (accessed December 15, 2003).

Oliveira, Luciano. 1994. *Do nunca mais ao eterno retorno: Uma reflexão sobre a tortura*. São Paulo: Brasiliense.

———. 1984. Sua excelência o comissário—Descrição e análise de práticas judiciais exercidas pela polícia na resolução de pequenos casos de natureza penal protagonizados pelas classes populares no Grande Recife. Masters thesis, Federal University of Pernambuco.

Paixão, Antonio Luiz. 1985. A distribuição da segurança pública e a organização policial. In *A instituição policial*, ed. J. Lemgruber, 167–187. Rio de Janeiro: Departamento de Publicações da Ordem dos Adogados do Brasil—Rio de Janeiro (OAB-RJ).

Paoli, Maria Célia. 1985. Mulheres: Lugar, imagem, movimento. *Perspectivas Antropológicas da Mulher* 4: 63–99.

Pateman, Carole. 1988. The patriarchal welfare state. In *Democracy and the welfare state*, ed. A. Gutman, 231–260. Princeton: Princeton University Press.

Philips, Lynne. 1998. Introduction: Neoliberalism in Latin America. In *The third wave of modernization in Latin America: Cultural perspectives on neoliberalism*, ed. L. Philips, xi–xxiv. Wilmington: Scholarly Resources, Inc.

Pimentel de Oliveira, Lucas. 1995. *Juizados especiais criminais: Lei n. 9.009, de 26.9.95*. São Paulo: Edipro.

Pimentel, Sílvia, and Maria Inês Valente Pierro. 1993. Proposta de lei contra a violência familiar. *Estudos Feministas* 1(1): 169–175.

Pimentel, Sílvia, and Sylma Corrêa. 1988. Women's police station: An innovation and efficient strategy against violence. Vienna: Vienna International Centre, United Nations. Photocopied.

Pinheiro, Paulo Sérgio. 1991. Violência fatal: Conflitos policiais em São Paulo (81–89). *Revista USP* 9: 95–112.

Pinto, C. R. J. 2003. *Uma história do feminismo no Brasil*. São Paulo: Fundação Perseu Abramo.

Pontes, Heloisa. 1986. Do palco aos bastidores: O SOS-Mulher e as práticas feministas contemporâneas. Masters thesis, Universidade Estadual de Campinas-UNICAMP, Campinas.

Rai, Shirin M. 1996. Women and the state in the third world. In *Women and the state: International perspectives*, eds. S. M. Rai and G. Lievesley, 15–22. London: Taylor & Francis.

Ray, R., and A. C. Korteweg. 1999. Women's movements in the third world: Identity, mobilization, and autonomy. *Annual Review of Sociology* 25: 47–71.

Ray, Raka. 1998. Women's movements and political fields: A comparison of two Indian cities. *Social Problems* 45(1): 21–36.

Rede de Informação Lésbica Um Outro Olhar. 1994. *Um outro olhar sobre a década 85/95: Uma visão lésbica*. São Paulo: Rede de Informação Lésbica Um Outro Olhar.

Reichmann, Rebecca. 1997. Mulher negra brasileira: Um retrato. *Estudos Feministas* 3(2): 496–505.

Research Centre for Women's Studies, Shreemati Nathibai Damodar Thackersey (SNDT) Women's University. 1999. *Responses to domestic violence in India: A study in Karnataka and Gujarat. Report-in-brief.* India: Research Centre for Women's Studies, Shreemati Nathibai Damodar Thackersey (SNDT) Women's University.

Ribeiro, Matilde. 1995. Mulheres negras brasileiras: De Bertioga a Beijing. *Estudos Feministas* 3(2): 446–457.

Rodrigues, Lígia, and Rita Andréa. 1984. SOS-Mulher do Rio de Janeiro: Uma entrevista. Interview by Maria Laura Viveiros de Castro Cavalcanti and Maria Luiza Heilborn (Rio de Janeiro, September 22, 1982). *Perspectivas Antropológicas da Mulher* 4: 109–137.

Rodriguez, L. 1994. Barrio women: Between the urban and the feminist movement. *Latin American Perspectives* 21(3): 32–48.

Roland, Edna. 2000. O movimento das mulheres negras brasileiras: Desafios e perspectivas. In *Tirando a máscara: Ensaios sobre o racismo no Brasil*, ed. Antonio Sérgio Alfredo Guimarães, and L. Huntley, 237–256. São Paulo: Paz e Terra.

Sader, Emir. 1995. *Quando novos personagens entraram em cena: Experiências e lutas dos trabalhadores da Grande São Paulo, 1970–1980*. Rio de Janeiro: Paz e Terra.

Saffioti, Heleieth I. B. 1978. *Women in class society*. New York: Monthly Review Press.

———. 1990. *Rearticulando gênero e classe social*. Paper presented at the Seminar Estudos sobre Mulher no Brasil: Avaliação e Perspectivas, organized by Carlos Chagas Foundation, São Paulo.

————. 1994. Violência de gênero no Brasil atual. *Estudos Feministas* 2(Special Number): 443–461.

————. 2002a. Violência contra a mulher e violência doméstica. In *Gênero, democracia e sociedade brasileira*, eds. C. Bruschini, and Sandra G. Unbehaum, 321–338. São Paulo: Editora 34 and Fundação Carlos Chagas.

————. 2002b. Violência doméstica: Questão de polícia e sociedade. In *Gênero & Cidadania*, ed. M. Corrêa, 59–69. Campinas, SP: PAGU/Núcleo de Estudos de Gênero, Universidade Estadual de Campinas-UNICAMP.

————. n.d. Violência doméstica: Questão de polícia e da sociedade. São Paulo: Conselho Estadual da Condição Feminina de São Paulo. Photocopied.

San Francisco Chronicle. 1993. All-woman police station for Pakistan. December 21, A-14.

Sant'Anna, Wania. 2001. Desigualdades étnico/raciais e de gênero no Brasil: As revelações possíveis do IDH e do IDG. Available at: http://www.mj.gov.br/sedh/cndm/artigos/wania.html (accessed March 31, 2003).

Santos, Cecília MacDowell. 2004. En-gendering the police: Women's police stations and feminism in São Paulo. *Latin American Research Review* 39(3).

————. 2001. Women's police stations in Brazil. In *Human rights in Brazil 2001: A report*, ed. Social Network for Justice and Human Rights in Partnership with Global Exchange, 163–171. São Paulo: Social Network for Justice and Human Rights.

————. 2000. Gender, the state, and citizenship: Women's police stations in São Paulo, Brazil. In *Irrumpiendo en lo público: Seis facetas de las mujeres en América Latina*, ed. Sara Poggio and Montserrat Sagot, 63–92. San José, C.R.: Maestria Regional en Estudios de la Mujer, Universidad de Costa Rica, Universidad Nacional, Latin American Studies Association.

Santos, Maria Cecília Mac Dowell dos. 1999a. The State, feminism, and gendered citizenship: Constructing rights in women's police stations in São Paulo. Ph.D. diss., University of California, Berkeley.

————. 1999b. Cidadania de gênero contraditória: Queixas, crimes e direitos na delegacia da mulher em São Paulo. In *O Cinquentenário da Declaração Universal dos Direitos do Homem*, ed. A. do Amaral Jr., and C. Perrone-Moisés, 315–352. São Paulo: Edusp.

————. 1995. Quem pode falar, onde e como? Uma conversa "não-inocente" com Donna Haraway. *Cadernos Pagu* 5: 43–72.

Schild, Verónica. 1998. New subjects of rights? Women's movements and the construction of citizenship in the "new democracies." In *Cultures of politics/politics of culture: Revisioning Latin American social movements*, eds. S. E. Alvarez, E. Dagnino, and A. Escobar, 93–117. Boulder, CO.: Westview Press.

Schumaher, Maria Aparecida, and Vargas, Elizabeth. 1993. Lugar no governo: Alibi ou conquista? *Estudos Feministas* 1(2): 348–364.

Scott, Joan W. 1988a. Introduction. In *Gender and the politics of history*. New York: Columbia University Press.

————. 1988b. Gender: A useful category of historical analysis. In *Gender and the politics of history*. New York: Columbia University Press.

Secretaria de Estado dos Direitos da Mulher–SEDIM, and AGENDE–Ações em Gênero, Cidadania e Desenvolvimento. 2002. *Direitos humanos das mulheres . . . em outras palavras: Subsídios para capactiação legal de mulheres e organizações.* Brasília, DF: Secretaria de Estado dos Direitos da Mulher–SEDIM, and AGENDE–Ações em Gênero, Cidadania e Desenvolvimento.

Shopping News, City News. 1986. Mais defesa para as vítimas de violência. March 16.

Silva Jr., Hélio. 1998. *Anti-racismo: Coletânea de leis brasileiras (Federais, estaduais, municipais).* São Paulo: Oliveira Mendes.

Silva, Kelly Crisitane n.d. As DEAMs, as corporações policiais e a violência contra as mulheres: Representações, dilemas e desafios. Unpublished. Photocopied.

Silva, Marlise Vinagre. 1992. *Violência contra a mulher: Quem mete a colher?* São Paulo: Cortez Editora.

Smith, Dorothy. 1987. *The everyday world as problematic: A feminist sociology.* Boston: Northeastern University Press.

Soares, Luiz Eduardo et al. 1996. Violência contra a mulher: As DEAMs e os pactos domésticos. In *Violência e política no Rio de Janeiro,* ed. L. E. Soares. Rio de Janeiro: Instituto de Estudos da Religião ISER/Relume Dumará.

Soares, Vera, Ana Alice Alcantara Costa, Cristina Maria Buarque, Denise Dourado Dora, and Wania Sant'Anna. 1995. Brazilian feminism and women's movements: A two-way street. In *The challenge of local feminisms: Women's movements in global perspective,* ed. A. Basu, 302–323. Boulder, CO.: Westview Press.

Soares, Vera. 1994. Movimento feminista: Paradigmas e desafios. *Estudos Feministas* 2(Special Number): 11–24.

Sorj, Bila. 2002. O feminismo e os dilemas da sociedade brasileira. In *Gênero, democracia e sociedade brasileira,* eds. C. Bruschini, and S. G. Unbehaum, 99–107. São Paulo: Editora 34 and Fundação Getúlio Vargas.

Sorj, Bila, and Paula Montero. 1985. SOS-Mulher e a luta contra a violência. *Perspectivas Antropológicas da Mulher* 4: 101–117.

Station, Elizabeth. 1989. Confronting an "invisible" issue. *Report on the Americas* 23(2): 10–12.

Sternbach, Nancy Saporta, Marisa Navarro-Aranguren, Patricia Chuchryk, and Sonia E. Alvarez. 1995. Feminisms in Latin America: From Bogotá to San Bernardo. In *Rethinking the political: Gender, resistance, and the state,* eds. B. Laslett, J. Brenner, and Y. Arat, 240–281. Chicago: The University of Chicago Press.

Suárez, M., and L. Bandeira. 2002. A politização da violência contra a mulher e o fortalecimento da cidadania. In *Gênero, democracia e sociedade brasileira,* eds. C. Bruschini, and S. G. Unbehaum, 295–320. São Paulo: Editora 34 and Fundação Getúlio Vargas.

Suplicy, Marta. 1995. Legislando contra o assédio. *Teoria & Debate* 8(29): 82–83.

Taube, Maria José. 2002. Quebrando silêncios/construindo mudanças: O SOS/Ação Mulher. In *Gênero & Cidadania,* ed. M. Corrêa, 167–201. Campinas, SP: Núcleo de Estudos de Gênero PAGU, Universidade Estadual de Campinas-UNICAMP.

Teles, Maria Amélia de Almeida. 1993. *Breve história do feminismo no Brasil*. São Paulo: Brasiliense.

Teles, Maria Amélia de Almeida, and Mônica de Melo. 2002. *O que é a violência contra a mulher*. São Paulo: Brasiliense.

Themis-Assessoria Jurídica e Estudos de Gênero. 1997. *Da guerra à paz: Os direitos humanos das mulheres: Instrumentos internacionais de proteção*. Porto Alegre: Themis-Assessoria Jurídica e Estudos de Gênero.

Thompson, Daniella. 2003. The herbal bath: How the young Ary Barroso found fame and fortune. Available at: http://www.brazzil.com/daniv/Texts/Ary_Barroso/Herbal_bath.htm (accessed March 28, 2003).

Tribuna Operária. 1985. Um dia na delegacia das mulheres. July 9–15.

Twine, France Winddance. 1998. *Racism in a racial democracy: The maintenance of white supremacy in Brazil*. New Brunswick, NJ: Rutgers University Press.

União de Mulheres de São Paulo. 1995. *A violência contra a mulher e a impunidade: Uma questão política*. São Paulo: União de Mulheres de São Paulo.

———. 2000. Projeto: Implantação do serviço de atendimento aos casos de violência doméstica: Relato sobre a experiência no Hospital Pérola Byington. São Paulo: União de Mulheres de São Paulo.

Veja. 1986. Feridas domésticas. April 23.

Verardo, Tereza. 1992. Violência. *Presença da Mulher*. October/November/December.

———. 1993. Do amor ao ódio. *Presença da Mulher*. January/February/March.

Vianna, Adriana de R. B., Ana L. Enne, Phillipe P. G. Leite, and Sérgio L. Carrara. 1995. Violência contra a mulher no Rio de Janeiro—Brasil: Relatório parcial de atividades (março-agosto/1995). Rio de Janeiro: Instituto de Estudos da Religião (ISER). Photocopied.

Viola, Eduardo J. 1987. O movimento ecológico no Brasil (1974–1986): Do ambientalismo à ecopolítica. *Revista de Ciências Sociais* 1(3): 5–26.

Walby, Sylvia. 1994. Is citizenship gendered? *Sociology* 28(2): 379–395.

War Against Rape. 2003. Pakistan's war against rape. Available at: http://www.ashrafs.org/ashrafstrpi/war.html (accessed December 15, 2003).

Waylen, Georgina. 1996a. *Gender in third world politics*. Boulder, CO.: Lynne Rienner.

———. 1996b. Democratization, feminism and the state in Chile: The establishment of SERNAM. In *Women and the state: International perspectives*, eds. S. M. Rai and G. Lievesley, 103–117. London: Taylor & Francis.

———. 1998. Gender, feminism and the state: An overview. In *Gender, politics and the state*, eds. V. Randall and G. Waylen, 1–17. New York: Routledge.

Winant, Howard. 1994. *Racial conditions: Politics, theory, comparison*. Minneapolis: University of Minnesota Press.

Wittner, Judith. 1998. Reconceptualizing agency in domestic violence court. In *Community activism and feminist politics: Organizing across race, class, and gender*, ed. Nancy A. Naples, 81–104. New York: Routledge.

Methodological Appendices

Appendix A: The Study

Research Methods

The field research for this book was conducted in the city of São Paulo from March to December of 1994, from June to December of 1995, in January of 1996, and in July of 2001. During different periods of research from January of 2002 to August of 2003, additional fieldwork was conducted by my research assistant in São Paulo, Adriana Carvalho. The field research was based on qualitative data gathering that integrated three techniques: participant observation, interview, and content analysis of documents.

The goal of the field research was to learn how state agents (here, policewomen working in women's police stations) related to civil society actors (here, feminists and female complainants) since the creation of the first women's police station in 1985, and how each group of women (policewomen, feminists, and complainants) contributed to the construction of gendered citizenship in São Paulo, Brazil. I was interested in understanding the dynamics of the relationship among these actors both at level of their everyday practices and within a historical and political context. Conventional sociological techniques—such as archival research and statistical analysis—seemed particularly hard-pressed to shed light on the interactions between state agents and civil society actors. Had I relied on these techniques I would not have been able to understand and analyze the significance of everyday work experiences. Participant observation, however, provides a unique mechanism for observing such phenomena. As an observer and participant both in women's police stations and in women's movements, I was able to concretely grasp the social relations between policewomen, feminists, and female complainants within the specific personal, social, and political environments that they operate.

From March to December of 1994, and from June to November of 1995, I visited all nine women's police stations located in the city of São Paulo. I also visited a regular police station located in the neighborhood of Butantã. In July of 2001, I returned to São Paulo and visited another regular police station, and the first as well as the third women's police stations. During ten months in 1994, six months in 1995, and one month in 2001, I regularly observed the interaction between policewomen and complainants at the women's police station located in downtown São Paulo. I went to this women's police station three to four times per week. There, I spent approximately four hours per day, either in the morning or in the afternoon, and observed how policewomen interacted with complainants on an average of three cases. As a licensed attorney in Brazil, I was able not only to observe the work of policewomen in this women's police station, but also to participate in their daily working experience by providing legal advice, on a volunteer basis, to female complainants. This gave me a relatively privileged position in which to relate to complainants, at the same time it affected their interaction with me in the women's police station, as I discuss further below.

In order to check whether there were significant differences between the first and the other women's police stations in the city of São Paulo, I regularly observed the interaction between policewomen and complainants in the women's police station located in the neighborhood of Butantã during three months in 1995. I went to this women's police station twice a week, either in the morning or in the afternoon. There, I spent approximately three hours per day, and observed how policewomen processed an average of two cases. I found that the behavior of complainants and female police officers in my selected women's police station mirrored that in others in many aspects. In 2001, I returned to the field to update the data and to observe whether the 1996 creation of small-claims criminal courts had affected the interaction between policewomen and their clients in the women's police stations. I did not find any significant difference in the ways they interacted with each other.

While observing the women's police stations, I was particularly interested in looking at how policewomen treated complainants (e.g., how much attention they paid to complainants, how seriously they took complaints); how they spoke of violence against women (e.g., as a crime, as a social problem, as women's rights); and how they registered or did not register complaints (under what criminal type).

With respect to female complainants, my observations focused on how they approached policewomen (e.g., with fear, respect, etc.); how they framed their complaints (e.g., as conjugal violence, sexual harassment, racial violence, etc.); whether or not they had a sense of rights and articulated a women's rights discourse; and what they expected from policewomen (e.g., to talk with the perpetrator, to register the complaint, or to put the perpetrator in jail).

In order to grasp the feminist discourse on violence against women, I also conducted participant observation research in women's movements. From March to December of 1994 I attended all meetings and workshops on violence against women led by governmental and non-governmental (NGO) women's organizations in the city of São Paulo. From July to December of 1995 I served as an intern with the feminist collective União de Mulheres de São Paulo, observing and participating in its activities regarding the issue of violence against women. These activities involved workshops, debates, and courses on violence against women promoted or attended by members of the organization. My internship with União de Mulheres de São Paulo helped me understand the daily experiences of feminist activists, as well as the dynamics of their relationship with policewomen and victims of violence. This internship and my close contact with feminists adversely affected my relationship with some policewomen in 1995, and illustrated the cold relationship between feminists and policewomen at the time. Since 1995, I continue to be a member of União de Mulheres de São Paulo. In July of 2001, when I returned to São Paulo, I participated in the activities of União de Mulheres de São Paulo and made two presentations, one about my Ph.D. dissertation (on which this book is based) and the other on my experience teaching sociology of gender in the United States.

As I was interested in examining the discursive practices of feminists, police-women, and female complainants—both at level of their everyday practices and within a historical and political context—I needed to supplement participant observation with other research techniques, particularly interviewing and the content analysis of documents. Interviewing was critical to understanding both present and past discursive struggles over the meaning of violence against women according to the terms of the actors involved in these struggles.

During different periods of research in 1994, 1995, 1996, and 2001, I conducted in-depth, tape-recorded interviews with 27 feminists involved with governmental and non-governmental organizations (NGOs) addressing the problem of violence against women in the city of São Paulo. In addition, I interviewed 28 police officers (23 female and 5 male) at various levels of the police organization in the city of São Paulo. With the exception of two male police officers, all of the interviewees were working or had worked for the women's police stations, or had coordinated these stations. I also had numerous informal conversations with feminists, policewomen, and complainants. Moreover, I interviewed three social workers and the psychologist working in the women's police station located in downtown São Paulo; the psychologist in charge of coordinating the only shelter (Centro de Convivência para Mulheres Vítimas de Violência Doméstica—COMVIDA) of the state of São Paulo (I also visited this shelter); Police Chief Jorge Miguel, the head of the police department at the time of my field research; and former Secretary of Public Security Michel Temer. Each interview took approximately two hours. I interviewed some feminists and policewomen twice. In 2002 and 2003 my research assistant, Adriana Carvalho, conducted additional interviews with one policewoman and two feminists.

The interviews with feminists were conducted either at their workplace or at their homes, with the exception of one interviewee who came to the apartment where I was living in São Paulo. I selected feminists who are, or had been, partici-pating in governmental organizations and/or NGOs addressing the problem of violence against women. I selected NGOs with different approaches to fighting violence against women, as well as feminists from different social, economic, racial, and sexual orientation backgrounds. Variations on these dimensions helped me understand the extent to which their discourse on violence against women shaped—and was shaped by—their socially constructed identities and interests.

Among governmental organizations, I interviewed members (or former mem-bers) of the Conselho Estadual da Condição Feminina de São Paulo (CECF) and Casa Eliane de Grammont. Among NGOs, I interviewed members (or former members) of the following organizations: the extinct SOS-Mulher, Pró-Mulher, Coletivo Feminista Sexualidade e Saúde, Geledés-Instituto da Mulher Negra, União de Mulheres de São Paulo, Casa da Mulher Negra, Coletivo de Feministas Lésbicas, Serviço de Orientação à Família-SOF, and CLADEM-Comitê Latino-americano para a Defesa dos Direitos da Mulher.

In terms of color and race, seven feminists identified themselves as *negras* (black)—four of these participated in black women's organizations; two identified themselves as *pardas* (brown); one as *semita* (Semite); one as *brasileira de origem indígena, africana e francesa* (Brazilian of indigenous, African, and French descent); fourteen as *brancas* (white); and one as *branca de descendência portuguesa e italina* (white of Portuguese and Italian descent). In terms of class origins, two said they come from upper–middle class families; eight from middle-class families; eight from industrial, working-class families; and seven from low-income or poor families. Despite their different class backgrounds, only one did not have a college degree. Regarding sexual orientation, three identified themselves as *lésbicas* (lesbians) and participated in lesbian organizations. All the others were heterosexuals and did not participate in organizations focusing on issues of sexual orientation.

As the attached interview questions show, I was interested in learning how feminists perceived the women's police stations; how they related to policewomen; and how they defined violence against women. Moreover, the interviews served to trace the history of feminist mobilizations to end violence against women. I would not have been able to find details of the history of these mobilizations in brochures and booklets.

The interviews with police officers (23 female and 5 male) were conducted at the women's police stations, with the exception of one interview conducted at the home of the interviewee. With the exception of two male police officers, all of the interviewees were working or had worked for the women's police stations, or had coordinated these stations. Among these, fourteen were *delegadas de polícia* (female police delegates), eight were *escrivãs* (female police clerks), and four were *investigadores* (investigators—one female and three male). As required by law, all *delegados* (police delegates) hold a law degree. In terms of class background, nine of these police delegates said they come from middle-class families, and five said they come from low-income families. In terms of color, ten police delegates identified themselves as *brancas* (white), and two as *morenas* and *brasileiras* (brown and Brazilian). In contrast, all eight police clerks and four police investigators whom I interviewed did not have higher education, only a high school degree. In terms of color and race of the female clerks and investigators, three identified as *negras* (black), two as *pardas* (brown), and three as *brancas* (white). The three male investigators identified themselves as *brancos* (white).

As the attached interview questions show, I was interested in understanding how policewomen viewed their work and the role of the women's police stations; how they defined violence against women; how they viewed complainants and perpetrators; and how they related to feminist organizations.

While conducting participant observation and providing legal advice to clients in the first women's police station in 1994, I had numerous informal conversations with and conducted in-depth tape-recorded interviews with 12 female complainants. In July of 2001 I returned to the same women's police stations and conducted two additional interviews with female complainants. Among the 14 complainants I interviewed, 13 complained about conjugal violence and 1 complained about sexual abuse of her daughter by a family member. Their age ranged from 21 to 48 years old. Twelve of them came from poor families, and only two from low-middle-class families. Half of them identified themselves as *brancas* (white) and the other half as *pardas* or *morenas* (brown). Ten of them worked outside home.

Five were migrants from the northeastern region. Their jobs ranged from domestic work, to shop assistance, to insurance selling, to coordination of a child care center. None had completed high school. Except for having a higher proportion of *pardas* women, the social and economic background of these complainants corresponds to the background of the majority of women who press charges in the women's police stations throughout the country.[1]

As the attached interview questions show, I focused on how female complainants defined violence against women; how they viewed the women's police stations and policewomen; how they compared the women's police stations with regular police stations; what they expected and learned from going to the women's police stations; and how they related (or did not relate) with feminists.

In order to examine the feminist discourse on violence against women and the formation of the first women's police station, I also collected legal documents, statistics, newspaper articles, booklets, and all types of materials on violence against women and on women's police stations published by the state and women's NGOs. Likewise, I collected videos produced by feminist organizations and by Brazilian television networks. These written texts and audio-visual materials were important illustrations of the hegemonic and counter-hegemonic discourses on violence against women as constructed by the state, the media, and feminist organizations. Finally, I gathered the available information on the number and types of complaints of violence against women reported to the women's police stations. This was important to find out not only the number and types of cases reported, but also under what criminal terms complaints were registered by policewomen.

Both Insider and Outsider: A Privileged Position?

During my research in the women's police stations, I constantly asked myself about the meaning of violence, where violence starts and ends, how we can address the problem of conjugal violence and other forms of violence against women, and to what extent we should, in the name of research, bother those facing the problem of violence either in their work experience or in their personal lives. These are empirical, ethical, and methodological questions. I do not intend to solve them, but rather to reflect on the issues that came out of my experience conducting participant observation and interviews in the women's police stations and in the women's movements.

Contrary to standpoint feminist methodology (Smith 1987; Keller 1985; Harding 1987; Hartsock 1987; MacKinnon 1987; Collins 1991), the fact that I am a Brazilian woman doing research in Brazil does not make unproblematic my position in relation to my subjects of study. Of course, in comparison to North American researchers, I already have the privilege of being positioned "within" Brazilian culture(s). In principle, this gives me a privileged position to produce a more accountable knowledge. But the production of knowledge does not come automatically from (essentialist) identity, as Haraway (1991b) persuasively argues in her formulation of situated knowledges. Moreover, to reclaim an epistemological privileged position on the basis of a national identity—without taking into account class, race, gender, sexual orientation, regional, and cultural differences— is a dangerous methodological and political mistake.

Nevertheless, identity plays an important role in the relationship between the researcher and his or her subjects of study. I am referring here to a conception of identity that is socially constructed. The process of constructing an identity always demarcates difference (see Trinh 1990; Santos 1995). In addition, both identity and difference are relationally and culturally situated. Consider, for example, my racial position in the United States and in Brazil. In the United States I gain an ethnic status of Brazilian, Latina, woman of color, or third world woman, whereas in Brazil these categories are not socially relevant or do not exist. In Brazil, I become a white woman from the underdeveloped northeast region of the country. I am also positioned as an upper–middle class female lawyer and sociology professor living in the United States. Thus, the way the researcher and his or her subject of study view each other both shapes and is shaped by an interlocking social process of identity and difference formation.

My social identification in Brazil, combined with my sociological feminist training in the United States, located me in multiple positions during the research, complicating the "outsider-within" stance reclaimed by researchers of color in the United States (see, for example, Collins 1991). Depending on the social position of my interviewees, I sensed that I was viewed as either a hybrid insider/outsider or as a complete outsider. In either case, I did not enjoy a purely "privileged" position to do research in the women's police stations and women's movements.

In relation to the middle-class feminists whom I interviewed, my status as a Brazilian feminist researcher trained in the United States positioned me as both insider and outsider. In the women's police stations, I was an outsider in several aspects (due, for example, to my class, race, political, and educational background), although in relation to policewomen with a law degree I was also viewed as an insider. In relation to complainants, I was always perceived as an outsider, regardless of any shared racial and regional origin. Apart from our clear-cut class and educational differences, we were also in different positions in the women's police stations. They were complaining about violence, whereas I was studying their actions and sometimes providing them with legal advice, which put me in a position of legal authority akin to the position of policewomen. Perhaps because I did not share any aspects of my social and economic position with complainants, I felt a great deal of inadequacy and awareness of our power differences when I was approaching them.

Every time I arrived at the women's police station that I regularly observed in 1994, I would first take a seat in the entrance hall to talk to complainants in an informal way. While sitting there, some complainants would start a conversation with me, usually talking about what had happened to occasion their visit. Then I would usually follow up some of these stories with inquiries about their experience in the women's police stations. In addition to providing some of them with legal advice, I would observe their encounters with either the social worker, the psychologist, or the police officer in charge of registering their cases. The head of the women's police station at that time, Delegada Izilda Ferreira, had authorized me to observe the work of all police officers, social workers, and the psychologist.[2] She had also authorized me to ask both the staff and female complainants to give me interviews. It was up to the individual to refuse or agree.

In addition, upon my request, I was authorized to provide legal advice to complainants. Ferreira unconditionally welcomed my participation in the women's police station. (Although complainants always need legal advice, there is no legal adviser in any of São Paulo's women's police stations.) I could provide legal advice in the same room where police officers registered the complaints, as long as this room was vacant. The police officer in the entrance hall was the one who would decide whether the complainant should receive legal advice. All cases she sent to me concerned conjugal violence. I would always introduce myself as an attorney and researcher conducting a study of women's police stations.

The kind of legal advice I provided depended on complainants' questions. Usually, complainants were concerned about their rights in case of divorce or separation. I would advise them to have their complaints registered in Bulletins of Occurrence before leaving their houses. This would serve as proof of not abandoning the family, which would prevent them from losing custody of their children. I would also explain that, in case they decided to divorce, they would not lose their rights to any property they had acquired with their husband or domestic partner. Finally, I would inform where they could look for public attorneys and what kind of documents they should take with them whenever they decided to consult with these attorneys and initiate a divorce suit. In case their partners refused to give them the necessary documents for a lawsuit (such as marriage certificate and birth certificate of children), they could order new copies from the register office where these documents had been originally registered. Usually, before and after giving legal advice, I would ask them whether they would give me an interview. Most complainants did not want to (out of over 40 women to whom I gave advice, only 12 agreed to be interviewed). In contrast, all feminists and policewomen whom I approached gave me interviews.

Because I was interested in learning about complainants' perspectives on the women's police stations, all interviews happened after complainants had talked with the female police officer in charge of registering their complaints. Some interviews also occurred right before I provided legal advice. Whenever possible, I did the interviews in a separate room inside the women's police station. Sometimes, we had to go to the patio in the back of the women's police station. At the beginning of each interview, they did not feel comfortable with the tape recorder; only after a while did they speak without noticing the recorder. All of them told me afterward that they were scared of talking about their situation with a stranger.

By the end of each interview, all interviewees expressed gratitude for the opportunity to learn from our conversation and to talk about their lives, especially after not receiving much attention from policewomen. In the women's police station, policewomen do not give complainants much time to talk about their feelings and do not spend enough time providing them with legal information. Whereas their meetings with policewomen did not exceed half an hour, my interviews took an average of one and one-half hours. Although I always explained that I was not part of the staff, I am not sure these complainants understood that, especially because some interviews followed my legal advice. They did not seem to understand the written "term of agreement" I had prepared, as required by the Committee for

Protection of Human Subjects at the University of California at Berkeley. All interviewees seemed scared by this term and none of them signed it.

It was difficult to interview complainants not only because of our different social positions. Due to their vulnerable situation and fear, just a few of them were willing to give me long tape-recorded interviews. I also hesitated in asking them to do that. Throughout my field research, I was observing women living through painful experiences, which made me constantly reflect on the violence they suffered and my relationship with them. I felt emotionally as well as intellectually affected by the situation of complainants and always questioned the extent to which I had the right to use their situation to write then a dissertation and now a book that they will never read. The fact that I could give them something back during the period of field research (e.g., legal advice) did not eliminate my question of why and for whom we do research and reconstruct theories.

How the production and distribution of knowledge affects and can be contested by subjects of study is not an issue for most, specifically positivist methods of scientific research and theory building. Feminist standpoint theorists have critically addressed the relationship between the researcher and her subjects of study (Smith 1987; Keller 1985; Harding 1987; Hartsock 1987; MacKinnon 1987; Collins 1991). Feminist postmodernist scholars, such as Donna Haraway (1991b), have also discussed the politics of the production of knowledge, advocating a politics of translation in the form of "situated knowledges." Yet this politics of translation does not solve the problem of how our research can benefit or be contested by our subjects of study. "Situated knowledges" are translated from the streets to the academy in a reflexive and critical manner. But we also need to be aware and practice a politics of translation that allows for the possibility of multiple contestations of knowledge from both inside and outside of academia. Since 1994 I have been struggling with this problem and have not been able to develop research in ways that can begin to address it. This is one among other limitations of my work.

Appendix B: Interview Questions

I asked all interviewees about their marital status, education, class, and racial background. But I formulated a different set of questions for different groups of women. Below are the questions asked in interviews with policewomen and policemen, feminists working for the Conselho Estadual da Condição Feminina de São Paulo (CECF), members or former members of feminist NGOs addressing the issue of violence against women, and female complainants.

Questions for police officers

(1) When did you start working for the women's police stations? How did you end up working here? Were you appointed? Did you choose? Why?

(2) Did you work in a regular police station before? After working in the women's police station, did your prestige in the police department change? How?

(3) How do you compare a regular police station with the women's police station?

(4) Why do you think the women's police stations were created? Were you in favor of their creation? Why?

(5) Did you have specific training for working in the women's police station? What kind of training?

(6) What do you think is the main role of policewomen and the women's police station?

(7) How do you define violence against women? Can you give me examples?

(8) Who are the women who usually come to the women's police station? Can you also give me examples of unusual complainants? Do they come alone? Who comes with them?

(9) How do you characterize your relationship with female complainants? How do you feel when you relate to these complainants who are also women?

(10) What kind of cases are usually brought to the women's police station? Can you also give me examples of unusual cases? What are your criteria to register the case?

(11) What do you think female complainants expect from the women's police stations?

(12) Do you think the women's police station helps the women who come here? How? Can you give me examples?

(13) What do you do when there is no legislation regulating the case?

(14) Have you had any contact with feminist groups and women's organizations? Which groups? What do you think about them? Do you consider yourself a feminist? Why?

(15) In your view, what are the major problems policewomen need to overcome to perform their tasks efficiently?

Questions for feminists working for the Conselho Estadual da Condição Feminina de São Paulo (CECF) and its Commission on Violence against Women

(1) When did you start working in the council? Do you work in another place besides the council? Where? What do you do?

(2) Are you a member of any feminist NGO? Which one? How long have you participated in the feminist movement? Have you always worked with the issue of violence against women? Have you participated in any campaign against violence against women? When? Can you describe this campaign?

(3) How do you define violence against women? Can you give me examples?

(4) Why do you think the women's police stations were created? Were you in favor of their creation? Why?

(5) Do the members of the council have meetings with policewomen? How do you characterize the relationship between feminists and policewomen? How do you characterize the relationship between other state agents dealing with violence against women and feminists in the council?

(6) What do you think is the main role of policewomen and women's police stations?

(7) Do you think policewomen should receive special training? What kind of training?

(8) Have you ever been in a women's police station? Why did you go there and what was your impression? If you were victim of violence, would you go to the women's police station? Why? What would you expect from policewomen?

(9) In your view, who are the women who can and actually go to the women's police stations? Why? What kind of cases do you think they report? How do you think they approach the women's police stations?

(10) Have you interacted with female victims of violence? How did you feel about your relationship with them?

(11) How do you think the women's police stations work? How do you think policewomen respond to the female complainants?

(12) What are the major problems the state council faces to change the situation of violence against women?

Questions for feminist activists who were members or former members of NGOs addressing the issue of violence against women

(1) How long have you participated in this group? Do you work in another place? What do you do?

(2) Have you participated in any campaign against violence against women? When and how? Can you describe this campaign?

(3) How do you define violence against women? Can you give me examples?

(4) Why do you think the women's police stations were created? Were you in favor of their creation? Why?

(5) Have you ever been in the women's police stations? Why did you go there and what was your impression? If you were victim of violence, would you report your case to the women's police station? Why? What would you expect from policewomen?

(6) What do you think is (or should be) the main role of policewomen and the women's police stations?

(7) In your view, who are the women who can and actually go to the women's police stations? Why? What kind of cases do you think they report? How do you think they approach the women's police stations?

(8) Have you interacted with female victims of violence? How did you feel about your relationship with them?

(9) How do you think the women's police stations work? How do you think policewomen relate to female complainants?

(10) What do you think the women's police stations can do to protect women against violence?

(11) What are the major problems feminist NGOs and grassroots women's groups face to change the situation of violence against women?

Questions for female complainants

(1) Where do you live? Do you work? What do you do? Are you married? Do you have children?
(2) Was it your first time in the women's police station? What happened to make you come here?
(3) How did you hear about the women's police station?
(4) How did you decide to seek the women's police station?
(5) Why didn't you look for the women's police station before?
(6) How did you feel about coming to the women's police station? Did you come alone?
(7) What did you expect to find in the women's police station?
(8) How was your experience in the women's police station? What do you think about policewomen, the psychologist, the social worker, etc.? What did you learn from them? How did you feel afterward?
(9) Have you been in a regular police station? How do you compare it with the women's police station? Why do you think the women's police station was created?
(10) Do you think the women's police station can help you? How? Would you come here again? Why?
(11) Have you had any contact with feminists and women's groups? Which group? What do you think about them?

Notes

Introduction

1 Translated by the author from the original Portuguese language. All quotes from texts and interviews are originally in the Portuguese language, and when cited throughout this book, were translated by the author.

2 See Cabral (n.d.) for a detailed biography of Ary Barroso, including the story of "Dá Nela" and Barroso's complete discography. See also Thompson (2003) for more details on the story of "Dá Nela." I should note that neither Cabral nor Thompson make any social commentary about gender relations and the violence against women that the song represents. Their focus is simply on Barroso's sudden success and fame thanks to the popularity of "Dá Nela."

3 Interview with Mila Duarte, São Paulo, September 22, 1994. Upon her request, I am not using the real name of this police officer.

4 The feminist reform of the Brazilian Penal Code proposes the abolishment of this rule. See Americas Watch Committee (1991a); Centro Feminista de Estudos e Assessoria (CFEMEA) (1993b, 1993c).

5 These countries are Argentina, Colombia, Costa Rica, El Salvador, Ecuador, Nicaragua, Peru, and Uruguay.

6 In the United States, women, working-class, poor, and less educated groups regularly use the lower courts to settle their grievances and resolve conflicts over personal relationships (Wittner 1998).

7 Similar findings have been reported by studies of women's police stations in other countries in Latin America (Jubb 2001; Jubb and Izumino 2002) and in South Asia (Research Centre for Women's Studies, SNDT Women's University 1999).

8 See Franceschet (2003) for an alternative argument on the positive effects of the Chilean national women's policy machinery on the women's movement.

9 See Haney (1996) for a similar argument regarding the literature on the U.S. welfare state.

10 I am borrowing Cohen's and Arato's (1997: ix) conception of civil society, but, unlike them, I am not including the family in the sphere of civil society.

11 See the Methodological Appendixes for details on the methods used to gather data for this book.

Chapter 1

1 See Arquidiocese de São Paulo no Brasil (1981); Alves (1987); and Oliveira (1994).
2 See Durham (1984); Sader (1995); Alvarez (1990); Teles (1993); Viola (1987); and Keck (1992).
3 See Alves (1986).
4 On the participation of feminist lobbies to influence the redrafting of the Brazilian constitution in 1988, see Centro de Estudos e Assessoria-CFEMEA (1993a).
5 See, for example, the Code for the Protection of Consumer Rights (Law 8,078/90) and the Statute for the Protection of Children and Adolescents (Law 8,069/90).
6 Sarney originally belonged to the rightist party PDS, which supported the military. He had to join the Partido do Movimento Democrático Brasileiro (PMDB) in order to run for vice president with Tancredo Neves (PMDB), the first civilian president selected by the Electoral College after the 1964 military coup. Due to health problems, Neves was hospitalized the night before taking office and died just over forty days later.
7 On the creation of this council, see Conselho Estadual da Condição Feminina de São Paulo (1984); Ardaillon (1989); and Alvarez (1990).
8 For details on the divisions among feminists regarding the creation of the Conselho Estadual da Condição Feminina (State Council on the Feminine Condition) (CECF), see Ardaillon (1989) and Alvarez (1990). See also *Folha de S. Paulo*, March 9, 1983a and *Folha de S. Paulo*, March 9, 1983b.
9 Interview with Michel Temer, São Paulo, October 17, 1994.
10 Ibid.
11 Ibid.
12 See Alvarez (1990) for the most comprehensive account of the Brazilian women's movement in transition politics. For accounts by local activists, see Teles (1993); Soares (1994); Soares et al. (1995); and Pinto (2003).
13 Wife-murderers were often acquitted by the jury on the basis of the "honor defense" argument—a throwback to Portuguese colonial law that allowed a man to kill his adulterous wife and her lover (Americas Watch 1991a). In 1991, the Brazilian Superior Tribunal of Justice (STJ) outlawed this argument, but later contradicted its own decision (Macaulay 2002). On the construction of the "honor defense" argument, see Corrêa (1981); Ardaillon and Debert (1987); Izumino (1998).
14 Quoted in Góes (1985a).
15 Quoted in Góes (1985a). Casa da Mulher do Centro was renamed in the late 1980s to Pró-Mulher, Família e Cidadania.
16 In the 1980s, for example, the sexist rule that protected the "honor of husbands" by not allowing married women to file a complaint of rape perpetrated by strangers without the authorization of the victims' husbands was still enforced. Moreover, adultery is still a crime according to the Brazilian Penal Code, in effect since 1941. In addition, sexual crimes are classified as "crimes against custom" rather than "crimes against the individual." Feminists have

been trying since the early 1980s to change these rules and other sexist legislation. For proposals of feminist congresswomen presented to the National Congress, see Centro Feminista de Estudos e Assessoria (CFEMEA) (1993b) and Centro Feminista de Estudos e Assessoria (CFEMEA) (1993c).

17 On the CECF's proposals to end violence against women, see Conselho Estadual da Condição Feminina de São Paulo (1984) and Conselho Estadual da Condição Feminina de São Paulo (1985a).

18 For more information on Centro de Orientação Jurídica e Encaminhamento à Mulher (Center for Legal Orientation and Guidance for Women) (COJE), see Conselho Estadual da Condição Feminina de São Paulo (1984) and Conselho Estadual da Condição Feminina de São Paulo (1985a).

19 Quoted in *Contigo*, August 5, 1985.

20 Unlike in the United States, police stations in Brazil specialize in certain crimes, such as homicide and drug trafficking. Therefore, Temer's proposal was not so different from the local legal tradition. During the redemocratization period, other secretaries of public security also proposed new police stations specializing in racial crimes, crimes against elders, and environmental crimes. The major novelty of these stations was the state's recognition of new social movements' demands, granting rights to social groups often excluded from access to justice.

21 See, for example, *Notícias de Itaquera*, January 10–16, 1986; *Contigo*, August 5, 1985; *Folha de S. Paulo*, August 12, 1985; *Tribuna Operária*, July 9–15, 1985.

22 Interview with Cida Medrado, São Paulo, October 19, 1994.

23 Interview with Michel Temer, São Paulo, October 17, 1994.

24 For a distinction between civil and military police, see Dos Santos (1985).

25 Regular police stations were not precluded from investigating these crimes, even when the victims were women. But in practice they have sent female complainants to women's police stations.

26 See Decree 40,693, March 1, 1996. In both cases of homicide and damage to property, the victim must know the perpetrator and the crime must take place within the domestic sphere.

27 Quoted in *Contigo*, August 5, 1985. See also *Folha de S. Paulo*, July 3, 1985; *Notícias de Itaquera*, January 10 through 16, 1986.

28 Interestingly, despite the existence of a police station specializing in crimes against children and adolescents, the jurisdiction of the women's police stations expanded in 1996 to include these crimes. See Decree 40,693, March 1, 1996.

29 See, for example, *Folha de S. Paulo*, August 6, 1985; *TV Manchete*, August 6, 1985; and *Notícias de Itaquera*, January 10 through 16, 1986.

30 Quoted in *Estado de São Paulo*, August 8, 1985. See also *Folha de S. Paulo*, August 6, 1985; *Folha de S. Paulo*, August 12, 1985; *Tribuna Operária*, July 9 through 15, 1985; *Jornal da Tarde*, August 6, 1985; and *Isto É*, February 5, 1986;

31 Decree 17,037/81 regulates the provision of social services in all regular and specialized police stations. In practice, however, most police stations do not offer social services. Moreover, this legislation does not make any reference to psychological services.

32 Besides the members of the CECF, members of the following organizations participated in this meeting: Casa da Mulher do Centro, Coletivo de Mulheres

Negras, Centro da Mulher Brasileira, SOS-Mulher, COJE, and União de Mulheres de São Paulo.

33 Conselho Estadual da Condição Feminina de São Paulo, "Letter to Secretary of Public Security Michel Temer," July 10, 1985.

34 Interview with Cida Medrado, São Paulo, October 10, 1994.

35 Interview with Rachel Moreno, São Paulo, November 21, 1994.

36 Quoted in *Shopping News, City News,* March 16, 1986.

37 Conselho Estadual da Condição Feminina de São Paulo, 1985c.

38 See, for example, *Folha de S. Paulo,* August 6, 1985; *Folha de S. Paulo,* November 5, 1985.

39 See Articles 1 and 5 of Portaria DGP-12, August 8, 1985.

40 A shorter version of this section also appears in an article published in *Latin American Research Review* vol. 39, no. 3 (October 2004).

41 Kant de Lima (1995, 246) argues that the application of "extremely general laws, usually federal ones, to the particular conditions of localities" is a problem, because the police lose discretionary power and "all the negotiations that ordinary police work involves are performed against the law." See also Paixão (1985) and Lemgruber (1985) for a critical sociological analysis of the police system in Brazil.

42 See Article 4 of the Brazilian Procedural Penal Code, in effect since 1941.

43 This legal change has had an impact on all police stations, leading, for example, to the enactment of a new legislation (Decree 40,693/96) expanding the jurisdiction of women's police stations to include crimes against children and adolescents. This legislation will be further discussed in chapter 4.

44 Interview with Iraci Medeiros, São Paulo, April 29, 1994. Unless indicated otherwise, throughout this book I use the real names of police officers.

45 For more details, see Ardaillon (1989, 97).

46 Góes (1985a).

47 See also the transcription of Blay's speech in Conselho Estadual da Condição Feminina de São Paulo (1985b).

48 On women's lack of access to the career of magistrates until the 1980s and the increasing "femininization" of this profession in the 1990s, see Avelar (1996) and Junqueira (1998).

49 See *Tribuna Operária,* July 9–15, 1985. There was only one *delegada* in the state of Rio de Janeiro when its first women's police station was created in September 1985 (*Jornal do Brasil,* September 4, 1985).

50 Quoted in *Tribuna Operária,* July 9–15, 1985.

51 Quoted in *Notícias de Itaquera,* January 10–16, 1986.

52 See *Isto É,* August 6, 1986; De Barros 1988; and *Informativo MB,* January 1988.

53 Of these, 16,690 cases concerned actual bodily harm (battering); 10,316 concerned threat of battering; 2,534 concerned verbal offense; 722 concerned rape; and 309 concerned attempted rape. See *Folha de S. Paulo,* May 12, 1990.

54 See "Primeiro Encontro Nacional de Assistentes Sociais das Delegacias de Polícias de Defesa da Mulher," 1990; and *Tribuna de Santos,* September 6, 1990. Studies of the role of social workers in women's police stations in Rio de Janeiro (Silva 1992) and Florianópolis (Knabben 1992) suggest that the

demand for more social workers in the women's police stations is not peculiar to the case of São Paulo.

55 See Grossi (1993) and Conselho Estadual da Condição Feminina de São Paulo (1994a). As revealed by feminists and policewomen in interviews, not all of them agreed that social workers should provide services in the women's police stations.

56 On the popularity of Corrêa in the mid-1980s, see *Afinal*, April 8, 1986; Góes (1985b); *Isto É*, August 6, 1986.

57 In Brazil, bachelors in law are called "doctors." Therefore, police delegates, who possess a law degree, are also called "doctors." This title is a sign of a hierarchical society in which few people have access to higher education. It is also a sign of relations of power and authority. For instance, it is common in Brazil to refer to a landlord or boss, as well as government officials, as "Doctor."

58 Interview with Rosmary Corrêa, São Paulo, June 16, 1994. Corrêa was also re-elected in 1998 and 2002.

59 See, for example, *Notícias de Itaquera*, October 12–18, 1986; *Jornal de Pinheiros*, October 6, 1986; 5th. Police Station in Defense of Women, "Ata de Reunião," May 4, 1986; and *Gazeta da Zona Norte*, March 7, 1987.

60 See Ações em Gênero, Cidadania e Desenvolvimento (AGENDE) and Comitê Latino-Americano e do Caribe para a Defesa dos Direitos da Mulher (CLADEM) (2003).

61 For details on the creation of this shelter, see *O Estado de S. Paulo*, August 29, 1991; *Diário Popular*, March 4, 1991; *Hora do Povo*, August 30, 1991; *Jornal do Brasil*, August 28, 1991; *Folha da Tarde*, August 28, 1991.

62 Social Democratic Party was created when the military regime initiated the *Abertura Política* (Political Opening) and changed the bi-party system to a multi-party system. PDS was rooted in ARENA-National Renovation Alliance, the party in power during the military regime. In 1993, PDS merged with PDC-Christian Democratic Party, which had been founded in 1988, and together they established the PPR-Progressive Reformist Party. In 1995, PPR merged with PP-Progressive Party and founded PPB-Progressive Brazilian Party. In April of 2003 PPB changed its name to PP-Progressive Party.

Chapter 2

1 See Jubb and Izumino 2002; Nelson 1996; Santos 1999a; Silva n.d.; Machado 2001; Massuno 2002; Vargas 2000; Jubb 1999; Muniz 1994; Conselho Nacional dos Direitos da Mulher 2001.

2 Some data and the arguments developed here appear in a shorter version of this chapter published as an article in *Latin American Research Review* vol. 39, no. 3 (October 2004). During different periods of research in 1994, 1995, 1996, and 2001, I conducted in-depth, tape-recorded interviews with 28 police officers (23 female and 5 male) at various levels of the police organization in the city of São Paulo. I also interviewed São Paulo's former Secretary of Public Security Michel Temer. With the exception of two male police officers, all of the

interviewees were working, or had worked for the women's police stations, or had coordinated these stations. Among these, 14 were *delegadas de polícia* (female police delegates), 8 were *escrivãs* (female police clerks), and 4 were *investigadores* (investigators, one female and three male). I also had numerous informal conversations with policewomen working in the nine women's police stations located in the city of São Paulo, all of which I visited in 1994. Moreover, I conducted in depth, tape-recorded interviews with 27 feminists involved with governmental organizations and NGOs addressing the problem of violence against women. Among governmental organizations, I interviewed members (or former members) of the Conselho Estadual da Condição Feminina de São Paulo and Casa Eliane de Grammont. Among NGOs, I interviewed members (or former members) of the following: the extinct SOS-Mulher, União de Mulheres de São Paulo, Pró-Mulher, Coletivo Feminista Sexualidade e Saúde, Geledés-Instituto da Mulher Negra, Casa da Mulher Negra, Coletivo de Feministas Lésbicas, Serviço de Orientação à Família-SOF, and CLADEM Brasil—Comitê Latino-americano para a Defesa dos Direitos da Mulher. In 2002 and 2003, my research assistant, Adriana Carvalho, conducted additional interviews with one policewoman and two feminists. In addition to interviews, this chapter draws on booklets, newsletters, and reports on violence against women and women's police stations published by the state and women's NGOs, as well as newspaper articles and legal documents.

3 See Conselho Nacional dos Direitos da Mulher (1986).
4 Interview with Heleieth Saffioti, São Paulo, March 12, 1994.
5 Conselho Estadual da Condição Feminina de São Paulo (1985b, 1).
6 See Conselho Nacional dos Direitos da Mulher (1986).
7 See Conselho Nacional dos Direitos da Mulher (1986, 3).
8 Conselho Nacional dos Direitos da Mulher (1986, 8).
9 Ibid.
10 Ibid.
11 Ibid.
12 Interview with Rosmary Corrêa, São Paulo, June 16, 1994.
13 Ibid.
14 Ibid.
15 Ibid.
16 Ibid.
17 As noted in chapter 1, the idea actually came from former Secretary of Public Security Michel Temer.
18 Interview with Rosmary Corrêa, São Paulo, June 16, 1994.
19 Ibid.
20 Ibid.
21 Ibid.
22 Ibid.
23 Ibid.
24 See also *Folha de S. Paulo*, September 7, 1985. Here Corrêa explains that she is a feminist as long as feminism means "to defend women's rights and to fight for the end of violence against women."

25 Interview with Rosmary Corrêa, São Paulo, June 16, 1994.
26 Ibid.
27 Ibid.
28 Ibid.
29 Ibid.
30 Ibid.
31 Ibid.
32 Ibid.
33 Ibid.
34 Ibid.
35 Ibid.
36 Ibid.
37 Ibid.
38 Ibid.
39 Ibid.
40 Ibid.
41 The term *capacitação* has no equivalent word in English. In Portuguese, *capacitação* derives from the verb *capacitar*, which means in English: 1. to capacitate, to render capable, to empower; 2. to enable, to authorize; 3. to convince, to persuade; or 4. to understand, to comprehend (*Random House College Dictionary*). For a discussion on the role of *capacitação* in women's NGOs training to make videos, see De Camargo (1995).
42 Interview with Heleieth Saffioti, São Paulo, December 3, 1994.
43 Interview with Maria Aparecida Schumaher, São Paulo, June 15, 1994.
44 Interview with Simone Diniz, São Paulo, November 12, 1992.
45 Structural adjustment policies (SAPs) are conditions attached to International Monetary Fund (IMF) loans and include four policy areas: currency devaluation; cuts in government expenditures; opening the economy to foreign capital; and export promotion development strategies (Benería 1996).
46 Collor was also the first Brazilian president to be impeached (due to corruption). His vice-president, Itamar Franco (PMDB), became the president in 1993.
47 This situation persisted under the Itamar Franco administration (1993-1994). State councils were openly critical of the Conselho Nacional dos Direitos da Mulher (National Council on Women's Rights) (Conselho Estadual da Condição Feminina de São Paulo 1993, 6).
48 Information provided by Carlinda de Almeida in an interview with the author, São Paulo, October 13, 1994.
49 Interview with Carlinda de Almeida, São Paulo, October 13, 1994.
50 Ibid.
51 Ibid.
52 Ibid.
53 Ibid.
54 Ibid.
55 Ibid.
56 Ibid.
57 Ibid.

58 Interview with Carlinda de Almeida, São Paulo, October 13, 1994.
59 Ibid.
60 Ibid.
61 Interview with Rosmary Corrêa, São Paulo, June 16, 1994.
62 Interview with Carlinda de Almeida, São Paulo, October 13, 1994.
63 Interview with Mila Duarte, São Paulo, September 22, 1994. Upon her request, I am not using the real name of this police officer.
64 Ibid.
65 Interview with Tereza Verardo, São Paulo, May 19, 1994.
66 Interview with Izilda Ferreira, São Paulo, May 5, 1994.
67 Ibid.
68 Ibid.
69 Ibid.
70 Ibid.
71 Ibid.
72 Ibid.
73 Ibid.
74 Ibid.
75 Interview with Tereza Verardo, São Paulo, May 19, 1994.
76 Interview with Izilda Ferreira, São Paulo, May 5, 1994.
77 Ibid.
78 Ibid.
79 Interview with Ivete Ramos, São Paulo, April 24, 1994. Upon her request, I am not using the real name of this police officer.
80 Ibid.
81 Ibid.
82 Ibid.
83 Ibid.
84 Ibid.
85 Ibid.
86 Ibid.
87 Ibid.
88 Ibid.
89 Ibid.
90 Ibid.
91 Ibid.
92 Ibid.
93 In the aftermath of Beijing, the Conselho Nacional dos Direitos da Mulher (National Council on Women's Rights) (CNDM) launched the National Program to Prevent and Eradicate Domestic and Sexual Violence. In 1998, the Latin American and Caribbean Committee for the Defense of Women's Rights (CLADEM) launched the campaign *Sem as Mulheres os Direitos Não São Humanos* ("Without Women, Rights Are Not Human").
94 Interview with Maria Inês Valenti, São Paulo, August 8, 1995.
95 Ibid.
96 Ibid.

97 Ibid.
98 Ibid.
99 Ibid.
100 Ibid.
101 Ibid.
102 In 1996, the jurisdiction expanded to include crimes of abortion, infanticide, homicide, and crimes against children and adolescents of all genders. See Decree 40,693, January 3, 1996.
103 Interview with Maria Inês Valenti, São Paulo, August 8, 1995.
104 Ibid.
105 Interview with Maria Inês Valenti, São Paulo, August 25, 1995.
106 Ibid.
107 Interview with Maria Tereza Gonçalves Rosa, São Paulo, October 23, 1995.
108 Interview with Maria Tereza Gonçalves Rosa, São Paulo, January 16, 1996.
109 See Conselho Estadual da Condição Feminina de São Paulo (1998b).
110 Notwithstanding this important achievement of the CECF in influencing the training of female police delegates, it is important to note that this ten-day course did not include police clerks and police investigators.
111 Interview with Maria Aparecida de Laia, conducted by my research assistant, Adriana Carvalho, in São Paulo, April 8, 2003.
112 Interview with Márcia Salgado, conducted by my research assistant, Adriana Carvalho, in São Paulo, July 26, 2002.
113 Ibid.
114 Ibid.
115 Information provided by my research assistant, Adriana Carvalho, based on a conversation she had with Márcia Salgado in São Paulo, June 18, 2003.
116 Information provided by my research assistant, Adriana Carvalho, based on conversations she had with two policewomen in São Paulo, June 18, 2003.

Chapter 3

1 For a detailed analysis of the emergence of the feminist and women's movements in Brazil, see Alvarez (1990 and 1994); Teles (1993); Soares et al. (1995); Soares (1994); Schumaher and Vargas (1993); Alves (1980); and Carneiro, (1993a). On the emergence and development of women's movements in other Latin America countries, see Sternbach et al. (1995); Lamas (1995); Escandón (1994); Chuchryk (1994); Chinchilla (1994); Feijóo and Nari (1994); Jaquette (1994); and Alvarez et al. (2003).
2 As Teles (1993, 114–115) recounts, in 1976 the leftist newspaper Movimento had one issue completely censored because it was dedicated to "women's work in Brazil." In 1978, many women metalworkers were fired for participating in the I Congresso da Mulher Metalúrgica (First Congress of Women Metalworkers), sponsored by the Sindicato dos Metalúrgicos (Union of Metalworkers) in the industrial city of São Bernardo do Campo.
3 See, for example, the testimony of released women political prisoners published in Brasil Mulher (4, no. 16, September 1979, p. 4–5).

4 This slogan appeared in 1980 on the walls of Belo Horizonte, capital of the southeast state of Minas Gerais, in response to the murder of two women by their husbands (see *Mulherio*, 1, no. 1, May/June 1981, p. 3).

5 The term *mulher honesta* (honest woman) appears in several articles of the Brazilian Penal Code, in action since 1940. Articles 215, 216, and 219, for example, require that the victim be an "honest woman" to complain against the perpetrator. In 2003 Congresswoman Iara Bernardi (PT) introduced a bill to the National Congress to eliminate this expression from the code (Law Proposal n. 117/2003). This bill has been approved by the House of Representatives and is now in the Senate.

6 In 1972, Roberto Lobato, member of a traditional middle-class family well known in Belo Horizonte, killed his wife, Josefina Lobato. His acquittal was applauded by the trial's audience (see *VEJA*, no. 215, October 18, 1972, p. 32–33).

7 *VEJA*, October 24, 1979, p. 112–114; *VEJA*, November 11, 1981, p. 20–25; *Jornal da República*, November 1, 1979; *Jornal do Brasil*, November 5, 1981; *Jornal do Brasil*, November 6, 1981; *Jornal do Brasil*, November 7, 1981; *Jornal do Brasil*, November 8, 1981; *O Globo*, November 3, 1981; *O Globo*, November 7, 1981; *Folha de S. Paulo*, June 7, 1981; *Folha de S. Paulo*, December 30, 1981; *Mulherio*, 2, no. 5, January/February 1982, p. 6–7.

8 Doca Street was found guilty and sentenced to two years in prison. However, the jury considered his crime a "non-intentional" murder (*homicídio culposo*) and, because he had never been convicted of a crime previously, he did not go to jail.

9 The Núcleo organized a demonstration in downtown Rio de Janeiro, distributed pamphlets in the streets, circulated an open letter, and organized a vigil in front of the court in Cabo Frio. Feminist groups in São Paulo also wrote a manifesto protesting the first Doca Street trial. Thanks to these feminist pressures on the court, Doca Street was sentenced to 15 years in prison at his second trial, and finally went to jail.

10 *Jornal do Brasil*, March 16, 1981; *Jornal do Brasil*, March 23, 1981; *Jornal do Brasil*, March 25, 1981.

11 *Mulheres contra a Violência*, "Basta", n.d. (flyer); "Todos à Missa de 7º Dia de Eliane de Grammont," n.d. (flyer); *Mulherio*, 2, n. 5, Jan./Feb. 1982, p. 6; *VEJA*, April 8, 1981, p. 24; *Folha de S. Paulo*, August 24, 1984; *Folha de S. Paulo*, August 26, 1984; *Folha da Tarde*, August 24, 1984.

12 Lindomar Castilho was sentenced to 15 years in prison.

13 The *Malu Mulher* broadcast was stopped because it was considered too advanced for Brazil at the time (Filho 1988).

14 The feminist reform of the Brazilian Penal Code proposes the abolishment of this rule. See Americas Watch Committee (1991a); Centro Feminista de Estudos e Assessoria (CFEMEA) (1993b, 1993c).

15 In Portuguese, *ronda* means to patrol, and *rondão*, the augmentative of *ronda*, means big patrol. Hence Rondão Operation can be translated as a heavy-duty patrol.

16 See, for example, *VEJA*, June 18, 1980, p. 29. See also the letters by Comissão Pró-Comando contra a Violência Policial, "Carta Aberta à População," São Paulo, 1980; and Grupo Somos, Grupo Eros, Grupo Libertos, Ação

Homossexualista, Ação Lésbico-Feminista, Grupo Nós Mulheres, Movimento Negro Unificado, Grupo Feminista 8 de Março, Associação de Mulheres, Núcleo de Defesa à Prostituta, "Comunicado à Imprensa," São Paulo, June 9, 1980.

17 See Alvarez (1990, 121–123) for details on the political divisions that surfaced during the Second Congress.

18 Other commissions were created during the same Congress, focusing on issues such as reproductive rights and communication.

19 See also *Movimento*, November 3–9, 1980.

20 See, for example, Ala Feminina do Grupo Negro da PUC/SP, "Apoio à Campanha contra a Violência à Mulher, Ato Público, 10 de outubro de 1980," São Paulo, October 1980. This pamphlet supported the feminist campaign to denounce violence against women, but specifying that black women were subject to a particular form of violence against women. However, the pamphlet took care in explaining that their struggle against violence was not a struggle against black men. See also Grupo de Ação Lésbico-Feminista, "Sobre Violência," São Paulo, n. d. This pamphlet was distributed at the feminist meeting in Valinhos in 1980, denouncing "discrimination against lesbians" as a form of "violence against women," and demanding that the feminist movement speak openly about this issue.

21 In the area of violence, the organization SOS Mulher was created; in the area of health, Coletivo Feminista Sexualidade e Política (today called Coletivo Feminista Sexualidade e Saúde); in the area of information, Centro Informação Mulher-CIM; and in the area of family advice, Casa da Mulher do Centro. Feminist organizations focusing on political mobilization also emerged in the early 1980s, such as União de Mulheres de São Paulo and Casa da Mulher do Grajaú.

22 Similar organizations also called SOS-Mulher were created all over the country during the same period, generally lasting an average of only three years, which were inspired by the French and North American movements to end violence against women. Only a few SOS-Mulher organizations are still active in Brazil, such as the one in the city of Campinas (Taube 2002). See Pontes (1986) and Gregori (1993a) for an anthropological analysis of the feminist discourse of the SOS-Mulher in São Paulo. See Grossi (1988) for an anthropological analysis of the feminist discourse of the SOS-Mulher in Porto Alegre.

23 See SOS-Mulher, "Dia Nacional de Protesto contra a Violência à Mulher" (Pamphlet, São Paulo, n.d.), "Mais uma Mulher Assassinada" (Pamphlet, São Paulo, n.d.), "Quem Ama Não Mata" (Pamphlet, São Paulo, n.d.), "Carta Aberta às Entidades Democráticas" (Open Letter to Democratic Organizations, São Paulo, n.d.), "Todos à Missa de 7o. Dia de Eliane de Grammont" (Pamphlet, São Paulo, n.d.), "Grite Fogo" (Pamphlet, São Paulo, n.d.), "SOS-Mulher: Contra a Violência de todo 'Santo' Dia" (Pamphlet, São Paulo, n.d.). Although emphasizing conjugal violence, SOS-Mulher also mobilized against rape and police violence against prostitutes. See, for example, "Mulheres Violentadas" (Pamphlet, São Paulo, n.d.) and "Carta Aberta à População" (Pamphlet, São Paulo, n.d.).

24 See SOS-Mulher, "Projeto SOS-Mulher," São Paulo, n.d. This conception of violence against women was articulated not only by the SOS-Mulher in São Paulo, but also by other SOS-Mulher groups and various women's organizations elsewhere in Brazil. See, for example, Franchetto, Cavalcanti, and Heilborn (1985); Chauí (1985); Paoli (1985); and Sorj and Montero (1985).

25 For similar statements, see also *Folha de S. Paulo*, January 14, 1981; *Folha de S. Paulo*, August 1, 1982.

26 See *Folha de S. Paulo*, January 15, 1981; *Folha de S. Paulo*, October 10, 1981; *Folha de S. Paulo*, August 28, 1981.

27 For more details on this campaign, see Gregori (1993a) and Pontes (1986).

28 This process has accelerated in the 1990s. As Alvarez (1997, 1998) points out, there has been an "NGO-ization" of Brazilian as well as Latin American women's movements. See Lebon (1996) for an analysis of the contradictions in the professionalization of women's health NGOs in São Paulo. Schild (1998) examines the contradictions in the professionalization of Chilean women's movements from a class perspective, calling attention to the production of and access to knowledge as constitutive of power differences among women.

29 See also Goldberg (1985a: 18–9).

30 Saffioti first developed her Marxist-structuralist approach to gender domination in her book, *A Mulher na Sociedade de Classes*, published in Brazil in 1968. The book's English-language translation was published in the United States in 1978 (Saffioti 1978). Since then she has devoted her attention to studies of violence against women and has published numerous articles on the topic. See, for example, Saffioti (2002a, 2002b, n.d.).

31 Quoted in Conselho Estadual da Condição Feminina de São Paulo (1994, 24–5).

32 Interview with Maria Amélia Teles, São Paulo, December 11, 1995.

33 Interview with Tereza Verardo, São Paulo, May 19, 1994.

34 See, for example, Casa Eliane de Grammont's (n.d.) booklets on sexual violence and conjugal violence.

35 Interview with Simone Diniz, São Paulo, November 12, 1995.

36 See Coletivo Feminista Sexualidade e Saúde, *II e III Cursos de capactiação para atendimento a mulheres em situação de violência*, 1995 (pamphlet).

37 In 1979, feminists protested the firing of five women who worked for the Rio de Janeiro's daily *Jornal do Brasil* because they had complained about *cantadas* (sexual harassment) at the workplace (Grossi 1994). In São Paulo, the first mobilization against *cantadas* at the workplace happened in 1985 in front of the metallurgist plant ECHLIN (see União de Mulheres de São Paulo 1995).

38 Members of the Workers' Party, however, were not unanimous on the criminalization of this issue. For debates within the party, see Kehl (1995); Mac Dowell (1995); and Suplicy (1995). In 1999, Congresswoman Iara Bernardi (PT) proposed another bill to criminalize sexual harassment (Law Proposal n. 61), which was approved by Congress in 2001 and became Law n. 10,224/01, adding Article 216-A to the Brazilian Penal Code. Defining sexual harassment as an act of constraining or threatening practiced by someone in a superior

position at the workplace to obtain sexual advantage from an employee, the new law established a penalty of one to two years of detention.

39 Interview with Heleieth Saffioti, São Paulo, March 12, 1994.

40 Interview with Maria Aparecida Schumaher, São Paulo, June 15, 1994.

41 For similar definitions, see Saffioti (1994) and União de Mulheres de São Paulo (1995).

42 This crime is defined in Article 146 of the Brazilian Penal Code as "the action of forcing someone, through the use of violence or threat, to do what is forbidden by law, or not to do what is allowed by law." The prison sentence corresponding to illegal constraint ranges from three months to one year, and it is not replaceable by fines.

43 For an excellent historical and sociological analysis of these arguments, see Guimarães (1999).

44 For a historical analysis of the black movement since the 1930s, see Nascimento and Nascimento (2000).

45 For a detailed historical account of the movement since the 1970s, see Mitchell (1991) and Gonzalez (1991). Since the 1970s, thanks to the expansion of the black liberation movement, the literature on race, racism, racial inequalities, and anti-racism in Brazil has grown considerably. On the construction of race, the denial of racism, and the politics of *embranquecimento* (whitening) in Brazil, see, for example, Guimarães (1995; 1999) and Twine (1998). For a pointed account of racism in the criminal justice system, see Adorno (1995). For an excellent overview of racial inequalities, racism and anti-racism struggles, see Guimarães and Huntley (2000).

46 Interview with Sueli Carneiro, São Paulo, January 15, 1996.

47 Ibid.

48 Interview with Maria Aparecida Schumaher, São Paulo, June 15, 1994.

49 In the 1990s, the state of São Paulo created specialized police stations to deal with racial crimes, which functioned like women's police stations. But while the latter expanded, the former were closed in 1999.

50 This convention was signed by then governor of São Paulo Luiz Antonio Fleury Filho (PMDB) on September 1, 1992.

51 See also Conselho Estadual da Condição Feminina de São Paulo (1992).

52 Interview with Maria Aparecida de Laia, São Paulo, July 3, 2001.

53 Interview with Lígia Santos, São Paulo, March 24, 1994.

54 Article 235 of the Military Penal Code refers to pederasty but establishes all sexual practices—homosexual or heterosexual—at military bases as crimes.

55 According to Coletivo de Feministas Lésbicas (1994), 74 city constitutions and 3 state constitutions explicitly prohibit discrimination on the basis of sexual orientation. At the federal level, however, despite the lobbying of gay and lesbian activists, the Brazilian Constitution enacted in 1988 did not explicitly condemn discrimination on the basis of sexual orientation. Contrary to racism, defined as a crime in the 1988 Constitution, homophobia is not mentioned in the constitutional text.

56 For a detailed analysis of the emergence of the Brazilian gay liberation movement, see Green (1981). For an account of hate crimes against gay men in

the late 1970s, see *Lampião da Esquina*, n. 20, January 1980, p. 3. On the subjection of lesbians to physical harm, imprisonment and psychiatric treatment imposed by their families, see *Lampião da Esquina*, n. 12, May 1979, p. 9–10. According to the gay organization based in Bahia, Grupo Gay da Bahia, violence against homosexuals increased in the 1980s. Between 1980 and 1993, 1,200 homosexuals were victims of hate crimes that resulted in death. Of these victims, 71 percent were gay men. See also "Carta Aberta à População" (1993), an open letter signed by gay and lesbian organizations, as well as the Human Rights Commission of the Bar Association in Rio de Janeiro, which demonstrated against a school that expelled a 19-year-old female student for kissing her girlfriend in the school cafeteria. This student was almost lynched by other students. Kissing in public still provokes homophobic reactions: a gay couple who kissed in a shopping center in São Paulo was barred from entering a movie theater in July 2003. In protest, gay groups mobilized over 2,000 people who met and kissed in the same shopping center the following week. The demonstration, known as "beijaço" (big kiss), received coverage by the media and inspired similar demonstrations in other cities (see *Folha de S. Paulo* 2003a, 2003b).

57 As reported by Rede de Informação Lésbica Um Outro Olhar (1994), the first Brazilian lesbian group, Ação Lésbico-Feminista-LF, was created in São Paulo in 1979, coming out of the gay and lesbian group Somos. In 1981, Ação Lésbico-Feminista was transformed into Grupo Ação Lésbica-Feminista-GALF. This was practically the only lesbian group in the country throughout the 1980s. In 1989, its name was changed again to Rede de Informação Lésbica Um Outro Olhar. Since 1990, new lesbian organizations have flourished in the country, especially in São Paulo, such as Coletivo de Feministas Lésbicas, Deusa Terra, Afins, and Estação Mulher. Along with Rede de Informação Lésbica Um Outro Olhar, some of them have published newsletters.

58 Coletivo de Feministas Lésbicas (1994, 21–22).

59 Since the early 1980s, feminist organizations dealing with sexuality, such as Coletivo Feminista Sexualidade e Saúde in São Paulo and SOS-Corpo in Recife, have limited this issue to reproductive rights.

60 The human rights framework was, and continues to be, adopted by the Brazilian gay, lesbian, bisexual and transgender rights movement. In 2003, the delegation of Brazil at the 59th session of the UN Commission on Human Rights in Geneva presented a resolution about "human rights and sexual orientation." Among other things, the resolution calls upon all States "to promote and protect the human rights of all persons regardless of their sexual orientation" (E/CN.4/2003/L.92).

61 Interview with Lígia Santos, São Paulo, March 24, 1994.

Chapter 4

1 Data provided by the Assessoria Especial das Delegacias de Defesa da Mulher do Estado de São Paulo (currently renamed to Serviço Técnico das Delegacias de Defesa da Mulher do Estado de São Paulo).

2 The meeting took place in Praia Grande, in the state of São Paulo, March 4–7, 1993. The campaign "Impunity as Accomplice to Violence" lasted over three years and it was carried out mostly by União de Mulheres de São Paulo and Casa de Cultura da Mulher Negra. In comparison with the feminist campaign of the early 1980s, this campaign did not seek to encourage victims to speak up and denounce the violence they had been suffering in silence. Instead, the campaign of the early 1990s targeted the criminal justice system and sought to denounce the disdain that police officers, judges and prosecutors emanated when dealing with cases of violence against women and especially wife-murder cases. For more details on this campaign, see União de Mulheres de São Paulo, *Boletim Informativo da Campanha contra a Violência à Mulher*, N. 0 (September 1993); N. 01 (November 1993); N. 2 (September 1994); N. 04 (May 1995); N. 05 (July 1995).

3 I also address these legal changes in Santos (2001).

4 Because I had received legal training and had practiced law in Brazil prior to coming to the United States, I was able to offer legal advice to clients on a volunteer basis, something the head of the first women's police station welcomed due to their lack of legal advisers.

5 According to the police department, there were 103 regular police stations in 1995.

6 While doing fieldwork in the first women's police station in 1994, I met journalists from two Brazilian television networks, Rede Globo and SBT. Policewomen told me that they had been interviewed by journalists from BBC and NBC as well. The American Consul in São Paulo had also visited the first women's police station.

7 Data provided by the Assessoria Especial das Delegacias de Polícia de Defesa da Mulher do Estado de São Paulo, currently called Serviço Técnico de Apoio às Delegacias de Polícia de Defesa da Mulher do Estado de São Paulo.

8 Interview with Rosmary Corrêa, São Paulo, June 16, 1994.

9 Interview with Izilda Ferreira, São Paulo, May 5, 1994.

10 Interview with Helena Siqueira, São Paulo, April 15, 1994. Upon her request, I am using a pseudonym for this police officer.

11 Interview with Rosmary Corrêa, São Paulo, June 16, 1994.

12 Interview with Mila Duarte, São Paulo, September 22, 1994. Upon her request, I am not using the real name of this police officer.

13 Ibid.

14 Ibid.

15 Ibid.

16 Interview with Maria Teresa Gonçalves Rosa, São Paulo, October 23, 1995.

17 Ibid.

18 Ibid.

19 Interview with Rosmary Corrêa, São Paulo, June 16, 1994.

20 Interview with Maria Cristina Mazzarello, São Paulo, July 17, 2001.

21 This is the first contact of complainants with a police officer in the women's police station. Complainants give this police officer their abbreviated stories, and the officer decides, based on instructions given to her by the police delegate,

whether or not the complaints must be registered. She may discourage complainants to have the complaints registered by sending them to another state service, without allowing complainants to see the police officer in charge of registering the complaint.

22 Interview with Helena Siqueira, São Paulo, April 15, 1994. On the differences between the military and civil police, see Dos Santos (1985).

23 Ibid.

24 Interview with Rosmary Corrêa, São Paulo, June 16, 1994.

25 Interview with Ivete Ramos, São Paulo, April 24, 1994. Upon her request, I am not using the real name of this police officer.

26 Ibid.

27 Interview with Izilda Ferreira, São Paulo, May 5, 1994.

28 By law, only female police officers are allowed to search women.

29 According to Brazilian criminal law, the difference between a *contravenção penal* (misdemeanor) and a *crime* (felony) relies on the severity of the punishment established by law. Misdemeanors carry less severe penalties than felonies, having the purpose to prevent the occurrence of a crime that would potentially become the ultimate result of a certain action considered dangerous. For further explanation on this difference, see Franco et al. (1995, 53–4).

30 For an analysis of this and other anti-racism laws in Brazil, see Silva Jr. (1998).

31 On the practice of *embranquecimento* in Brazil, see Guimarães (1995) and Twine (1998).

32 Interview with Helena Siqueira, São Paulo, April 15, 1994.

33 Interview with Ivete Ramos, São Paulo, April 24, 1994.

34 Ibid.

35 Interview with Carlinda de Almeida, São Paulo, October 13, 1994.

36 Interview with Iraci Medeiros, São Paulo, April 29, 1994.

37 Interview with Maria Inês Valenti, São Paulo, August 25, 1995.

38 Interview with Maria Cristina Santos, São Paulo, April 29, 1994.

39 Interview with Rosmary Corrêa Sãa Paulo, June,16,1994.

40 Ibid.

41 Interview with Ivete Ramos, São Paulo, April 24, 1994.

42 Ibid.

43 Ibid.

44 Interview with Márcia Salgado, São Paulo, August 2, 1994.

45 Law No. 8,072/90 increased the prison sentence assigned to this crime. By doing so, the legislator attempted to make a parallel between *atentado violento ao pudor* (violent sexual molestation) and *estupro* (rape), considering both equally serious. See Franco et al. (1995, 2464) for a critique of this legal change.

46 Interview with Iraci Medeiros, São Paulo, April 29, 1994.

47 Ibid.

48 Interview with Mila Duarte, São Paulo, September 22, 1994.

49 Interview with Maria Teresa Gonçalves Rosa, São Paulo, October 23, 1995.

Chapter 5

1 To protect the confidentiality of complainants, I do not use their real names throughout this chapter.

2 In 1994, I conducted in-depth, tape-recorded interviews with twelve battered women who reported cases of conjugal violence to the first women's police station located in downtown São Paulo. I also had informal conversations with several battered women to whom I provided legal advice on a voluntary basis at the same women's police station. In July 2001, I returned to this police station and conducted interviews with two additional clients.

3 On a similar conception of complainants' agency, see Wittner (1998).

4 See Wittner (1998) for similar findings in a domestic violence court created in Chicago in 1984.

5 Camargo, Dagostin, and Coutinho (1991) examine Bulletins of Occurrence concerning cases of conjugal violence in one women's police station in Florianópolis, and argue that the visibility given to these cases is "partial," because complaints are registered based on bureaucratic formalities without taking into account the complexity of the grievances.

6 A similar argument has been made in post-industrialized countries. For an analysis of racist practices by police in their responses to domestic violence involving black families in England, for example, see Mama (1989).

7 Interview with Lucinda Barbosa, São Paulo, July 7, 2001.

8 According to the report of the National Congress Commission to Investigate the Issue of Violence against Women (Congresso Nacional 1993), 45.90 percent of the victims who press charges in the women's police stations are *brancas* (white), whereas 33.10 percent are *negras* (black), and 21.00 percent are in a category of *outros* (others), which may include *pardas* (brown), *amarelas* (yellow), and so on. The report concludes that violent behaviors are not associated with a specific race and color.

9 Interview with Aparecida Andrade, São Paulo, September 22, 1994.

10 Ibid.

11 Ibid.

12 Ibid.

13 Ibid.

14 Ibid.

15 Ibid.

16 Ibid.

17 Interview with Rosenete Campos, São Paulo, May 23, 1994.

18 Ibid.

19 Ibid.

20 Ibid.

21 Ibid.

22 Ibid.

23 Ibid.

24 Ibid.
25 Interview with Marta Silva, São Paulo, August 31, 1994.
26 Ibid.
27 Interview with Lucinda Barbosa, São Paulo, July 14, 2001.
28 Ibid.
29 Ibid.
30 Interview with Lucinda Barbosa, São Paulo, July 14, 2001.
31 Ibid.
32 Ibid.
33 Ibid.
34 In the women's police station of Rio de Janeiro, for example, over 70 percent of women who press charges against their male partners ask to close the police investigation (Brandão 1998, 53). See Brandão (1998) for an insightful anthropological analysis of the reasons why women who complain about conjugal violence ask to close the police investigation later.
35 Interview with Delegada Izilda Ferreira, São Paulo, May 5, 1994.
36 Interview with Aparecida Andrade, São Paulo, September 22, 1994.
37 Ibid.
38 Ibid.
39 Ibid.
40 Ibid.
41 Interview with Lindalva Macedo, São Paulo, November 14, 1994.
42 Ibid.
43 Ibid.
44 Ibid.
45 Interview with Hortência Santana, São Paulo, August 10, 1994.
46 Ibid.
47 Ibid.
48 Interview with Rosenete Campos, São Paulo, May 23, 1994.
49 Ibid.
50 Interview with Lucinda Barbosa, São Paulo, July 14, 2001.
51 Ibid.
52 Ibid.
53 Ibid.
54 Ibid.
55 Ibid.
56 Interview with Eliene Souto, São Paulo, July 9, 2001.
57 Ibid.
58 Ibid.
59 Interview with Rosenete Campos, São Paulo, May 23, 1994.
60 Ibid.
61 Interview with Marta Silva, São Paulo, August 31, 1994.
62 Ibid.
63 Ibid.
64 Ibid.
65 Interview with Margarida Lapenda, São Paulo, October 10, 1994.

66 Ibid.
67 Interview with Anastácia Leite, São Paulo, October 10, 1994.
68 Ibid.
69 Ibid.
70 Interview with Lucinda Barbosa, São Paulo, July 14, 2001.

Conclusion

1 See Walby (1994) for an elaboration and discussion of the concept of gendered citizenship.
2 Information provided by the Serviço Técnico de Apoio às Delegacias de Polícia de Defesa da Mulher do Estado de São Paulo.
3 See Hancy (1996) for a similar observation regarding the feminist theorizing of the U.S. welfare state.
4 See Mouffe (1992) for another critique of gendered citizenship. According to Mouffe (1992), this concept is problematic because it relies on an essentialist notion of women's identity, therefore not considering women's multiple and fluid subject positions.
5 The leaders of this campaign included the following feminist NGOs and networks: União de Mulheres de São Paulo, Centro de Promotoras Legais Populares de São José dos Campos—DANDARA, and Marcha Mundial de Mulheres. The following non-govenrmental organizations of legal professionals also led this campaing: IBAP—Instituto Brasileiro de Advocacia Pública, Movimento do Ministério Público Democrático, and Comissão da Mulher Advogada da OAB/SP. All of these groups signed the two letters sent to the presidents of the Tribunal of Justice of São Paulo in 2001 and 2002, respectively. For more details about their reasoning, see the pamphlet "Violência contra as Mulheres: Campanha pela Criação do Juizado Especial para Crimes de Violência de Gênero" (União de Mulheres de São Paulo et al. n.d.).

Methodological Appendixes

1 Except for having a higher proportion of *pardas* (brown) women, the social and economic background of these complainants corresponds to the background of the majority of women who press charges in the women's police stations throughout the country (see Congresso Nacional 1993).
2 This was the only women's police station in the city of São Paulo with a psychologist and social workers providing services within the police precinct. Since 1996, psychological and social assistance has not been offered within this women's police station.

Index